THE SOFTBALL COACHING BIBLE

National Fastpitch Coaches Association

Project coordinated by
Jacquie Joseph
Michigan State University

Human Kinetics

Library of Congress Cataloging-in-Publication Data

The softball coaching bible / National Fastpitch Coaches Association ; project coordinated by Jacquie Joseph

    p. cm

  ISBN 0-7360-3827-2

    1. Softball--Coaching. I. Joseph, Jacquie, 1962- II.
National Fastpitch Coaches Association

  GV881.4.C6 S64 2002
  796.357'8--dc21

    796.357
    SOF
              2001039841

ISBN: 0-7360-3827-2

Developmental Editor: Cynthia McEntire; **Assistant Editor:** John Wentworth; **Copyeditor:** Scott Weckerly; **Proofreader:** Erin Cler; **Graphic Designer:** Robert Reuther; **Graphic Artist:** Francine Hamerski; **Photo Manager:** Tom Roberts; **Cover Designer:** Jack W. Davis; **Photographer (cover):** Bongarts/SportsChrome USA; **Art Managers:** Craig Newsom and Carl Johnson; **Illustrator:** Keith Blomberg; **Printer:** Bang Printing

Human Kinetics books are available at special discounts for bulk purchase. Special editions or book excerpts can also be created to specification. For details, contact the Special Sales Manager at Human Kinetics.

Printed in the United States of America   10   9   8   7   6   5   4   3   2   1

Human Kinetics
Web site: www.humankinetics.com

United States: Human Kinetics
P.O. Box 5076
Champaign, IL 61825-5076
800-747-4457
e-mail: humank@hkusa.com

Canada: Human Kinetics
475 Devonshire Road Unit 100
Windsor, ON N8Y 2L5
800-465-7301 (in Canada only)
e-mail: orders@hkcanada.com

Europe: Human Kinetics
Units C2/C3 Wira Business Park
West Park Ring Road
Leeds LS16 6EB, United Kingdom

+44 (0) 113 278 1708
e-mail: hk@hkeurope.com

Australia: Human Kinetics
57A Price Avenue
Lower Mitcham, South Australia 5062
08 8277 1555
e-mail: liahka@senet.com.au

New Zealand: Human Kinetics
P.O. Box 105-231, Auckland Central
09-523-3462
e-mail: hkp@ihug.co.nz

THE SOFTBALL COACHING BIBLE

National Fastpitch Coaches Association

CONTENTS

iv

INTRODUCTION

Learning From the Best

Jacquie Joseph

For as long as I can remember I have been fascinated by and studied coaches. What makes one better than the other? Is it just getting better players? Do you have to scream and carry on, or, if you're a more reserved type, can you just be yourself?

For the first time in the sport of fastpitch softball, we have a book that addresses these issues. In *The Softball Coaching Bible*, many of the finest coaches in the country share their principles, insights, strategies, methods, and experiences. Topics range from teaching the best skills and drills to many subjects rarely written about, such as developing responsible athletes and building character and loyalty in players.

When I started my coaching career, I took every opportunity to observe coaches in action. One of the greatest qualities of our sport is the willingness of coaches to share their knowledge of the game. In my first year as a head coach, I flew to Arizona State University over Christmas break to spend time with a legend in the game, Linda Wells. She let me hang around her preseason practices to observe and learn. Each May, I would head out to the College World Series two days early to catch the teams practicing. I stood as close as I could to the fence, hoping to learn as much as I could from the great ones. I would also sneak into the pressroom for the pregame and postgame interviews with the coaches.

That experience observing Linda and many others like her over the past 15 years revealed several commonalties in the approaches taken by coaches who have achieved at the highest level. The best coaches I've known share these traits.

These coaches live their own values and are authentic. Being authentic is more than just being yourself. Authenticity means that your actions are consistent with your words. Authentic coaches are able to communicate a genuine sense of caring. That, in turn, nurtures trust among the coaching staff, team, and parents.

The best coaches are driven by their desire for personal excellence and are technically competent. Technical competence means knowing the Xs and Os in addition to being able to communicate and teach them. It also means knowing how to use motivational and problem-solving skills to put in sufficient practice time and overcome challenges that inevitably confront coaches and athletes.

Great coaches exude enthusiasm for the game, their teams, and coaching. They have the ability to unite people as a team to work toward a common goal. Although they set their expectations high and are demanding in performance, they encourage and support their teams and staff, maintaining discipline and giving constructive feedback. Even when they are faced with tough decisions, the best coaches persevere. They have a sense of competitive greatness and can make people believe in themselves.

It may be impossible to achieve the highest level in all of these areas, but the best coaches have competence in most, and they never stop learning and growing in the sport.

The coaches in this book not only continue building upon their vast coaching knowledge, they also make the effort to share what they know with other coaches so that they may use their newfound understanding and tools to enhance the experience and development of their athletes. *The Softball Coaching Bible* is a shining example of such knowledge sharing. Soak it up, enjoy the stories, and appreciate the wisdom of our sport's finest mentors.

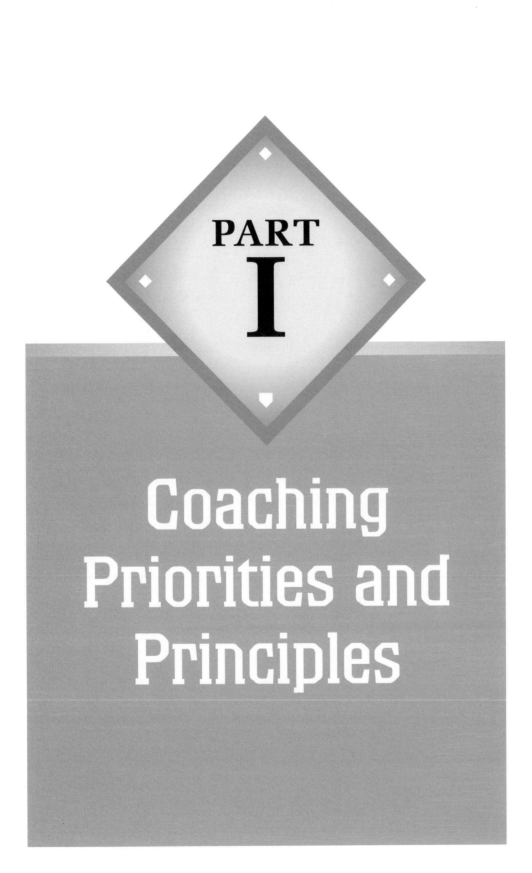

PART I

Coaching Priorities and Principles

Sharing a Love for the Game

Dianne Baker

My life's passion has always been playing and coaching softball. I truly love every part of the game. I am a fierce competitor and make no excuses for it. I played the game hard; I coach the game even harder. I enjoy coaching young people and trying to bring the best out in them. To me, there is something exciting about facing an opponent and finding the edge my team needs to win the game. My athletes keep me young, and nothing makes me happier than listening to them laugh and share their enthusiasm for softball.

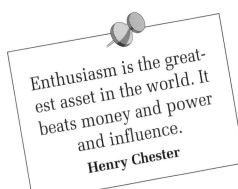

Enthusiasm is the greatest asset in the world. It beats money and power and influence.
Henry Chester

When I started coaching softball 25 years ago, I thought I would stay a few years, then move into the corporate world. But coaching got into my blood, and now I cannot get enough of it. When I am not coaching softball, I am usually speaking about, writing about, or promoting the game. I live it every day. My passion for the game keeps me going after a loss, when the weather doesn't cooperate, or at the end of the season when I'm so tired that I can barely move. I just can never wait for the next game or the next season.

There is no magical formula for my passion. I believe that when you really love what you do, it shows in your language, actions, and attitude. When you commit yourself to something, you owe it to yourself and others to give your very best. Take how you feel about softball, add your team to the mix, and together you will enjoy the game more than you ever thought possible.

I am an all-or-nothing kind of person. The things that are important to me get my complete focus and commitment and are driven by my own set of standards. This set of standards makes me go and gives me the energy to work hard. Coaches have to define their personal standards to discover what turns their passion into action. For me, 10 simple statements define my professional makeup:

1. Respect your profession.
2. Give credit to your colleagues who have helped the sport prosper, and mentor those who are just beginning.
3. Do not be afraid to show your emotions.
4. Stand for something. It's okay to disagree with the majority.
5. Be honest and accept responsibility for your actions.
6. Never be outworked, outprepared, or have your team outhustled.
7. Keep coaching in perspective. Softball is a game, and it should be fun.

8. Keep your energy high.
9. Have the best interest of your athletes at heart at all times.
10. Loyalty to your program is of the utmost importance.

Baker's Dozen

The way you express your expectations to your team is important in the process of sharing your love of softball. You want *your* vision to become *their* vision. Your team embraces your passion by what you say and how you say it. In my first team meeting, I share my blueprint for success, which I call the *Baker's Dozen.*

First, I tell my team to *expect to win.* I do not *hope* they will win; I *expect* them to win. I do not *hope* my athletes will be committed; I *expect* them to be. My athletes meet my expectations, so I want my expectations to be set high. As Dr. Preston Bradley once said, "Expect victory and you make victory."

I encourage my players to *recover quickly from a loss* and move on, but this closure is something coaches need to learn, too. It has always amazed me how athletes recover more quickly from a loss than their coaches. Many coaches take the losses personally. It is not about our success—it's about our players' success. We must understand why we are coaching and keep the sport in perspective.

Plant the seeds of greatness. Athletes must believe that they each have the ability to achieve greatness in their lives. I tell my team that each of them has a choice: You can become great or remain good. This is often decided by work ethic, commitment, and attitude as much as it is by talent. "The difference between great and good is a little extra effort" (Clarence Munn).

I tell my players to *put themselves on the line.* I want my athletes to believe that there are no limitations to what they can accomplish when they work hard and work smart. It bothers me that some athletes limit themselves. It's my job to show them there doesn't have to be any limits to what they can achieve. After all, "Until you try, you don't know what you can do" (Henry James).

Surround yourself with excellence and you become excellent. This saying is one of my all-time favorites. I strongly believe that people act like their environment. Proverbs 13:20 reads, "He that walketh with wise men shall be wise." Hopefully, you can put yourself in an environment that allows you to prosper.

Do not be afraid to succeed. Growing up, I would hear the phrase *afraid to fail,* but I personally believe that some people are afraid to succeed. When you succeed, there is so much more responsibility thrust upon you, and you must be willing to welcome that responsibility. Teach your athletes not to be afraid to be at the top.

Dreams can come true, but it takes work. You can dream all you want, but it's the hard work that makes dreams come true. Hard work builds confidence, and playing with confidence creates success.

You cannot fake confidence. You either believe in yourself, or you do not. As Ralph Waldo Emerson said, "Believe in yourself, and what others think won't matter."

Judge a player's strength on how she acts when things are going wrong. We have all heard the expression, "When the going gets tough, the tough get going." When the game's on the line, you really find out who rises to the challenge.

Do the little things right. A reporter once asked the great baseball player Ty Cobb, who held the record for most stolen bases for nearly half a century, why he nervously kicked first base when he was on the bag. Cobb replied, "Son, let me explain something to you. I was definitely not nervous when I was on first base. But very early in my career, I discovered that if I kicked the first base enough times, I could move it a full two inches toward second base, which gave me that much of a jump towards stealing the base!" It is the little things done right that make a big difference in softball.

Keep pressure on your opponent. When you leave your door open, people walk in. The same holds true in softball. When you let your opponent back into the game, you find yourself asking, *What happened?* Don't give them the opportunity.

Welcome pressure. Go through life welcoming tough times and tough situations for they make you stronger, better adjusted, and more successful. I want athletes who want the ball hit hard to them with bases loaded, two outs, bottom of the seventh with a big game on the line. Talk about having fun!

Build a team of players who complement each other. John Wooden once said, "There is no limit to what can be accomplished when no one cares who gets the credit." Softball is a team sport that relies on everyone being good at what they do to be successful. No team wins without the help of everyone.

Coming Full Circle

Coaching is a tough business. It is one of the few jobs in the world where your livelihood depends on someone else performing well. My relationship with my sport has always been one of give and get. I have always tried to give my best and, in turn, have been rewarded with so much. I am not saying there have not been some hard times, but these have been overshadowed by the joy the sport has given me. In coaching, every day is different, every team is different, and every player is different. These differences present new opportunities and challenges, and you continue to coach because of the sheer joy of the sport's unpredictability and the hope that comes with the next day.

Consider the number of softball coaches who have stayed in the sport 25 years or more. There haven't been that many. The ones who have lasted are the ones who really love what they do and appreciate the special relationships that the sport brings. They are the ones who have gone full circle in their lives.

I've enjoyed an outstanding coaching career because of a simple concept called the circle of success (see figure 1.1). The top of the circle represents the ultimate in coaching, such as winning a national championship or a state title. The bottom of the circle represents a place where no coach wants to be—coaching a losing team. The left side of the circle represents a climb to the top, and the right side is a slide to the bottom. The sides of the circle are where most coaches spend much of their careers. They are either trying to reach the top or stop the fall to the bottom. What you come to realize in coaching—if you stay in this business long enough—is that you do not remain on the top forever and you do not stay on the bottom forever. Every coach comes full circle. It comes with the territory. When you realize and accept all of it, you enjoy the ride much more. My advice is to learn as much at the bottom of the circle as you do at the top. The circle is part of the process that all successful coaches understand and appreciate.

Coaching has been a wonderful and exciting ride for me. Relish the before, during, and after of every game. Few people can call themselves "coach," and what a wonderful ring that title has. Keep your passion alive!

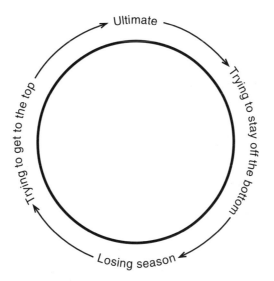

Figure 1.1   The circle of success.

CHAPTER TWO

Making Softball Fun

Margo Jonker

Photo by Robert Barclay, courtesy of Central Michigan University

Making softball fun is easy. Fastpitch softball is fun; it is the greatest sport. Let there be no doubt in anyone's mind. Think of the thrill—the rush when the ball is hit to the center fielder with a runner on second base. The outfielder attacks the grounder, picks it up cleanly as the runner rounds third, fires a strike to the catcher just in time for the catcher to tag the sliding base runner for the third out in the bottom of the seventh inning to ensure the victory for the team. The sound of the crowd, the excitement—what more is there in the world of athletics? Softball is fun.

Having the opportunity to coach young women in the sport is a treasure in itself. It is what the game is truly all about—the people. So I asked my players what makes softball fun for them, and I used their responses throughout this chapter.

Everyone views fun in a unique way, but most define fun as enjoyment or pleasure. How does the game of softball elicit such responses?

First of all we must remember that the game of softball is just that: a game. We must keep it in the proper perspective. As coaches we should always remember that softball is a part of life, often a huge part of life, but not life itself. The lessons our players' learn from softball will help them in the game of life. For example, a great lesson we learn through sport is to realize and identify what we can and cannot control. In softball, some things we cannot control, some we can influence . . . but others we have no influence over. We can teach our players to control their reactions to conditions, but we cannot control the conditions, whether it is a teammate's play, an umpire's decision, or the weather itself. Our players will learn to control what they can and to handle uncontrollables with class and poise. Our own attitude is one item that we can definitely learn to control—although it is often difficult.

Cheering on your teammates is fun.

Attitude

Our attitude, as coaches, makes a major difference in our players having fun. Our enthusiasm is vital. We need to have a passion for the game and for coaching young people. How can we *not* be excited about coaching softball to young people? Working with motivated, quality people in the greatest sport makes it easy to be enthusiastic most of the time. Our athletes need to see that in us.

We must respect the game. It is unfathomable to coach young people in a game and not know that the game is bigger than we are. To make it fun, we must hold the game in highest regard and truly enjoy it. We must value our athletes and enjoy their successes.

How we go into each practice, each drill, and each game makes a difference. We all hope to win every game, but in reality 50 percent of the teams lose. Winning is definitely more fun than losing (a subject we'll go into in more detail later), but we want the whole experience to be enjoyable, win or lose. Look at a team that has lost some games. Is that team still having fun? Are we still excited when our athlete makes a great play?

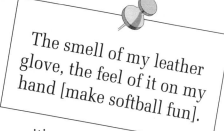

The smell of my leather glove, the feel of it on my hand [make softball fun].

We need to remember what is important at the moment, go into each practice or game with new positive energy. That is our immediate task; our personalities don't matter. High positive energy in every practice and game interaction helps our players have the most fun. We should all coach within ourselves and not try to be someone else. The enthusiasm is shown in our own unique way.

The Game

The actual game—knowing the game, playing the game, being a part of something bigger than we are—now *that* is fun. We need to know as much as possible about the actual game. We need to know all the rules and how they can help us win. Respect the game enough to honor the rules, but do everything within the spirit of the rules to help your team win.

Skills are a major part. Skills combined with strategy executed to perfection bring a new level of enjoyment. Successful athletes usually mean a successful team and fun.

Different coaches have different philosophies. Some coaches play a conservative game: With a runner on first base and no outs, expect the bunt or just hit away. Others have a more aggressive style of play: If the team has the personnel to run, doing so always adds excitement. Throwing in the unpredictable keeps everyone on edge and in the game, but of course, we must coach within our philosophy and our players' abilities. There comes a time, no matter how good a team is, when the sticks are not coming through and we must create runs.

Being alert on the base paths puts pressure on the defense, and taking the extra base when able keeps everyone in the game. With the correct people in the right places, the suicide squeeze gives an element of excitement. Of course, the home run ball is always thrilling; power is a plus for every team and player. Power cannot, however, always be relied on.

Add the hit-and-run, the bunt-and-run, the safety squeeze, the suicide squeeze, the straight steal, and the delayed steal to the power game; *that* keeps every player and every fan in the game and having fun.

The Team

Each member of the team must feel she is an important part of the whole. Each individual has to buy into the team's goals for the year. The team needs to know what the yearly goals are.

Often goals can be reached by different methods. An analogy of travel can explain our path to our goals. When traveling, we have to know the starting point and the destination—but the ways we get there can be very different. We can go by alternate modes of transportation. We could all agree on taking a car, and yet there are choices after that decision. Which route is the best route? Some drivers may opt for the interstates to arrive at their destination faster. Others may choose back roads for a more scenic route. The same is true with a team. There are many ways to do something, but one way has to be agreed on by the team.

> Softball is fun because of the relationships formed on the field, the team unity, being able to accomplish common goals together.

Team personnel need to know each other, trust each other, and be able to depend on each other. How do we do this? Some teams use ropes courses; others have camping trips and tell stories by the campfire; others have a motto for the year. The options are numerous. Finding a route for the year is crucial for the enjoyment of that year's athletes.

If a motto is used, we need to keep returning to it throughout the year and not let it drop. A team that was rebuilding used the video about building the Hoover Dam. They used this theme throughout the year. At different times during the season, different elements of the video were shown, depending on situations that materialized. It was something all the players could relate to. They could all come back to it, relate to it, and draw from it.

Knowing Roles and Responsibilities

To help each member of the team truly enjoy her experience, each must know and accept her role. That is true for the coaches, managers, trainers, and all support staff as well as the players. Each must feel a sense of belonging and importance. Each must have a feeling of ownership.

Because of their positions and skill levels, players automatically fall into different roles. These differences only make the unit stronger. In most games, a pitcher is in the limelight more than an outfielder. A hitter who comes to bat with a runner on second has a more visible role when she gets an RBI than the person who moved the runner to second via a sacrifice bunt. The roles are different, but each depends on the other to reach the goal. Each was essential. Our players must understand and embrace this.

For starters, what are their roles? Is the leadoff hitter expected to come back to the dugout and give her teammates information she may have picked up regarding the speed of the pitch or if she was able to pick a certain pitch? Or is that not in the coach's philosophy? Does the on-deck batter have a role? Each has to be informed of the coach's desires.

All players desire to start, but it's not possible for everyone to start in every game. Nonstarters need to know their roles just as starters should understand theirs. Take our bull pen catcher, for example. Hers is not a glamorous role, but it is essential to our pitchers and to our overall success. She takes pride in making sure the pitchers are both mentally and physically ready to go into the game. Before the game, she goes to the coach and asks who is in relief and in which order. She takes it upon herself to understand that day's plan for the pitching rotation so she can make sure the pitcher is ready if called on.

Everyone needs to know the team is behind her. The atmosphere created on the bench is an especially significant factor for team unity. Each player needs to be into the game. Everyone—starters and nonstarters—must always know the outs, what the defense is doing, and so on. Some players may have the assignment of watching where the middle infielders go on a first and third situation. Other players take great pride in stealing the coach's signs, whether it is the signals to the hitter or to the catcher when the coach is calling the game.

Some players may be called on to keep charts. Charts can be very helpful if they are used. It can be frustrating for a player to keep a chart if it is never used. Someone on the staff may be in charge of making sure the player calls out the information to the appropriate people. The keeper of the chart needs to know it is helpful in reaching the team's ultimate goals. Everyone has to be on the same page with these roles.

The bench players need to know they are an important link. They should be informed when they are doing a good job—that it is expected and appreciated when they are ready to go into the game, that it helps when they support the starters. The starters need to know if the expectations we have of them have been met.

It's fun being in a situation where people are depending on you and you come through for them. Then if you don't come through that one time, they will be there to pick you up.

Each player needs to know her teammates' needs. Some athletes like a teammate coming up to them immediately after an at-bat or a play on defense. Others like to be left alone. Coaches and teammates alike need to know the player well enough to know her wishes. That doesn't mean it is always adhered to—at times it is in the best interest of the athlete not to go with her wishes. But knowing is still

13

important. Then you can make a decision on which course of action to take for the desired outcome.

Communication

Good teams gel, which is a product of honest communication. Communication is a two-way street. Listening is as important, if not more important, than talking. Too often, both parties don't listen to each other. Rather they interrupt or are just waiting for their chance to talk without really listening to what is said. Listening to what is said and how it is said is essential to fully understand the person you are communicating with.

Players need to know they can trust the coach to listen to their concerns, to know their conversation is confidential unless, for the team's or athlete's benefit, there is a need to share the information. The trust factor is huge in a player having a positive experience. An open-door policy allows the player to come in and discuss things with the coach.

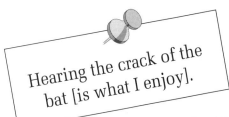

Hearing the crack of the bat [is what I enjoy].

People don't care how much you know until they know how much you care. Listening and getting to know the athlete indicate the coach really cares about her as a person and not just a means to a win/loss record.

There are always conflicts in a group of people who work closely together. How we deal with these conflicts dictates our success. Putting out brushfires before they become forest fires helps. We need to confront issues when they first come up to keep them from getting out of control.

Honest Positive Reinforcement

Whether in a practice setting or in a game setting, players should receive honest positive reinforcement. When a player makes a good effort, whether she succeeds or not, let her know. When a player makes a good play, has a great hit, or does something well, let her know. The danger is in positive reinforcement that is not honest. The key to positive reinforcement is that it is honest; it must be genuinely earned.

An athlete usually knows when she is being told the truth. Telling someone she is doing a good job when she isn't undercuts your credibility and doesn't help anyone. Coaches often say *good job,* but they don't say at what. Was it good effort? Were the hands in the right place on the swing? To tell someone she had a nice swing when it was a poor one is worse than giving no feedback at all. To tell someone a great pitch was thrown when it was a meatball makes the pitcher wonder if the coach is knowledgeable; future advice may be questioned.

The flip side of positive reinforcement is negative reinforcement. When a softball player performs poorly, her self-worth shouldn't be threatened by the coach's comments. Comments should be directed at the performance, not at the player. Indicating only that it was a poor job leaves the athlete short. Unless she has been instructed numerous times before, there needs to be a follow-up session. She needs to know what was done poorly and how it can be corrected.

The Softball Family

The team is all about people. Softball is great because of the people. There are none greater than those who are part of the softball family. When there is a crisis, we need to look no further than our softball sisters and brothers to be there for us. It is truly a family.

Players

Players learn this early. When recruits come on campus, it is so important that they enjoy the people, that they enjoy their future teammates. Often that initial bonding is the main reason a recruit chooses one program over another, an indication how important the people really are.

Players come from different backgrounds, different locations, and different beliefs, but all come together to form a team. It is exciting when players come from different parts of the country or different cultures. They can learn about the differences and likenesses of all involved. How many times are there van conversations that discuss how different words and phrases are said in the different parts of the country? How many times are life questions discussed that truly broaden the educational experience? Players learn to accept and, yes, even embrace differences. What better education is there? What can be more fun, more rewarding than that? What can be better than these individuals with all their differences bonding together into one unit with common goals?

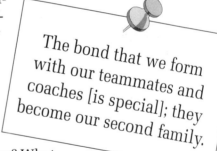

The bond that we form with our teammates and coaches [is special]; they become our second family.

Many of the best life friendships are formed within the team. We learn to depend on our teammates in crucial situations in games. We also learn to depend on our teammates in crucial situations in life. Quantity and quality time is spent together in practice, in rehab, on the road, and in social settings.

Team chemistry often determines if the team is successful or not. A lesser-talented team can defeat a more highly skilled team if the chemistry is there. That is why we play the game on the field. Isn't it so much more fun in life when we enjoy each other's company? People enjoy sharing things with others. That is why team sports are great. We depend on the others and they depend on us.

Alumni

The family goes beyond this year's team; it includes the alumni. Many programs have alumni games. The alumni enjoy coming back and seeing what this year's team has. They love reminiscing about the great times they had.

The current team players watch the fun the alumni has. The seniors often comment on their anticipation of being on the other side of the field the next year. It shows everyone involved that it is bigger than the current team. There is a bigger family out there.

To make a connection to the alumni and the program's history, some teams have current players research the players who wore their numbers before them. The coach gives the current players the names and addresses of the alumni with their common numbers. The players write the alumni and ask about their experiences and the significance of the number to them. It helps connect the past with the present.

I love the traditions.

The current team should know the history of the program. They should know who went before them and what was significant to them. It makes them appreciate what they have and identify with the alumni. It is significant for us all to know how those who came before us helped build what we have, to appreciate efforts that were made. The traditions of a program are thus carried from year to year. Tradition.

Fans

The softball family extends to the fans—the fans who are friends and relatives of players, the fans who are true to their team with no direct connection to a particular player but just enjoy watching the game. A higher level of energy is present when there is a large attendance. The electricity is enhanced when the stands are full of fans cheering on the plays and players, sighing on any misplay. These sounds all add to the overall experience of making the game fun.

To get fans to the game, there needs to be a plan to market softball as well as all the other sports. We have a great product. The word needs to get out. Once fans come, they are often hooked for life. Being at the game is great for the players' and the fans' enjoyment, but promoting softball is also a must for the future of the game.

Support Staff

We depend on our support staff. Look at all the people who help our games run smoothly. A good grounds crew, one that takes pride in the field, enhances the experience for players, coaches, and fans alike. Players enjoy it when the field is in great shape—when the outfield grass is cut in a certain pattern, when the edges are sharp. Having a quality field to play on adds to the quality of play and the aesthetics. Our grounds crew takes pride in how well the team does. The players appreciate the grounds crew and the great job they do. The athletes need to let them know how much their work is appreciated, as they are also a part of the family.

Whoever else works to support the team—the video people, the sport information people, the trainers—it is important that the players acknowledge their work. It makes for a close-knit family and adds to the overall experience for all involved. To say *thank you* only takes a minute, but it means the world.

Competition

People love to compete. To have a great experience, it is essential that the players love to compete. That is usually not a problem—even bus trips often include card games. Athletes love to compete.

It's fun to compete!

Schedule

To enhance the experience, careful consideration should be given to the schedule. Too easy a schedule takes away the excitement of winning, the anticipation, and the need to prepare in the best possible way. Too difficult a schedule is frustrating, defeating, even demoralizing at times. A good schedule is a mix.

Set a schedule that allows the team to gain confidence while being totally challenged. The strength of a schedule may be different from year to year, depending on the strength of the team in a particular season. In a rebuilding year, the schedule isn't going to be as difficult as in a year the team is anticipating competing for the championship. When the team travels and when the team is at home helps dictate a quality schedule. Most players enjoy playing in front of the home crowd. Bring in a talented team, one that is a rival, and play the game in front of the home crowd. Now that adds a level of excitement and fun!

Within the Team

How does each player reach her potential? For many players it means being pushed by someone. With no one competing for her position, the player can become complacent. She can settle for something less than her best.

Competition within the team affects how each player prepares for position play, how she conditions, and other intangible areas of her game. It is healthy for a player to be challenged within her position. If that's not possible in a given year, each can still be inspired to be her best in other ways. For example, give her challenges in the conditioning program; pair her with someone who is a step faster; encourage her to pick up her intensity and get one step quicker. Not all players are in the starting lineup, but all can compete for a position. This concept illustrates roles and knowing the importance of those roles.

Trips

Trips that teams make, whether near or far, give an opportunity for players and staff to build relationships because of time spent together and experiences shared. These trips to other cities, states, and possibly countries can be tremendous fun.

It's a chance to travel, to visit different places, places I wouldn't have gotten a chance to experience in another way.

Organization

Organization is key in making a trip all it can be. Pay attention to details. It is helpful for everything to be prearranged so that the athletes know everything will go as smoothly as possible. Of course, no matter how well it is planned, something unexpected is bound to come up. This is when flexibility is needed.

When the players know that everything was planned and there was a glitch in the plans, they often take it in stride. Not only do they take it in stride, but it may be something to talk about years later when they get together at those alumni events.

An itinerary handed out before departure helps answer everyone's questions and makes things go smoother. Have maps for the drivers in case someone gets lost or stopped at a light, and develop a plan for how the vehicles are to follow one another. Have a plan at the airport that everyone knows about. (Cell phones sure are helpful in this area.) Upperclassmen can assist here. They have been in these situations before, so they can address questions from the younger players. Make meal arrangements so that the team doesn't have to wait for hours to be served. Make sure athletes have the proper nutrition options and can time their meals appropriately for competition.

If the schedule allows, it is great to do other things while on a trip. If there is a day off on the spring trip, a side trip to Disney, Busch Gardens, or anything unique enhances the experience and adds fun!

Parents and Families

Each coach has a different philosophy regarding how much interaction players and their families are to have during softball trips. The key is to make sure everyone is informed. Is there time for the players to go to dinner with their families? Is there a set time for meetings every night, making sure the players are back and ready to prepare for the next day's activities? Can the parents and families join the team at the restaurants? Are the parents to stay in the same hotels as the team? Some don't allow parents, families, friends, or anyone other than team personnel in the players' rooms. The players are allowed to go to a parent's room or the lounge, but players' rooms are off-limits for all nonteam members. As long as it is mapped out in advance, there should be no problems.

Some send parents local maps to the game fields, motel lists, a general departure schedule, and a game schedule for the year. That way they can make arrangements and be able to cheer their daughters to victory. As long as everyone works within the perimeters established by the coaching staff, everything should run smoothly.

Success

What is success? Certainly part of success is determined by the win/loss record of a team.

How do you make softball fun? That's easy—*win*. Everyone loves to win. But not every team that wins has fun. There is more to it than that. And how do we win? The key is being willing to work hard enough and prepare well enough to win.

It's fun to win!

Part of winning is attitude. You have to believe you can win. Create an environment in which the softball player can be successful. She has to be comfortable enough to reach her potential within the framework of the team.

If we can help each individual reach her potential, we certainly have won. If we can help players improve each year and come closer to their peak performance on a regular basis, that is success. Therefore—fun!

When each student athlete reaches her potential, when the team is always put first, and when each player knows and accepts her role on the team, the team will reach its potential. The only way for each player to reach her potential is by productive practices.

A great deal of time is spent in practice each year. Consequently, for softball to be fun, practices have to be fun. Practices should be organized yet flexible, intense yet relaxed, competitive yet set in a learning environment.

A practice plan is helpful, but the practice plan shouldn't be so rigid that it can't be changed. If learning a skill needs more time, we need to make adjustments to the predetermined schedule. Each coach needs to be utilized to the utmost to make practice beneficial for each athlete and the team as a whole. In practice, we must attempt to strengthen a player's or team's weakness but not spend all our time on that one weakness. We also need to spend quality and quantity time on the athlete's strength. It's fun to attempt to get better at both weaknesses and strengths.

During practices, there are many times when a great deal of intensity is essential. We want to practice as we play, but if something funny happens it should be relaxed enough for the players to feel free to laugh. Afterward, it's time to get back to business. Just like in a game, the players have moments of higher levels of concentration and intensity versus other moments. When a batter is in the batter's box and the pitch is on the way, the concentration is going to be greater than when the defensive team is running off the field. Make practices as gamelike as possible. Since most players enjoy competition, incorporate competitive drills into each or most practices. When players lack competition, these drills intensify their competitiveness.

Our practices are fun.

Each practice should have a purpose; therefore, all the practices as a whole need to cover every situation that is found in the game. At the beginning of the year, the practice environment is more of learning than of drilling. The closer to the competitive season, the more competitive the drills are. Practices can be fun. Practices must be fun.

A team needs discipline to be successful—discipline in practice, in games, on the field, and off the field. Practice is the best place to make sure players know the expectations. The difficulty with discipline is how to be consistent. Consistency is so difficult and so important.

Every situation—on or off the field—is handled differently for each student athlete because no two situations are identical. But discipline must be handled consistently. The players need to know what to expect. The players want discipline, and they want it to be consistent.

Pride and Tradition

The players who play the game, the umpires who officiate, the fans who follow each game, the coaches—they all take pride in softball's strong traditions. I relish days when I see athletes take pride in their performance, when athletes take pride in the team they are part of—*wow*—now that's fun!

Look on the field and see your players with the gleam in their eyes when they come to third base after a stand-up triple. See the excitement when the team turns the double play to end a rally. Watch the runner jump up into the arms of her teammates after sliding in safely on a perfectly executed suicide squeeze that wins the game. Now you know you have succeeded in making softball fun!

CHAPTER THREE

Competing With Class

Carol Bruggeman

Photo courtesy of Christy Connoyer

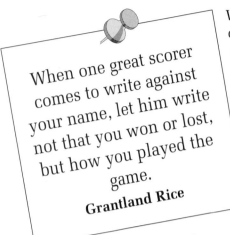

When one great scorer comes to write against your name, let him write not that you won or lost, but how you played the game.

Grantland Rice

We have all heard the comment, "Wow, that coach sure has class!" An image of a certain coach comes into each and every one of our minds when we read this statement. But why do some coaches fall into the classy category and others do not? What is it that a coach does or says that makes him or her classy? And how on earth does a coach *compete* with class? After all, competition is hard, where lines are drawn and winning is the only thing that matters, right?

Competing with class is a choice, and coaches who choose to do so are the biggest winners of all. Competing with class has its foundation in sportsmanship. At the heart of sportsmanship, *how* one goes about winning and losing is just as important as winning and losing itself. This process can be a better measure of who we really are as coaches than the outcome. At the core of every coach who competes with class are basic beliefs and philosophies about the game, the coaching profession, and ultimately, how life should be lived. Standards are written down, believed in, committed to, and lived every day with no exceptions.

To compete with class means to treat others with respect. It means maintaining a positive attitude with players, staff members, opponents, umpires, and fans. It means accepting the fact that a coach is a role model with an image to uphold—24 hours a day, 7 days a week, 365 days a year. It means believing that coaches represent not only themselves during competition but also their players, schools, and staff. It means treating others the way one would like to be treated in return. Most of all, it means having the will to compete and win, and doing so in a way that makes everyone associated proud.

It is important to remember that class is a subjective concept. People perceive situations differently. For example, if a coach is emotional and yells a lot and the team wins, he is a great motivator. If the coach yells a lot and the team loses, he is too tough on the team. If a coach is laid back and the team wins, she is a great player's coach. If a coach is laid back and the team loses, she is not enough of a disciplinarian. The bottom line is that when a coach wins, what the coach is doing is perceived to be right. A coach must trust his or her instincts, experience, and preparation. Do not change for the sake of changing. Trust yourself as a coach and always keep the faith in what you are doing and believe to be right.

Competition

Competing with class does not mean being soft; it simply means you do everything in your power to win while maintaining the core values in which you believe. Typically, these core values include integrity, honesty, selflessness, respect, and love.

An example of a coach competing with class and holding onto core values is exemplified by John Thompson, former men's basketball coach at Georgetown. In an NCAA men's basketball tournament game, Georgetown was ahead by one point with only a few seconds left in the game. A Georgetown player made an ill-advised pass that allowed the opponent to win the game, preventing Georgetown from going to the Final Four. Coach Thompson, a legendary role model and successful man, could have hung his head, screamed at the player, and pouted off the court. Instead, without hesitation, he ran onto the court and wrapped the sobbing player in his arms. "Son," he said, "if that's the worst thing that ever happens to you in your life, you'll be just fine." Wow. That's class. Coach Thompson never lost sight of his values and the lessons he wanted to teach his players, even in the heat of one of the biggest moments of his coaching career.

Competition can bring out the best and worst in people. As coaches, we have all gotten a little hot under the collar at times. Some equate being competitive with being a jerk and accept behaviors during competition that would never be accepted elsewhere. However, coaches who compete with class remain the same before, during, and after competition. They are prepared and therefore more relaxed when competing. Who they are carries over into all facets of their lives, including game competition. There is no Dr. Jekyl and Mr. Hyde.

Probably the most important factor in developing class is to acquire a healthy attitude about competition. A coach stands a good chance to be successful and reliable if he or she can master such a healthy attitude. Coaches must respect both themselves and the opponent, and they must remain composed in difficult situations. During competition, look for ways to improve a situation. Ask not Why did this happen? but rather How should I respond? Level-headed decisions under stress are valuable in situations far beyond the sport itself.

Practices are for coaches; competitions are for players. My idea of a perfect game is one in which only the players and the game itself are noticed. The coaches and umpires seem to disappear. Too often during competition, coaches try to control everything happening. Let the players play! Sure, some adjustments need to be made and strategies developed. However, if coaches have truly done their job at practice, their role during competition should be to motivate, encourage, and guide. Then your players, your staff, the fans, and the umpires have the opportunity to see you compete with class.

Image and Appearance

The old truism states, *You never get a second chance to make a good first impression.* Think of how easy it is to judge people from one glance or one conversation. Coaches who have class consistently are aware of their appearance. Their appearance is always neat and appropriate for the situation. They pay attention to detail. Therefore, if you want to compete with class, first sell yourself through your appearance. Two things happen: one, you feel better about yourself and, thus, more confident about your coaching. Two, your team, the media, the fans, and the opponent immediately offer you a level of respect as you set the tone with your appearance.

Whether we like it or not, image does matter. A coach who portrays an image of confidence, grace, poise, and competitiveness earns many supporters; a coach who portrays an image of arrogance, incivility, panic, and rudeness does not. By exuding a positive, confident image, you have positioned yourself to succeed.

Body language plays a significant role in appearance. As a coach, exude confidence and energy for your team. Your team can read you like a book and feed off your emotions. When you are tight, they play tight. When you are confident, they play confident. When you are relaxed, they become relaxed. The challenge is to be intense without being tense. Coaches with class do not slouch, throw their heads into their hands after an error, or shake their heads with every pitch. Every now and then a smile is exactly what a team needs. Remember, we do play a game. If something funny happens during competition, go ahead and laugh! Competition should not change who you are or how you act to an extreme.

Two well-respected coaches in women's basketball are Nell Fortner, head coach of the WNBA's Indiana Fever, and Carolyn Peck, head coach of the WNBA's Orlando Miracle. (Both served as head coaches at Purdue in the late '90s.) Ask anyone who knows anything about women's basketball, and they will tell you Coach Fortner and Coach Peck are two of the classiest coaches in the business. They will also tell you they are the most driven and competitive, and both hate to lose. Coach Fortner and Coach Peck are consistently aware of their appearance, and they each work with their staff, the media, and the officials with respect. They both understand how a positive image can develop a favorable rapport. Coach Fortner and Coach Peck are composed, committed, honest, and embrace sportsmanship. In winning at every level, they have represented themselves with style, poise, and confidence.

Do these two successful coaches know how to win? Yes. Do these two successful coaches love to compete? Yes. Do these two coaches compete with class? Absolutely. Not once have Coach Fortner or Coach Peck publicly lost their love for the game or their staff and players; not once have they belittled their opponents; not once have they lost sight of their core values; and not once have they demanded anything but the best from their players. They are living proof that you can compete with class and truly be successful.

Katie Crabtree, one of our most talented players at Purdue, taught me a rewarding lesson in image and the importance of presenting the image you desire. It was May 1997 (the third year of conference play for our new program), and our team was competing in the Big Ten tournament in Iowa City, Iowa. Katie, a junior in high school, was being recruited by several Big Ten schools and attended the tournament to see the teams in action. I had never talked to her prior to that tournament. Despite two tough one-run games, the Boilermakers ended on the short side of the score and lost both contests. Although disappointed, our team played hard and I was proud of their effort, attitude, and competitiveness.

In July of that same year, Katie committed to an official visit at Purdue during my first phone conversation with her. I was thrilled at the thought of her becoming a Boilermaker, but I had to ask her why she was so confident in making us one of her top five choices. She excitedly told me how she had watched us at the Big Ten tournament and was impressed with our hustle, attitude, and fight. She also had noticed and appreciated my coaching style. After watching us for two games, which we lost, she knew she wanted to play for Purdue. Amazing. That true story illustrates how important image can be to you and your program.

Attitude

Attitude is a choice. One can choose to be positive or negative in any situation. As coaches, we continually ask our players to control the things they can. Players cannot control the umpires, the weather, or the fans. Therefore, we try to guide our players to focus on the things they can control. Coaches should heed their own advice.

We all have a choice on how to act and react every day. Every choice has a consequence. For example, if a coach composes an organized, detailed practice plan (choice), then practice runs more smoothly and more is accomplished (consequence). If a coach wings it at practice (choice), then practice is more likely to be chaotic, and no goals are achieved (consequence). Choices made with a positive and productive attitude prepare a coach to be ready to compete with class. When a coach has a negative attitude, his or her mind is cluttered with negative thoughts that ultimately affect coaching decisions. It is a challenge to remain in control of our thoughts, attitudes, and actions, but the more we strive to achieve some success in this area, the better the outcome. A positive attitude is contagious and powerful.

Players

Competing with class means treating your players with respect on and off the field. Long after eligibility is exhausted, players seldom remember every pitch or at bat of every game of every season of every year. What they do remember is how they were treated and how they developed and whether or not their coach really cared about them. Take the time to let them know you care!

A coach must assume many roles. Coaches must inspire, counsel, motivate, discipline, explain, and teach. Of all the things a coach must do, communication is the most important. If a coach can effectively communicate with players, half the battle is won. Too often, we tell and direct without explaining why. As the teacher's creed states, "I hear and I forget, I see and I remember, I do and I understand." It is important that your players understand what is expected of them, both on and off the field.

Coaches who compete with class accept the responsibility to their players of being a solid role model. Coaches can and do affect lives. Before we demand effort, punctuality, commitment, and class from our players, we must lead and motivate by example. Coaches are role models both at and away from the softball diamond. Respect is earned when team needs are placed in front of any individual needs. Win or lose, you should always be there for your team. I would even suggest that coaches be more demanding after a win than a loss. This approach challenges your team as you continue to push them when they are successful. After a loss, your team feels bad enough as it is, and they typically need support rather than an earful of reprimands.

Teaching and discipline can be done with class. The appearance and attitude of your players and staff are direct reflections of you. A coach must take responsibility for how a team looks on the field and in public. Every aspect of a program starts at the top, and accountability must be accepted. A coach should also be organized and knowledgeable.

Most coaches develop a set of rules, guidelines, or a code of conduct for their teams. At Purdue, we have several items that we all must adhere to and believe in to ensure a successful year. Instead of simply writing these rules down or having the players sign a copy, we try different methods. One year we wrote the rules on a white, spongy, 12-inch softball. Each player wrote items on the ball as we discussed each one in detail. Words like *honesty*, *academics*, *respect*, and *loyalty* all appeared on the ball, one by one. Each player signed it, then I passed around a blank ball for them all to sign so that I could keep one in my office. Our theme for the year was *Take care of the ball.* That theme applied to our action on the softball diamond as well as off the diamond. Anytime we had a problem with a player, we would take out the softball with our rules on it and discuss where the breakdown occurred.

Another year, we spray painted a set of eight keys, representing our keys to success, for each team member. Each key was a different color and had its own unique meaning. For example, the blue key represented respect; the yellow key, attitude; the red key, love. We all felt the importance of having and showing respect for one's teammates, the coaching staff, the softball program, Purdue University, the media, fans, and self. If an athlete was late to a training room appointment, all we had to do was take out the blue key and begin the discussion about respecting other's time. It was a fun way to commit to our rules.

Staff

Coaches who compete with class remain loyal to their staffs and value their input, abilities, and talents. Everyone on your staff must believe in your philosophies. Your staff is an extension of you, so it is imperative that you teach them the hows and whys of your program.

Surround yourself with staff members who have strengths different from yours. Communication with your staff is vital to success, as open lines of communication can keep your program flowing smoothly. Have regular staff meetings to discuss the direction and status of your program and players. Everyone must be on the same page. When conflicts emerge, remember this: There is a time and a place for discussion, and in front of your team is never an option. Your team should feel a sense of togetherness from your staff at all times. Having a staff that competes with class can be an extremely powerful tool.

Get to know your staff members, both on and off the field. Do little things for them that show how much their hard work is appreciated. When is the last time you did something out of the ordinary for your staff? The more they feel valued and appreciated, the harder they work for you. Develop their individual skills and assist them in their professional endeavors.

Opponents

Do you ever look at your schedule, see a particular opponent, and cringe? In general, there are two reasons for cringing. One, the opponent is very competitive. The team is ranked in the top 10, works hard, and is loaded with talent. You know it will be a tough game, and your players will have to be at their best to compete. Two, you know the team is unsportsmanlike. The team will be mouthy, dirty, or rude and it will not be fun to even play the game.

Coaches who compete with class treat opponents with respect, realizing that the treatment of others far outweighs a win or loss. I have seen coaches criticize the opposing team, yelling obscenities and derogatory comments. Worse, some coaches allow or teach their players to have the same behavior. Trying to rattle an opponent or win the game this way is a waste of time. Disciplined teams are not fooled one bit, and you, as the coach, have ultimately lost. You have lost respect, credibility, and probably the game. When coaches use those tactics to win, I question their core values and whether or not they really belong in coaching as role models.

Umpires

My father was a softball umpire, and I learned at an early age that not many people appreciate or like umpires. Some fans attend games simply to see how far they can push an umpire. Coaches who compete with class realize that umpires are human beings, too. Various coaches whom I respect have told me it helped them to remember that an umpire is someone's dad or mom, brother or sister. In addition, we would not be able to have a fair game without umpires.

We all have witnessed coaches spend the entire competition badgering the umpire. They try to intimidate or work the official. When a call goes against them, they fly onto the field with a red face, veins bulging, screaming one inch from the umpire's face about their displeasure with the call. Two things happen when yelling at an official: One, they tune you out just as you would do with someone yelling at you. Two, you as a coach look ridiculous and class goes right out the door.

We all believe in standing up for our players. It may be much more effective to hold a directed conversation with an umpire. Asking questions is much more effective than questioning calls—for example, try asking, "Where was that last pitch?" versus "How could you miss that call?" You may or may not get that particular call, but you are certainly taken more seriously and are listened to more closely on the next one. On the other hand, umpires may test a coach throughout a game with unnecessary comments. Be the bigger person and walk away. At times, by saying nothing you can speak volumes to your players.

Umpires and Coaches

Kathy Strahm

Coaches cannot work with umpires. To *work with* implies that the two parties have a common goal. Umpires and coaches do not. The umpire's goal is to ensure that neither team gets an unfair advantage over the other. The umpire is neither team's ally or enemy. Umpires judge their own success on whether they were able to conduct a fair and impartial game in which the teams' skills determined the winner.

The coach's goal, on the other hand, is to fight for every possible advantage for her or his team and to direct the team's talents toward victory. Coaches cannot work with umpires to achieve these goals. Doing so would mean one team would gain an unfair advantage over the other.

Although coaches cannot work with umpires, they can improve their communication with them. Some techniques work and some do not. The key for coaches is to make certain the lines of communication remain open. Once the communication line between the coach and the umpire is damaged or severed, the game is a long one for everyone involved.

What Works

Take control of your players. If your pitcher is whining and begging in the circle, take control and stop it before the umpire does. You can expect better communication with the umpire when you assume responsibility for your players. Show the umpire that you recognize your job and are willing to do it while letting the umpire do her or his job.

Teach your catchers how to respect the umpire. Holding the pitch is a blatant attempt to show up the umpire and only mangles the possibility of your catcher doing the very best job for your pitcher. Teach your catchers how to communicate with the umpire without turning around, drawing lines in the dirt, or holding pitches.

Ask questions when you do not understand a ruling. If, for example, you want to know why the call was obstruction and not interference, wait for a dead ball and ask the umpire who made the call. Remember: There is a difference between asking a question and voicing an opinion. If you sincerely want a question answered, ask it professionally, then give enough time for the umpire to answer it. If all you want to do is express your displeasure with the call, then say what you want to say and leave.

Make a conscious effort not to let the fans know you disagree with the call. If you have a serious problem with the balls and strikes that have been called, instead of shouting and demonstrating your displeasure from the coaching box for all the world to see, call for time. Pull out your lineup card, turn away from the spectators, and stand next to the umpire as though discussing your lineup. From this position, you can tell the umpire exactly what you think of those last calls and still keep the lines of communication open.

What Doesn't Work

Arguing every call that goes against you doesn't work. Asking the umpire to go for help on every judgment call does nothing but destroy your credibility and damage communication. Crying wolf works the same on the ball field as it does in Aesop's fable. Similarly, constant complaining that every pitcher and every pitch is illegal damages your ability to communicate with the umpires on genuine pitching issues and on all subsequent matters.

Throwing things never works. Whether it's throwing equipment or temper tantrums, throwing needs to be limited to balls on the diamond. Losing control of yourself or allowing your players to lose control shows the umpire that attempts to communicate with you may be a waste of effort.

Don't try to intimidate the umpires, and don't ever, under any circumstances, touch them. Intimidation tactics sever the communication line, and physical contact with the umpire sends the coach directly to the parking lot. Neither situation helps your team. Instead of taking a confrontational in-your-face position, stand next to the umpire or at a distance just outside the umpire's personal space. Keep your hands down and never threaten the umpire. The coach who resorts to threats can expect that the word will get around. That coach will continue to have a difficult time communicating with fellow umpires in a way that could have benefited the team.

Again, coaches cannot work with umpires, but they can work beside them. Coaches have the job of leading their teams to victory, and umpires have the job of administering the game fairly and impartially. Bad communication between coaches and umpires makes it difficult for coaches to obtain every possible advantage for their team. In turn, effective communication between the two parties makes it easier for both to do their jobs and achieve their respective goals.

Kathy Strahm has umpired every major fastpitch event in the world, including the Women's College World Series, the NCAA Division II and III National Championships, the Pan Am Games, the Women's World Championships, and the 1996 Olympic Games. Formerly the ASA Umpire-in-Chief of Indianapolis, she is currently the umpire coordinator for the Big Ten Conference and an NCAA Softball Umpire Advisor.

Parents

Ah, parents. Parents are here to stay. They can be your biggest support group or your biggest nightmare. For some reason, everyone feels they can coach and knows how to coach. Many of them have no problem telling you this at any time, at any place, or in front of any one. Not many people tell a plumber, or an accountant, or a stockbroker how to do his or her job. For some reason, coaching is different.

Competing with class means addressing parents with class. I am fortunate at Purdue to have a terrific, supportive group of parents. However, we have all observed the overbearing dad or mom who sits (or hangs) right behind the home plate fence and screams, grimaces, or cries with every pitch his or her daughter throws. We have also seen parents yelling at coaches from the stands with regard to coaching or decisions about playing time.

Parents are serious about their daughter's softball career. Before the season begins, let them know your coaching philosophies and goals for the team. This information can be shared at a formal meeting or through a letter. Remind parents you are available to discuss any issue but that there is an appropriate time and place.

One idea I have found helpful over the years is to welcome conversations with parents at any time, except when it concerns playing time issues. Before I discuss playing time, I invite the parents to attend practice for one week. Now they have the opportunity to witness the same work ethic, attitudes, and performance levels that the coaching staff sees every day. It is only natural for parents to arrive on game day and want to see their daughter play. However, we all know playing time is earned in practice.

Get parents involved in feeling a part of the team. Include them in potluck dinners, promotional activities, and end of the year banquets. Giving parents a clear understanding of what you believe in as a coach and where you are going is important in preparing to compete with class.

Recruiting

This topic is near and dear to my heart. Recruiting is one of the most important things we do. Whether you are a high school, travel ball, or collegiate coach, we all do some form of recruiting. We do our best to find young women who fit our programs. We are excited when they join us and disappointed when they do not.

Class plays a huge role in recruiting. There is no place for cheating or for negative recruiting. Concentrate your efforts on selling your program, not bad-mouthing another. Unfortunately, negative recruiting happens more than we would like to believe, but I have found that eventually negative recruiting catches up with coaches.

Sometimes when an athlete tells a coach she is not going to his or her school, the coach is rude and mean. This does not make anyone feel better and nothing positive happens. Additionally, young players talk to each other about recruiting. It hurts you to be derogatory to a prospect when at a later time you are recruiting a teammate of that prospect, and she is seriously considering your program.

It is equally important to be yourself when recruiting. Be careful not to have a recruiting personality and a coaching personality. I have heard many travel ball coaches tell their high school seniors that they will have two coaches in college: the one who recruited them and the one who coaches them. Coaches who are themselves, both in recruiting and on the field, have more realistic relationships with their players. The players also are not surprised by the coach's behavior once at the school. Coaches who compete with class believe in consistency.

Final Thoughts

Coaching is an extremely volatile profession with personnel changes nearly every year. One way to gain some stability is to surround yourself with successful, quality people. Do this in both your coaching profession and in life. Do not make time for anything negative in your coaching preparation. You can control whom you listen to. Sport psychologists suggest that we get exactly what we expect. Expect success. Set your standards high so that you can achieve great things. Surround yourself with the people in your life who can take you where you want to go.

Competing with class is important because of the life lessons involved. Coaches affect lives. Make it your challenge to leave the field a better coach every day. Also, challenge your players to leave the field as better players and better people every day. Success can be measured in many ways. One of those ways is through wins and losses; however, sometimes winning and losing are out of our control. We do control our attitudes, actions, and decisions. We are successful if we can compete with class and teach our players valuable life lessons along the way.

CHAPTER FOUR

Outhustling Your Opponent

Teresa Wilson

Photo courtesy of the University of Washington

When told that hustle and the University of Washington softball program are synonymous, I was honored, yet my first reaction was "Is there any other way?" We all know that games are often won or lost because of hustle, either directly or indirectly. I tend to look at hustle as the norm. I often notice the teams that don't hustle and wonder why.

Hustle is a pretty obvious trait. Run out the ground balls and the pop flies. Dive and slide on anything close. Sprint on and off the field. Go hard all the time, whether practice or a game, even when it looks like it won't matter and even when no one else is watching. These are the obvious, outward signs of hustle, what we perceive as the basic definition. But when you look deeper, you find that hustle isn't something you turn on and off like a faucet. It's an attitude, philosophy, personality, and approach that become the foundation for everything you do. If you understand the foundation, then the reason for hustle as a by-product also becomes obvious. But with this knowledge comes responsibility. It's not enough to simply give your team the command to hustle. You must provide the foundation, set the table, and lead patiently until your team accepts ownership and adopts the philosophy as their own.

Hustle is born of a team made up of mentally tough players with one mind and one mission who are motivated to succeed. The challenge for the coach is to get the team to that stage.

Motivation

I think of motivation as the fuel in the gas tank. Without it, you aren't going far. Of course, there are different types and qualities of fuel. As a college coach, I am very fortunate. The athletes I coach most likely would never have reached this level without being highly motivated. Motivation has two sources—internal and external.

Internal Motivation

Internal motivation can be identified, almost exclusively, as a product of an individual's personality. Internal motivation can be affected or enhanced by knowledge, environment, circumstances, maturity, or forms of external motivation, but my first indication of an athlete's level of internal motivation is based directly on identification of certain personality traits.

Although athletes possess different personality traits, certain personality traits are more common in elite athletes. The most coachable athletes tend to be open-minded, eager to learn, curious, hard working, and in possession of a high level of respect for themselves, others, and the game they play. They typically set high standards for themselves and have a deep sense of pride and a high level of perseverance. They also can remain objective. They differentiate between the person off the field and the athlete on the field. The person off the field has emotions associated with that individual's personality; the athlete on the field has one mission—to win. The most coachable athletes welcome feedback, love to be challenged, and possess a passion for the game that motivates them to become students of the game at a high level.

Internal motivation is the drive that separates the good athlete from the great athlete. It provides the athlete with the discipline (the term I most often associate with internal motivation) to train hard and the desire to maintain her high standards while playing the game year after year. Internal motivation, most often, is the key to longevity and the avoidance of burnout.

To inspire internal motivation, I have found the most effective tool to be the sense of accomplishment, discipline, and pride followed by the reward of responsibility and ownership. If you can convince the young mind that the sense of achievement she feels when she knows deep inside that she has given her best and has done the task the right way, you have effectively instilled ownership. This ultimately is the most powerful sense of internal motivation.

We talk to our team at length about the difference between a good athlete and a great athlete. Great athletes find a way to get the job done right when they least feel like being there. Only the student athlete knows if she has given everything she has. Others can guess but never know for sure. Ownership is the lesson you want them to exercise once they enter the real world. It will serve them well for the rest of their lives.

External Motivation

External motivation is any form of motivation that comes from outside the body, such as games on TV, highlight reels, or other videotapes. Some players are motivated by another athlete and the admiration for her skill level or the desire to be more like her. External motivation could also be in the form of a reward for an excellent performance, and discipline often motivates a driven athlete, as does both success and failure, each motivating her to try again. Quotes, speakers, books, teammates, discussions—all of these forms as well have their place during the course of the year to provide any additional external motivation.

Over the years, I have found yelling and screaming to be the least effective form of motivation. Today's athletes simply don't respond to that type of motivation. Certain actions may merit a firm discussion, with the motivation being to avoid those types of discussions in the future, but that is the exception and not the rule. Use yelling and screaming too much, and the only thing coaches accomplish is getting tuned out. With today's athletes, we must find a different way.

The most effective form of external motivation is, without a doubt, positive reinforcement. The word of praise or the pat on the back for the mental, physical, emotional, or skill-related task still elicits the most immediate and satisfying form of external motivation.

Learning

Motivation and learning go hand in hand. Our learning process involves exploring and ultimately becoming comfortable with new methods and levels of problem solving. Many people are negatively affected by the pressure of time lines and the task of finding a solution because they think there is only one way to solve a problem and only one correct answer. A student of the game must accept the fact that often there is not a single way, a single answer, or even a correct answer to solve a problem within a time line.

When players become more familiar with problem solving at a higher level and learn to apply different methods to different situations with different time lines, they open up a whole new dimension of doing things. During this process, we eliminate failure as we know it from the equation. Failure simply becomes part of the process and is perceived as a challenge and not an outcome.

The process becomes a lesson in perspective. Many times, players feel like giving up, but through life—and softball—they learn to persevere. Through success, failure, hardship, motivation, and challenge, we learn to become better athletes, then ultimately, better people.

Successful people do not set easy goals; they set goals that challenge themselves. We challenge our team daily throughout the year to push themselves, set high goals, be willing to risk failure—then we can put ourselves in a position to succeed. Improvement is a process. Through failure, evaluation, adjustment, and repetition, we eventually reach levels of success we would initially not have thought attainable.

We must first reach and affect the individual, then the group. How does this concept evolve to affect the many, instead of just the one?

Team Chemistry and Cohesion

Each and every member of your team must establish her own learning curve, and each will inevitably struggle to gain confidence and motivation throughout the learning process. The team becomes stronger as the players grow as individuals. Team cohesion and team chemistry are two of the major factors in determining whether a team is successful. Many times people consider cohesion and chemistry to be the same thing. I believe they are related, yet quite different.

Team chemistry as a product of the team that has set a mission statement for themselves and the team. They don't have to be the closest team off the field, but once they walk into that locker room or step across that white line, their mission is singular. They function as one unit with one heartbeat and one mindset. The respect and unity they have for each other as teammates and athletes serve as the driving factor during their quest to achieve their mission.

In the physical sense, team chemistry is timing. In softball, the team that has chemistry is the team that seems to be in sync, whether they are on offense—stealing bases, situational hitting—or defense—fielding a base hit, a bunt, a ground ball, or turning a double play. Softball is all about timing. To spectators, it seems as if a player's movements are seamless: She doesn't have to look up to see the individual she is throwing to nor does she have to see the outcome of the throw. She just knows. Players are fluid in their movements, timing, and communication. They function as one unit. This is a beautiful sight to behold and the result of months of hard work and commitment.

Cohesion is the bond that makes a team stick together. It is an achievement, indeed, to bring together 20 people from every walk of life, every background, and every part of the country, and develop this cohesion that enables them to function with complete chemistry as one.

Cohesion begins with the recruiting process and involves identifying what your team needs to achieve a balance of personality types. We strive for a mix of personality types. A good, lively mix is a combination of natural leaders, vocal leaders, leaders by example, feisty players, calm players, good mom/sister figures, listeners, regulators, motivators, stabilizers, and even one or two instigators. They complement and play off each other. They begin to become a family. Families take care of each other and they take care of business.

This sense of family has probably been the biggest non-skill-related factor leading to our success. Our players know that they may never again work so hard with one group of people to achieve a common goal. In the best scenario, the team develops a unity that bonds them on and off the field. Examples of how our teams develop unity: We do ropes courses; we do sports psychology sessions, where we identify each player's personality type and preferred method of feedback and source of motivation; we host guest speakers; and we participate in other team-building progressions and identification drills throughout the year.

As the cohesion, the mission, and the ownership develop, the chemistry becomes more apparent. Players feed off each other, and the program's philosophy comes full circle. Once the chemistry develops, the actions and reactions become automatic.

Discipline

Over the years, discipline has been the benchmark of our program. Discipline provides the foundation on which our program develops, but it is even more encompassing than that. Discipline is a trait that transcends athletics. Discipline is the one characteristic necessary to achieve success in all aspects of life. We strive to achieve success as students in the classroom and athletes on the field, as teammates, friends, and family members, and as people who will make a significant contribution to society. Our philosophy suggests that you cannot have discipline in only one of these areas and still be complete.

Discipline and pride provide the internal motivation to do things right all the time, even the little things. Doing things correctly all the time leads to success in achieving muscle memory in skill-related tasks. This is a must for the efficient development of every player.

A motivated team provides most of its own discipline. Anything else would be a loss of focus and would lead to a path away from the mission. At this point, the coaching staff provides only information, support, and guidance. During our program's inception, the guidance and most of the discipline had to be provided by the staff. As the program developed, the team adopted the philosophy and accepted ownership. Now they take care of everything except rare cases of discipline. The team's desire to accept ownership of the program is a true sign of maturity.

Mental Toughness

Mental toughness takes on many definitions in different situations. For me, mental toughness, ultimately, is the ability to stick with the plan in the face of adversity. A team develops into one mind. With that one mind comes consistency. With consistency comes confidence, which leads to success.

As the team accepts the philosophy, goals, and standards of the program and as they develop pride, discipline, responsibility, and ownership, mental toughness develops as well. *Believe in the process*—that's the central theme to develop mental toughness in players. When the going gets tough, go back to the fundamentals. The solid foundation is our source of strength. Like muscle memory in a skill-related task, consistent repetition and reinforcement during preseason and all of the regular season lead to confidence in the process. If you don't develop the philosophy in practice, don't expect it to show up come game time.

The challenges to mental toughness are pressure, failure, the feeling of being overwhelmed, unfamiliar territory, and distraction. Mental toughness develops when we learn to work through these challenges. Softball is a game of failure; learn to deal with it. Have you ever heard of a major league baseball player who never experienced a slump? The more positive the attitude, the more stable and consistent the plan, the more calculated the approach, the quicker the solution.

The more a player actually practices problem solving and achieves success, the more mentally tough she becomes. Even seeing teammates succeed provides positive reinforcement, creating a feeling of being in control and having a plan.

Players who possess metal toughness don't allow themselves to become upset by an umpire's call. By looking at them you wouldn't know if they were hitless or 4-4 on the day. Their leadership qualities don't change based on their success on the field. They maintain focus and stability. They consistently maintain composure in difficult situations. They deal with adversity. When panic and chaos develop, they are the ones who stick with the game plan. It takes time, patience, discipline, and belief to achieve mental toughness.

Final Thoughts

At the end of the year, players look back and reflect. For the freshmen, their careers are now one-quarter complete. A few short months ago they were wide-eyed sponges soaking up all the information they could hold, but they lacked experience. Now, they have an entire season under their belts and suddenly feel very wise. The sophomores have completed half of their college education. They will soon go from the second year players trying to apply all they learned as freshmen to the upper classmen who are responsible for helping educate the newcomers. The juniors, who felt like they had plenty of time to reach their goals, now stand at the threshold of their final season. Soon, they will realize the sense of urgency felt by seniors for generations before them. The seniors wonder Where did the time go? How can it be over? As coaches, we ask ourselves How did they end their careers? and What marks did they leave for future generations?

When you work to put yourself in a position to succeed, success tends to find you. We talk to freshmen about what kind of athletes, students, and people they want to become during their college careers. We talk about how success is synonymous with giving it their all and doing their very best each day. We explain that the very best you can do in life is to put yourself in the best possible position to succeed in everything you do.

We also ask them to look ahead four years. How do they want others to describe their careers? How do they want to be remembered? And, most of all, when they walk off the field for the last time, will they be able to look back on their careers and say, "I have no regrets"?

The lessons learned during their time at Washington—motivation, discipline, ownership, responsibility, and mental toughness—echo throughout the rest of their lives. Hustle is the easy part.

CHAPTER FIVE

Coaching With Integrity

Marge Willadsen

Photo courtesy of Buena Vista University

There can be no victory without integrity.

What could be more important in the coaching field today than coaching with integrity? Teaching players how to hit, field, and run are important, but teaching our players how to play and compete with integrity is even more critical as we prepare them for life after their playing days end. Our society needs a sport that is willing to model what is good, what is valuable, and what is important about being involved in sport. I challenge us as coaches to accept the responsibility of making softball the model that others want to emulate.

The organization Citizenship Through Sports Alliance (CTSA) promotes values of citizenship that are realized through sportsmanship and ethical play in athletics. Their concern regarding the current sports culture is reflected in the following statement taken from a CTSA brochure: "Alliance members have noted a worrisome decline in sportsmanship and ethical conduct in athletics, a deterioration that permeates sports competition from the youth leagues to the professional leagues. The breakdown in sportsmanship extends beyond the courts and fields."

According to *Webster's New World Dictionary*, *integrity* is "the quality or state of being of sound moral principle; uprightness, honesty, and sincerity." Translated into coaching terms, integrity means doing what is morally right. Jim Webb, head coach at Lake City Community College, believes that "integrity is loving the game so much that playing right is more important than winning games, and teaching that to young folks." Susan Craig, head coach at the University of New Mexico, offers another point of view: "There is the letter of the law and there is the intent of the law. The questions that must be addressed are: Is it right? Is it fair? Is it honest? We are not selling used cars. The lives of the athletes we deal with are greatly impacted by our actions and our words. The end does not justify the means. Winning that compromises the lives of those who trust us is always tainted."

Coaching with integrity is conceivably more important than any other area when educating coaches. It may also be the most neglected area. Coaching theory courses typically focus on skills and strategies, while topics such as integrity and ethics receive minimal discussion if any at all. Because coaches have such a profound impact and influence on the lives and dreams of young athletes, it is imperative that coaches conduct themselves with impeccable integrity. Integrity, however, is often compromised. The pressure to win, to be the best, and to gain the competitive edge has replaced the more important moral and ethical goals once thought sacred in sport.

To gather material on the topic of integrity, I developed a *Coaching With Integrity* questionnaire and sent it to a small number of colleagues who coach at the high school, junior college, and NCAA Division I, II, and III levels of play. The responses to this questionnaire provided me with many of the statements and insights in this chapter.

Pressures, Temptations, and Compromises

The ultimate goal in the sports world is to win. Winning an Olympic gold medal or an NCAA championship is the dream of both coaches and athletes. Wanting to win and striving to win are worthy goals that serve to motivate coaches, but when the pressure and insatiable desire to win overshadow all else, coaches may compromise integrity. When this happens, the game and those who play it are also compromised.

Where does pressure come from, and how does it influence our decisions? Coaches receive pressure from a variety of internal and external sources. The greatest pressure is often self-imposed, as the majority of coaches are competitive in nature. For some, winning may become an obsession, and losing a game implies failure. Those who are unable to recover from defeat or a losing season may look for shortcuts to success. These shortcuts can lead to unethical or unfair practices by coaches who fall victim to the temptations.

A high school coach who had been coaching for 27 years gave an excellent example of a recent situation in which he was tempted to compromise his integrity. He had promised his number-two pitcher that she would pitch in rotation, alternating with the number-one pitcher. The rotation worked out so that the number-two pitcher was scheduled to pitch in the final regional game. Winning this game meant a trip to the state tournament. The coach knew that his number-one pitcher had a better chance of winning. He ultimately made the difficult but ethical decision to go with number two. This particular coach indicated that, earlier in his career, he might not have made that same decision. Being a person of your word develops trust and respect from players. (Note: The team did win the game.)

As softball programs have gained in popularity and prestige, the aspiration to field national contenders has intensified. To accommodate the growing number of fans and spectators, many new stadiums have been constructed. These factors have created additional pressure and placed unrealistic expectations on the coaches. In a recent conversation, Jay Miller, head coach at the University of Missouri, indicated that today's coaches are receiving more pressure to produce winning programs, and those who don't produce find themselves looking for employment.

> Our greatest contribution is in teaching young people the values of competition: to make a commitment, to work hard, to strive for excellence, to sacrifice to make the team better, to be the best you can be as a person and an athlete.
>
> **Susan Craig**

Recruiting the most talented players is paramount in the mind of every college coach who wants to develop a successful program. There is overwhelming pressure to land these top recruits, which has intensified the recruiting battles now being waged among coaches.

Head coach Gina Loudenburg, Wheaton College, indicated that she is tempted to compromise her integrity when she wants to recruit a great player against another coach when an intense rivalry exists, or against other coaches who have done things that aren't right. Sharon Panske, head coach at the University of Wisconsin-Oshkosh, feels tempted when her opponent has no integrity and no matter what she does, she can't win.

Always remember what is important and never lose sight of your coaching philosophy. Respect the game, the officials, and everyone involved.

Sharon Panske

Incredible time demands are made on coaches as they feel the necessity to attend all of the major recruiting camps and tournaments held throughout the summer. The coach who does not attend runs the risk of losing the star recruit to the opposition. I suspect that many NCAA recruiting violations occur during these periods of competition.

Coaches who lack the courage and conviction to withstand pressure and temptation may be more apt to compromise integrity. Let us now examine the most troublesome areas that plague the integrity of coaches.

Areas of Concern

It is probably not too surprising that recruiting is the area of most concern, especially negative recruiting. The all-too-common practice of negative recruiting may be one of the gravest issues facing our profession. It is difficult to prove or prevent and as a consequence may have damaging implications for a program.

Negative recruiting is the practice of communicating negative or false statements about another coach's program, team, institution, or personnel to a potential recruit, her parents, or a coaching colleague. For example, a coach from one institution may falsely claim that an opposing conference school has been known to lie to recruits about playing time or that the opposing institution has a poor academic reputation.

Opposing coaches may be unaware of these tactics or feel powerless to counteract them. We must find ways to prevent or punish coaches who practice negative recruiting tactics. Even though confronting colleagues may be difficult, Dianne Baker, head coach at Texas Women's University, believes that coaches should go directly to the source of the allegations and talk honestly about their concerns. Most problems can be handled with communication between both parties. I would also advocate reporting violations to the opposing institution's athletic director as another avenue to remedy the situation. If the problem remains unresolved, coaches have the option to report recruiting violations to the NCAA or unethical practices to the Ethics Committee of the National Fastpitch Coaches Association (NFCA).

The second area of most concern deals with general recruiting. As competition for top recruits has escalated, so too have the temptations for coaches who lack integrity to circumvent recruiting rules and regulations. Susan Craig believes that "The most serious issue of integrity in recruiting is the handling of athletes by coaches both during recruitment and once on campus. Athletes are constantly lied to and pressured to make quick decisions on selecting programs. Once at school, they are sometimes mentally and physically abused with no protection. Sometimes a coach may make promises to a player knowing full well that he or she is unable to keep those promises."

A willingness by coaches to do whatever it takes to win was the third area of most concern. This might include intimidating players and officials, misrepresenting scholarships, influencing financial aid packaging, teaching players unethical tactics, or bending the intent of the rules of the game. Coaches who are willing to compromise integrity in these areas in the name of victory have lost sight of the important values that can be taught on our playing fields.

The fourth area of concern regards coaches who disregard integrity because they don't think they will be caught, or they feign ignorance once detected. They are only cheating themselves, their teams, their opponents, and the system. The coaches who choose to follow this path may win, but at whose expense? A better philosophy to follow is one offered by Simpson College's head coach Henry Christowski: "Make sure that your mother would be proud of the manner in which you have conducted yourself." Ashland University head coach Sheila Goulas also had a good suggestion: "If you can look at yourself in the mirror and know that you made the correct decision, that is all that matters."

> Your job is to develop the total person, not just the athlete. Have respect for the game and all involved. Do not look for the easy way.
> **Sheila Goulas**

The last issue of concern deals with the much larger issue of practices that are permissible in sports but are not tolerated outside the sporting arena. Sport mirrors many of the same moral and ethical problems present within society. Some people lie on their income taxes, steal, or assault another individual. Coaches, too, may lie, cheat, break rules, or they may have pitchers purposely throw at batters, ask players to slide with cleats high, or have runners charge into an opponent with such force that injury is likely to occur. However, unlike society, these behaviors are often over-looked because they are interpreted as being a part of the game.

"In the sporting world, some lapses in integrity are accepted because they are in sport not in life," says Beth Kirschner, head coach at the University of Kentucky. "Although sport is not the real world, lessons in sport are often applied to the real world, and I am disappointed in some of the lessons some athletes learn." We must refuse to condone unethical and dishonest practices in our sport that would not be tolerated in the world outside of sports.

> When faced with a difficult decision, try to eliminate all the emotions that surround the situation. Try to take a step back, add some perspective, and maybe bounce ideas off people you respect who are not involved in the situation.
>
> **Beth Kirschner**

Susan Craig believes that the solution to solving the integrity issue lies with the administration: "They are the ones who are ultimately responsible for the actions of their coaches. If they tolerate coaches who have no integrity, there is no solution." The University of Indiana recently applied what they termed a "zero-based tolerance" policy to dismiss one of the most successful coaches in basketball history who had exhibited coaching behaviors that were deemed inappropriate. The decision of this university to apply such a policy may signal an end to accepting behavior in sports that would not be tolerated in society. As important role models for young people, coaches must be held accountable for their behavior. Winning championships cannot be offered as an excuse for tolerating abusive and unprofessional behavior.

Integrity in Relationships

A coach's integrity, or lack thereof, extends beyond the playing field to the relationships he or she develops with others involved in the sport. How a coach communicates and treats players, colleagues, parents, family members, and officials reflects on the program as a whole.

Player-Coach Relationships

Treating players with integrity, respect, honesty, and fairness seems like an easy thing to do. Gretchen Weibrecht, head coach at John Carroll University, believes that coaches should treat players as people with feelings. This is difficult when the motivation to win games is such a strong force in the competitive nature of a coach that players' feelings may be the last priority.

Jim Webb stated, "Values and ethics are as important as hitting and catching. Don't worry about what others think; do right. In the end, who you are is judged by your conscience, not by your record. Be a good person first and then you can be a good coach."

Many coaches enter the coaching profession because they enjoy working with student athletes. Although there are many challenges, frustrations, and some disappointments, the rewards and personal satisfaction far outweigh the negatives. Day-to-day teaching offers opportunities to develop close relationships with the players. An analogy written by Henry Christowski is an excellent example for coaches to remember: "I have always dealt with coaching as teaching and the game as the unit test. To see how well I had taught, some units were more difficult than others, but the challenge was always the same: to have my students (players) prepared to succeed. If I, in any way, tried to unfairly affect the outcome of the game, I would have invalidated the test, thereby never really knowing what kind of teaching job I had done."

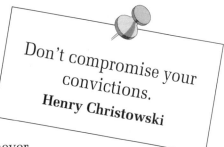

Don't compromise your convictions.
Henry Christowski

Developing lifelong friendships with players, I believe, is what inspires many coaches to thrive in this profession. The wins and losses may be forgotten with the passage of time, but friendships are never forgotten. Young athletes admire, respect, trust, and emulate their coaches. Coaches should also show admiration, respect, and trust for their players. We have the opportunity to teach many valuable lessons through the medium of our playing fields. While teaching players how to execute double plays may be an easier task than teaching them the values of honesty, fairness, trust, and respect, these values are the most worthwhile goals that our players can attain.

Personality differences, a lack of playing time, unclear expectations, or broken promises may lead to conflicts between coaches and student athletes. The stress and disappointment created by these conflicts may cause players to drop out of softball or lose all enjoyment for the game. For others, the love of the game or the possibility of losing a scholarship may cause players to ignore abuse from coaches. However, knowing how to handle scholarship athletes may work in reverse by clouding a coach's decision-making ability.

A coaching colleague shared an incident in her career when she tolerated behavior from one of her scholarship athletes that was detrimental to the team. The coach allowed the scholarship athlete to remain on the team longer than she should have because the player was such a talented athlete. This, she said, compromised her integrity as a coach. The team atmosphere improved significantly once she dismissed the player from the team, a decision she wishes she had made sooner.

Coaches who use intimidation tactics or who attempt to play mind games with team members are manipulative individuals. They are not only attempting to psychologically control players, they may also use the same tactics with opposing players, coaches, and officials. Intimidation by embarrassing players in front of their teammates seriously damages any respect between coaches and athletes. Using fear, intimidation, or mind games to control the thinking and actions of players is a perilous breach of coaching with integrity.

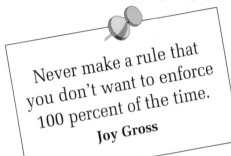

Never make a rule that you don't want to enforce 100 percent of the time.

Joy Gross

A more positive method of treating athletes is offered by Joy Gross, head high school coach at Irwin-Kirkman-Manilla, who believes that you should act as if every player is your own child and treat her as you would like your child to be treated.

Occasionally a coach knowingly compromises the health of an athlete if it means the difference between winning and losing—for example, playing an injured athlete who has not been cleared to play or teaching players unsportsmanlike techniques designed to injure or take out opponents. Coaches who are willing to jeopardize a player's health are few in number. There can be no excuse for compromising the health and well-being of our players.

The relationship between coach and athlete is a precious commodity that should be nourished and protected. Our role is to help athletes develop their playing skills, of course, but the more important role is that of teaching them to become responsible citizens, leaders, and individuals of integrity and honesty. Coaches who rob athletes of this opportunity are cheating the ones who trust us most. Gerry Pinkston, NFCA Hall of Fame coach from Central Oklahoma, shared some valuable advice: "Hopefully when your players are finished with their softball career, they will be glad they came to play for you."

Colleague-Coach Relationships

Just as coaches make lifelong friends with players, so do lifelong friendships develop between softball coaches. A fellow colleague and I have been coaching against each other for over 20 years. Throughout this period, I have always enjoyed playing her team because I know that she coaches with integrity. Whoever is victorious on that given day has scored more runs than the other. This makes the competition fun and enjoyable for both players and coaches.

The increasing popularity of softball over the past 10 years, coupled with the pressure put on coaches to win a national or conference championship, may cause friction between coaches who once competed as friendly rivals. Recruiting wars, pressures to win, striving to gain an edge, and the temptations to retaliate against coaches who win by unethical means may produce cancers that slowly erode the ethical values coaches once thought important.

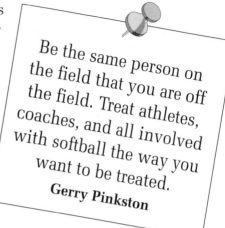

Be the same person on the field that you are off the field. Treat athletes, coaches, and all involved with softball the way you want to be treated.
Gerry Pinkston

To combat this erosion, older coaches who have experienced and overcome the obstacles to integrity should mentor younger coaches, who may not know how to resist the temptations. Often the experience and wisdom of the mentor can be a guiding force when it is most needed. Newer coaches should not be afraid or embarrassed to ask for advice. Sharing concerns with coaching colleagues you admire and respect can help alleviate many anxieties and stresses of coaching.

Sharing information with colleagues during roundtable discussions at the NFCA Convention has allowed coaches to get to know one another in a noncompetitive atmosphere. I think this would work well for coaches at the high school and ASA levels of play as well.

Parent-Coach Relationships

Parents can and should become the coach's best allies. However, they can also be a source of extreme tension, especially at the high school level. When parents feel that a coach is mistreating their child, their natural instinct is to protect their child. A breakdown in communication between the parents, the child, and the coach often is to blame when parents perceive that the coach is intimidating or treating their child unfairly.

Coaches may be able to prevent problems by conducting parent-coach preseason meetings to set and establish goals for the program. Clear guidelines for parent-coach discussions should also be established at this time. Table 5.1 lists some issues and concerns parents should and shouldn't discuss with coaches.

Some situations may require a conference between the coach and the parents. When this happens I suggest you establish the following guidelines:

- Do not have a confrontation before or after a game.
- Set up an appointment to meet with the parents, the coach, and the athletic director.
- Listen to the parent's concerns.

- Stay calm.
- Explain your actions based upon your honest and ethical evaluation of the situation.
- Work together for a solution that is equitable and fair.

TABLE 5.1

Issues for Parents and Coaches to Discuss

Appropriate issues that parents may discuss with coaches	Inappropriate issues that parents should not discuss with coaches
• Mental and physical treatment of player	• Playing time
• Ways to help player improve	• Team strategy or play calling
• Concerns about player's behavior	• Other student athletes

I encourage our players' parents to travel with us during our spring trip. This opportunity allows them to support the team and make friends with the other parents. We also set aside one night for coaches and parents to have dinner together so that we can get better acquainted in an informal setting. Some of the friendships I have made with parents became as long lasting as those made with the players. Encouraging players, parents, and coaches to bond together much as families bond together is more enjoyable and rewarding for all involved. It may also lead to better team cohesion and a winning effort on the field.

Family-Coach Relationships

Coaching often leads to difficult decisions that can have a profound impact on your own children. For example, several years ago I had to decide whether to coach my team during an NCAA championship series or attend my daughter's college graduation. My daughter, who had previously played for me and understood the thrill of both playing and coaching at a national championship, assured me that it was okay if I missed her graduation. At the time, I was torn between my loyalty and obligation to the team and the desire to show support for my daughter's accomplishment. However, with a guilty conscience, I decided to coach my team.

I have always regretted that decision and looking back now, I realize that my family should have taken priority. This is especially true during important milestones in the lives of our children. Too often we allow family matters to take a backseat to our coaching duties. We must remember that there is always another game to coach, but there may only be one chance to experience our children's dreams and aspirations.

Although difficult, a coach should try to maintain balance between job responsibilities and family obligations. It is easy to become so wrapped up in our coaching duties that we end up compromising the time spent with our families and our friends. Having balance may also be a deterrent to burnout, which affects many coaches.

Official-Coach Relationships

The official's job is to maintain the integrity of the game by ensuring that the players and coaches follow the rules. The integrity of the game is seriously damaged by coaches who badger officials through acts of intimidation or loud and abusive confrontations, and the increase in physical attacks on officials by coaches is frightening. What message are we sending our youth when coaches are ejected from games during ugly confrontations with umpires? Sanctions against coaches for unsportsmanlike conduct in NCAA championship play have increased. This is an embarrassment to the coaches, the institutions, the student athletes, and to our sport.

There is nothing more important than your reputation and self-respect. Do everything to secure these.
Sandy Jerstad

The umpires I have met and worked with during the NCAA Division III National Championship have been most professional. They take pride in their work and continually seek ways to improve techniques. Umpires' goals are much like our own—to be the best. Respecting officials only enhances the coach-umpire relationship, helping make our game more enjoyable for those involved. Adhering to the rules of the game as well as complying with the intent of the rules would be a model worth emulating to coaches in other sports.

Safeguarding Academic Integrity

As coaches with integrity, we must always support the educational mission of our institutions and seek to recruit student athletes who are capable of succeeding academically at the college level. Coaches with questionable ethics might pressure recruits to sign letters of intent, pressure recruits to accept scholarship offers, mislead recruits concerning academic majors, or make promises that are not kept. Exploiting the academic integrity of student athletes under the guise of winning is unacceptable. Championships

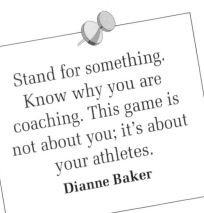

Stand for something. Know why you are coaching. This game is not about you; it's about your athletes.

Dianne Baker

won by these means are contaminated by these dishonest acts and unethical practices.

Ensuring academic integrity must be a top priority for both the coach and the administration. The philosophy and goals of the athletic department should be compatible with the educational mission of the institution. Monitoring the academic progress of student athletes, providing academic counseling, and holding coaches accountable for the graduation rates of their athletes help to ensure the academic integrity of the athletic program and its coaches. The popular statement *Student first, athlete second* must guide the actions of those involved in the educational process.

Final Thoughts

It takes courage to stand up for what you believe to be right and just. Many pressures and temptations confront us throughout our coaching careers, but we must remain steadfast to our moral obligation to teach and coach with integrity. The athletes we have the opportunity to influence deserve no less than our best. To compromise that goal is to cheat in the more important game—the game of life.

Next time you are tempted to compromise your integrity, ask yourself the following questions: Is it right? Is it fair? Is it honest? When you can look yourself in the mirror and answer yes to all four questions, your integrity is on solid foundation.

PART

II

Program
Building and
Management

CHAPTER SIX

Organizing and Orchestrating a Winning Program

JoAnne Graf

Photo by Tom Casazza, courtesy of Florida State University

The foundation of any program is its philosophy. All those involved in the program—coaches, administrators, trainers, sports information personnel, marketing personnel, players—must be committed to this philosophy so that everyone is working toward a common goal. Decisions are made with regard to the philosophy of the softball program.

The head coach should set program goals with input from assistants and administrators. If a conflict exists between what the coach wants to achieve and what the administration is willing to fund, success is unlikely. The coach then endures stress and frustration while trying to achieve goals that are not supported.

For example, let's say the head coach sets the goal to win a national championship, but the administration only wants the head coach to compete at the regional level. Therefore, funding, building facilities, and assigning support staff are done to keep the program competitive regionally but not nationally. The coach grows increasingly frustrated with the reduced ability to beat certain teams that would be beatible if the administration had the same goal and provided the appropriate support. The coach either leaves this program or lowers his or her goals to those of the administration.

As the director of the softball program, the head coach must demand excellence from all those who work with the program. When you do not have high goals, no one else does. When you don't work hard for your program, don't expect others to.

The assistants hired should reflect the same philosophy as the head coach. A shared vision ensures that all the coaches are leading the players in the same direction. Players must know what the coaches expect. The players who are recruited should also want the same goals as the coaches. This compatibility increases the probability that everyone will make the sacrifices and work at the level needed to achieve the program's goals.

Hire a Loyal Staff

Hiring a competent and loyal coaching staff is one of the most important steps in organizing a successful softball program. Work with the administration to ensure that you have the maximum number of coaches your governing organization allows. Salaries must be competitive with other schools. Benefits and perks factor in any employee's decision and must also be competitive.

Use every available resource to determine the best assistants for your program. Check references carefully and ask others who know both you and the applicant. This insight helps you determine if the qualifications and personality of the applicant fit. Check with the personnel office to make sure you are aware of all rules pertaining to employee hiring. Hiring assistants who complement the head coach and other assistants strengthens the overall ability of the staff.

A strong work ethic is a must for an assistant coach. Coaching requires a great deal of personal sacrifice. Not everyone is willing to give up as much time as is required to have a successful program. Hire people you trust and make sure they feel comfortable enough to speak their minds, even if they disagree with you. Hiring yes-people does not help you improve as a head coach.

While you may not have a direct say in the hiring of other support staff, try to have as much input as possible. If you are assigned a trainer or sports information person, make sure that individual works hard to help your program achieve its goals. Work with the supervisor who assigns certain support staff to voice your expectations.

Staff longevity also is important to a winning program. If your staff changes every year, your program suffers from a lack of continuity. Your time is spent training new staff, and you increase the chance of hiring someone who does not agree with your philosophy. Spending time training staff takes away from time you can spend on other duties. Treat staff as you wish to be treated. Work to ensure that they receive adequate raises. Keep the administration current with added benefits that other staffs across the country receive and work to see that your staff receives these benefits.

As the head coach, elect not to care who gets the credit. Always credit your assistants and staff for the work they do. They always appreciate when their hard work is noticed. A compliment and pat on the back mean a great deal. Remember that head coaches are not successful without quality assistants.

Recruit Solid Student Athletes

In any successful program, recruiting is a priority. Great players make great coaches. Great players make for long coaching careers.

A coach must recruit student athletes who fit the program's philosophy. Players must be placed in an environment where they can be successful. When a recruit ends up at a school where she is unable to find success either athletically or academically, chances are she does not stay at the school. It is only fair to give recruits the opportunity to achieve their goals, just as the team would like to achieve its goals.

One of the hardest decisions to make is to pass on a player who is a great athlete but a weak student. As a recruiter, you must determine why the student athlete is a weak student, then decide if she has the potential to be successful at your school. You must also know if you have the academic support system to assist the student athlete. The primary mission of each program should be to graduate all players; thus, a coach cannot recruit too many poor students.

Checking the background of prospective athletes is important in weeding out players with potential problems. Remember the saying One bad apple can spoil the bunch. Spend time talking to others who know the player to gain their insight. This network can be summer league coaches, high school coaches, guidance counselors, and so on.

It is important for coaches to know and follow their governing body's recruiting rules. While the majority of coaches are ethical, some are not. Shortcuts may bring success in the short run, but it won't last. Coaches who break rules do not have the player's best interest at heart; they are interested only in winning. You can't teach values if you aren't a role model. Coaches who believe in winning at all costs usually do not stay in coaching for long because they are in it for the wrong reason.

Know the Rules

The rules regarding recruiting are often the ones that cause problems for athletic programs. If you are going to have a successful program, it is imperative that you know the rules. Follow both the letter of the law as well as the intent, and you earn the respect of your colleagues and others you deal with. Too many coaches try to figure out ways around the rules when it's much easier to follow them.

Each governing body has its own set of rules. A coach needs to know the rules that apply to his or her institution. If any rules are unclear, get a clarification from the compliance office, conference office, or governing body. There is no excuse for not knowing the rules.

Conference rules can differ from national rules and can be more restrictive. Be sure that you are aware of any differences that exist and apply all rules to your softball program.

Academic and eligibility rules are also important for coaches to know. Academic performance is ultimately the responsibility of the coach. Even if an academic advising office oversees academic progress, you need to meet with them on a regular basis to know exactly what your athletes must do to remain eligible. Unfortunately, strong students can be found to be ineligible because the rules were not understood.

As should all employees, coaches should understand the personnel rules of their institutions. You should know how much sick leave and annual leave you and your staff can accrue. You should understand your institution's contractual obligations to you.

Naturally, knowing the rules of the game benefit the team on the field. However, not only should the coach know the rules of the game, but he or she should also know how the umpires are going to enforce the rules. Make sure your players know the rules. Since rules can change yearly, keep up with current decisions.

Coaches must learn to police themselves. Although coaches are understandably reluctant to turn in those who break rules, they must if coaching is to be a profession everyone can be proud of. The pressure to win often causes coaches to feel they must do anything to win, but that is no excuse. Other coaches have a responsibility to the profession to make sure the rules are followed. When you know a rule is being broken, talk to the offending coach directly. If this doesn't work, inform your compliance office of the problem or go directly to the appropriate governing body. Many coaches are reluctant to get involved in reporting violations by their colleagues, but they need to remember that coaches who break rules reflect badly on the entire profession.

Develop Booster and Fan Groups

Developing a booster or fan group helps a coach build and sustain a winning program. These groups help raise money to provide extra revenue, and they increase your fan base by creating interest in your program.

Schools form fan groups in different ways. Some have one booster group that may separate into men's and women's sports; others form friends, a special group of boosters who tend to support one particular sport. Be sure to find out what your restrictions are as a coach.

While booster groups are formed to be helpful to a program, care must be taken to ensure that they do not try to be too helpful. Educate your boosters as to the rules of your governing body. The National Collegiate Athletic Association (NCAA), for example, prohibits boosters from contacting potential recruits. However, most boosters do not know these rules and can cause players to be ineligible or a program to be put on probation when they think they are only helping. Education assures that everyone knows the rules and their roles.

Maintaining communication with boosters requires time and effort. A newsletter is an effective way to keep your fans updated with team information. You can include things such as player bios, upcoming events, results, player honors, alumni updates, and so on. This keeps the boosters updated, and they feel a part of the program.

Players and coaches should always take time after games to talk to the fans. Signing autographs is very popular, especially with children. Giveaway items are used to increase fan support at certain games. Include the sponsor's name on the item given away to promote the sponsor. Giveaway games are used to increase attendance and to advertise the sponsor's business or product. It is a win-win situation. If you are fortunate enough to have a marketing/promotions department, they can help you target certain games for promotion.

Kathy Veroni

Parents are a critical factor in the success of a softball program. They can be your greatest, most loyal fans, but also your strongest critics. How a coach works with parents has an effect on the long-term success of the team.

When we recruit an athlete, we actually recruit her entire family. Even though our relationship with the athlete could last five years, our relationship with the family may be ongoing. If you take a good look at the family when you are recruiting and realize the athlete is a product of that family, you should be happy with your athletes and parents.

Parents can be your best fans before their daughter attends, during her time at your school, and after she graduates as well. They become ambassadors of your university and your program. Depending on their perception of your program, their comments to others can be positive or, unfortunately, quite negative. This influence is why it is so important to work with parents and make them feel a part of the team.

On the Sunday before the school year begins, I host a team cookout and potluck for the players and their families. It is a great time for the coaches to meet the new families and for the parents to interact with everyone. Through this event, we are able to start the year off with everyone on the same page. School administrators, support staff, and each team captain are given the stage to welcome everyone as well.

Guidelines for Coaches

Speak to parents truthfully, answer their questions honestly, and give them time to express their views. Work with parents and see them as part of the team rather than as critics to be avoided.

Parents must be able to approach you and talk to you about their daughters. They should be able to discuss their child with you, and they want you to take the time to answer their questions. In most cases, all they want to know is that their child is doing well and that she is in good hands. Take the time to approach the parents, too. It is a nice feeling when the coach initiates the conversation and lets the parents know that their child is a fine young athlete.

One of the issues that often causes conflict between parents and coaches is playing time. I know that parents want their children to play. It is easy to see their disappointment when their daughter is not in the starting nine or not performing well. I do not avoid the issue, and if the parents ever want to talk with me about the *whys,* I am willing to do so.

Guidelines for Parents

If I could speak to all parents, one guideline I would ask them to follow is to not criticize your daughter, the other players, or the coaching staff. Too often, we criticize others when we do not know all of the facts or circumstances. Try to communicate rather than criticize. Allow your daughter to make her own choices; don't push her into it, and do not make her hurry her decision as it relates to playing.

I have overheard the tone of voice some parents use with their daughters. Sometimes that tone is used as punishment when it really can be used to build self-esteem. I admire the parents who are positive and tell the athlete, "Yes, you can do it!" Before and after the game, parents must think about what they are going to say before they say it.

Don't criticize your daughter in public; it makes you look mean and hostile. Praise in public. This makes you, the parent, look good and builds confidence in your daughter. Remember the times you tried to do difficult things. How did the person who taught you treat you? Were you taught with patience and understanding, or did your teacher scare you so much you were not able to perform at the necessary level?

Along with not criticizing, learn to take a compliment and enjoy your daughter's success. When the game ends, the coach needs to talk to a lot of people. Parents may have one minute with the coach after the game, and what the parents and coach say to each other is very important. I like to congratulate the parents on the job their daughter did. Many parents respond, "All the players did well" or something similar, but I truly wish they would allow this compliment on their daughter's behalf and bask in her glory. This time is opportune for parents to thank the coach for coaching their daughter and to speak about their child and how proud they are of her.

Once I complimented a player's parents, and they remarked that I had to keep her confidence up for the next weekend. The opportunity was lost for them. It was a time for them to enjoy the moment and trust that the next game would be equally successful without placing that doubt out there for the child or the coach.

College is a time for the athlete to take responsibility for her actions. Parents should not call the coach when the issue relates to the athlete's responsibilities. The athlete is the one on the team and on campus. It is important for the parent to let the child take care of herself and to assume responsibility for her career and life.

I wish all parents would follow the example of Mr. Joseph Martin, whose daughter was a pitcher. Before the last inning of our conference championship, Melissa did not feel as sharp as she had earlier in the game and suggested we put in a relief pitcher. We made the change, but unfortunately lost the game. The season and the seniors' careers came to an end. Bob hugged me and said, "I will always be thankful you recruited my daughter and selected her to play for you." Years later, I remember that conversation and am thankful for the coaches, players, and parents who have been and are on my team.

Kathy Veroni served as head softball coach at Western Illinois University in Macomb, IL. She has won over 1,000 women's premier and Division I college games. A former president of the National Fastpitch Coaches Association and United States Fastpitch Association, Coach Veroni is a member of the National Fastpitch Coaches Hall of Fame, the Illinois State University Hall of Fame, and the Illinois Amateur Softball Association Hall of Fame.

Photo courtesy of Western Illinois University

Communicate Effectively

Communication seems to be an obvious factor in building and continuing a successful softball program. Although it is one of the most important factors, it is one of the hardest to maintain, often because of a lack of staff and time. However, any extra effort pays significant dividends.

Keep parents up-to-date with the team's schedule and travel plans. Send them a copy of your hotel list, so they can plan to attend your events. Parents are an important part of your program. Communicating team rules to parents ensures that they are knowledgeable about the standards of behavior expected from team members.

During the season you receive requests from fans and boosters, ranging from questions about game times to requests for you to speak at functions. Answer requests promptly. If you cannot personally answer every request, be sure that someone from your staff does. This communication enhances community support for your program.

Make sure that all communication outlets for team information and score reports are kept up-to-date. This timely maintenance helps the public know how your team is doing. Work with the sports information department to make sure information is forwarded promptly. When the papers write a nice story about your program, let the reporter know that you appreciate the publicity. Answer questions from the media honestly, respecting the job they have to do. Establishing a rapport with the media increases your coverage.

When you are asked to do a TV or radio interview, say yes. I do interviews even if they interfere with practice. Reporters appreciate the fact that I value their time and deadlines. See exactly what they want to film and then set it up when they arrive, so they can film and move to their next assignment. When you make their job easier, the coverage for your program increases.

Trust your instincts about what is right for your program. You are the expert about what it needs, and you should not hesitate to let administrators know. Sometimes coaches fear approaching those in charge. However, administrators want your input on how to improve the program.

Work With Summer League and High School Coaches

Summer league and high school coaches can be invaluable in helping college coaches gather information needed to form recruiting lists. Summer league and high school guides should include pertinent data for each player—including name, year in school, address, phone number, grade point average, SAT/ACT scores, coach's phone number, and playing schedule. Accurate information is a must, as coaches use these guides to evaluate players based on their criteria and needs.

Summer league and high school coaches help both coaches and recruits. They can let a college coach know what factors are important to the recruit. For example, when the student wants to stay close to home, those schools that are far away may decide to stop recruiting that player. When a player wants to be guaranteed a starting position and a college coach does not do that, then recruiting that player will not be successful, and both individuals should look elsewhere.

The recruit's coach can also let the college coach know if the interest is sincere. This communication is important because of the amount of time spent recruiting a player. No one wants to waste time if one of the parties is not interested.

Scholarships are a big investment. Coaches want to know about the recruit's work ethic and attitude. It is important to find this information out from a variety of sources. If you only ask one person, you risk getting inaccurate information. There may be a personality conflict or another problem that you are unaware of. However, if you hear the same thing from several sources, pay attention.

Summer league and high school coaches are there to help. They do not make decisions for the college coach, nor do they tell the college coach whom to recruit. They are, however, an aid to help the player find the right place to continue her education as well as continue playing softball.

Create a Tradition

Establish a winning attitude as soon as you begin coaching your team. The team must believe it can win against any opponent. When you do not believe that you can beat a team, chances are you won't. Part of beginning to establish a winning attitude comes from establishing traditions.

Players can be involved in creating traditions by coming up with pregame and postgame rituals. Student athletes tend to hand these traditions down from year to year, and they can characterize your team. Returning players can teach the rituals to new players, creating a sense of generational pride. The rituals can be changed as the makeup of the team changes. Involve your players and listen to their suggestions.

Championship awards and tournament trophies show both past glories and demonstrate future expectations. Display these trophies and awards for All-American, All-Conference, All-Region, All-Academic, and any other important awards your program earns. In seeing their names displayed, players feel a sense of pride that lasts a lifetime. Young players work hard to get their names displayed on the wall, plaque, or trophy. Graduated players come back and show their children, husbands, and friends where their name is displayed. Fans also enjoy learning about the program by viewing these displays.

Final Thoughts

An administrator once said that I looked at the glass as if it were half-empty. I explained that I looked at it as half-full but felt there was no reason that the glass could not be completely full. You should always work to fill the glass completely so that you can achieve your goals.

Building a successful softball program takes time and commitment. To spend the time, you need to love the sport. Keep priorities in a proper order, remembering that players come first. While winning is important, it is not the most important thing. Build excellence into all aspects of your program, and the winning follows. Coach with your heart and you can always be successful.

CHAPTER SEVEN

Mentoring Within Your Staff

Gayle Blevins

Photo courtesy of the University of Iowa

In the coaching profession, the mentoring exchange may be the single most powerful means to make a positive difference in the lives of others. When we flourish as mentors, we affect the lives of our assistants, our athletes, and all those with whom we closely interact. There is perhaps no greater calling than to pass on our most precious personal and professional values.

When first presented with this subject, I chose to change the title from "Mentoring Your Staff" to "Mentoring Within Your Staff." My reasoning is simple: The mentoring spirit flows multidirectionally. A young child can mentor an adult; a first-year assistant can mentor a seasoned coach; and a freshman can mentor an All-American. To allow exchange in only one direction is shortsighted. All with whom we come in contact have the capacity to mentor. Some assume that only coaches with a national championship or a top four NCAA Division I program have the ability to mentor. What a huge oversight! All situations, be they great or small, provide us with opportunities to mentor and be mentored.

In *Mentoring: The Tao of Giving and Receiving Wisdom* (1995), authors Chunglian Al Huang and Jerry Lynch traced the word *mentor* back to ancient Greece, when the hero Odysseus entrusted his son's education to his friend Mentor. The practice itself has existed in virtually every culture, and today mentoring is practiced in many facets of life, from education and sports to business, organized religion, parenting, and friendships.

Whether we realize it or not, mentors have been guiding our lives even without our conscious awareness. A personal example is my family. My parents' example was to do your best with whatever you are given. Mom made raising her five children her life's mission. Dad spent his life's work laboring in a thankless factory job. Both showed my siblings and me how to commit to a task and do an honest day's work for an honest day's pay.

With our myriad of responsibilities as coaches, we often ironically discover that the areas in which we spend the least amount of time are the things we enjoy doing the most and the things most important for us to do. And so it is with mentoring. It is one of our greatest responsibilities, yet it is one to which we seldom deliberately commit our time and energy.

Mentoring is difficult to define and measure, yet it is so powerful and enriching to those who receive it. In an effort to suggest an easy way to remember some elements of mentoring, I take the letters of the word MENTOR and share what they represent to me: Model, Empower, Nurture, Teach, Observe, and Risk.

Model

Being a role model is no small undertaking. Role models are not gods or saints, nor are they perfect; but I believe mentors must be people with strong ethics, moral fiber, integrity, and passion. The expression "Attitudes are contagious; is yours worth catching?" makes a simple but important point. When you're a role model, be worthy of the title.

My dad has often reminded me what a blessing it is to be able to earn a living doing what I love to do and have a passion for. Passion is the single most energizing ingredient in anything we do. Passion adds energy, meaning, and purpose. A life without passion is empty—it lacks the sparkling of water or the glistening of the sun. Passion makes a good coach great. Let your staff see your enthusiasm for the game, the players, and your job.

An effective role model must walk the talk. When we say one thing and do another, our behavior becomes meaningless and does more harm than good. The discrepancies we show may make others cynical and reluctant to be receptive in future mentoring situations. We must be what we profess to be. In *The Mentor's Spirit* (1998), Sinetar says, "What you are speaks so loudly, I cannot hear what you say." No one is perfect, and that is okay. Our assistants realize that we, too, are human just by being around us every day. However, what is important is to stand for something. When push comes to shove, we must demonstrate that we are people of high ethics and moral character. The life lessons we pass along leave indelible marks on future coaches, so we must make these marks the kind of which we are proud.

Recently in completing our recruiting class at Iowa, we were presented with some ethical choices. Holly Killion, my newest assistant, was experiencing recruiting for the first time as a coach. We had offered a scholarship to a student who shortly thereafter committed to another school. We moved on in our recruiting and brought in another student who made a commitment to us. The day after this student committed, the first student we had recruited phoned our office. Her summer coach approached us the next day to inform us the student felt she had "made a mistake, chosen the other school for all the wrong reasons, and wanted to come to Iowa" and asked if our scholarship was still open. Obviously, we were stunned by the news but informed her summer coach we had received a commitment from another student and the scholarship was no longer available.

After returning to campus, I talked with Holly about the original recruit's change of heart. Her question was "Now what do you do?" I told her there was nothing *to* do. We had made our offer, it had been accepted, and unfortunately the first student simply waited too long to have a change of heart. This was a perfect opportunity to teach an important lesson to Holly. We could have pulled our offer from the second student, making up some excuse, then gone back to the student who was our first choice, but I believed we needed to stay true to our word. And so we did.

Assistants face the same dilemmas we encounter and hopefully they, too, make their decisions with integrity. If Holly chooses to remain in the coaching profession, she may experience this situation again someday as a head coach. I'm sure this experience will remain with her, and I feel confident she will make a decision based upon ethics and integrity.

Empower

Empower assistants and team members to take ownership in your program. A significant turning point in my coaching career came when I examined my leadership style and consciously changed it to better empower my assistants and team to take ownership. A book I read, *The Flight of the Buffalo* (1993), forced me to review how I led.

Authors Belasco and Stayer describe the old leadership style as "the head buffalo and the herd." Buffalo, fiercely loyal to one leader, do whatever the head buffalo wants and go wherever the leader wants them to go. The weakness of this style is that the herd stands and waits for the leader to show them what to do and where to go next. They only go where they are led and no farther. In fact, if the head buffalo jumps off a cliff, the whole herd follows. Essentially, the leader makes all the decisions. As head coaches, we know this becomes exhausting work.

In comparison, a new leadership style mirrors a flock of geese. This style encourages all members of a group to be responsible and interdependent. If you watch a flock of geese traveling together, you notice the leadership changes frequently with different geese taking the lead. As one leader tires, it moves back, drafting off other members of the flock, and another leader emerges. Each, then, serves a role as leader, follower, and occasionally scout. It is a proved fact that a flock can travel farther than one goose flying alone.

Belasco and Stayer sum up their leadership principles in four basic steps, which I apply to coaching. First, transfer ownership to the people who do the work. This philosophy applies to assistant coaches, trainers, and even players. Second, the environment you create should encourage each member of your staff to embrace responsibility. Third, help assistants develop their personal abilities. Fourth, learn quickly and assist others in learning.

Once I stepped back and gave more control and responsibility to the staff and team, I began to see people taking initiative, holding themselves accountable, solving problems, and thinking analytically. Our beginning-of-the-year meeting now sets the tone for group ownership. Our team determines its own mission statement and goals and sets its own rules and procedures.

When she was an assistant at Iowa, I asked Jenny Allard, now head coach at Harvard, and another assistant their opinions of a graduate who wanted to become Iowa's volunteer assistant. Jenny was surprised I had asked for their opinions, thinking I would make the decision alone. However, I valued their input and believed it was important to involve them in the decision, thereby empowering them to take ownership in the makeup of our staff. Jenny said this left a strong impression on her and is something she has reflected upon in the selection of her own coaching staff at Harvard.

As we empower our staff and team, we need to hold them accountable to fully complete their responsibilities. One way to empower involves recruiting. After we determine whom we are recruiting, we delegate responsibilities to all staff members. Our phone log is assigned weekly, and our assistants know it is their responsibility to make the call. This means reaching the recruit. An excuse of "I couldn't reach the student" or "I called twice and did not get her" flies once at best. Assistants must realize their contributions are critical and that we value their work.

Nurture

Huang and Lynch (1995) describe nurturing as "instilling courage, giving us permission to follow the heart, our passion, in all that we do amid life's tests of patience and trust." Nurturing is a give and take. Caring for our staff's emotional well-being is of equal concern as assisting them in learning the tools of the trade.

One of the greatest challenges in our profession is negotiating the highs and lows. When things are going well, recognizing and crediting the staff and team are critical. We motivate our assistants to give greater effort when we recognize their contributions. As head coaches, it is crucial to be aware of and utilize humility in our daily work. Media interviews provide perfect opportunities to acknowledge the solid work of our staff.

On the flip side, we must be steady during the low points—a disappointing performance, a loss, bad news from the administration regarding a project, losing a recruit, and so. Everyone is disappointed with failure, loss, or a setback and, as a result, may be sensitive to criticism. One thing I recommend is to take time to assess a disappointment. When participating in staff conversations about disappointments, sharing and discussing are important versus placing blame and accusing. This is a crucial distinction. Also, let go of the loss. Every year I try to do better with this, and I can honestly say this is where many of my colleagues continue to mentor me. Staying on a more even keel is a great approach to longevity and happiness in our profession.

One of the best ways to deal with the highs and lows is to work at maintaining perspective. Examine all that is important in your life. Our families and our faith are of far greater value than winning a ball game, capturing a title, securing a facility, or landing a recruit.

Maintain your self-worth. Early in my career, my total identity was wrapped up in our team's performance. If things were going well, great. If not, I really had difficulty feeling good about myself. It took me a long time to separate the two concerns, coaching my team and doing my best with them while feeling good about my identity apart from my team's performance.

If our assistants are going to stay in the coaching profession and have happy and healthy careers, we must pass along this lesson. The better they maintain a distinction between the two—the team's performance and their self-worth—the healthier and more satisfied they can be with their own lives. This lesson is also critical for our players to accept. Our players may struggle with their self-worth if they are not playing well or not playing. We must constantly remind them with our words *and* with our actions that we value them every bit as much when they fail as when they succeed.

Take time away from work. Volunteer with an outside group or organization. We all have opportunities to help organizations in our communities. It is one thing to give money, something else to give our time. Habitat for Humanity provides a great opportunity for reflection, team building, and appreciation for what we have in our lives. Hospitals teach us to value the one gift we all hope to possess—good health. Organizations such as the Ronald McDonald House, soup kitchens, and nursing homes need our help and also can help put us back on track. These are great experiences to share with assistants and team members.

Have fun. Eugene Lenti, head coach at DePaul University, has been an excellent mentor to me in demonstrating the great joy in coaching. He has shown he can keep things in perspective and see the bright side of a disappointing moment. I remember competing against his DePaul team in the NCAA regionals in Iowa City in 1997. We were on offense, and I sent our runner from second base to the plate, where she was thrown out by almost 30 feet. I was visibly disappointed in my decision. As Eugene walked toward the third base box, he came over to me and encouraged me, saying, "We have all made those kinds of decisions. Obviously you have made far more than a few great ones to get where you are today." Eugene did not want me to be upset. He genuinely wanted me to enjoy the moment and not allow one bad decision to take away the pleasure of the competition. I have never forgotten this.

Often we have chances to plug humor into our daily lessons. Ruth Crowe, a former assistant and now head coach at Iowa State, recalled an Iowa practice on mental training where we introduced a fun skit to our team. I asked my players to write down on a card every negative thought that could enter their heads before or during competition. I collected their cards, and we started talking about them. Assistant coach Pam Lee then arrived dressed like a cockroach. Her clothes were tattered and torn, she had a lit cigarette in her mouth, and she carried herself in a slumped and slovenly manner. Pam raced in, ripped the cards away from me, and announced how much she loved *fear, apprehension, failure,* and *uncertainty,* all of the negatives the team had written. She told them she thrived on the negatives they allowed themselves to focus on.

I explained to our team that they did not have to allow the negatives to control them, they could control these thoughts. As soon as I said this, Ruth marched around the corner dressed in her running shirt and tights, an Iowa softball helmet, and a pair of sunglasses with a Hawkeye on the lens. She carried a plastic Wiffle ball bat. Ruth got into a verbal exchange with

Pam the cockroach, and a physical battle ensued, with Ruth eventually beating Pam to the ground with the bat. As Pam lay on the ground, Ruth put her foot on top of her, raised her Wiffle ball bat, and proclaimed that she was "Hawkeye Woman!" When our team needed to control the negatives, we encouraged them to envision Hawkeye Woman beating the cockroach. The team obviously enjoyed this session. Furthermore, they enjoyed our enjoying it with them.

Choose your battles. To stay healthy and fresh we must selectively choose our battles, an important concept in all walks of life. We cannot be in constant conflict with the world. There is not enough time or energy to do everything.

Diane Stephenson, head coach at Indiana University and a former player and assistant of mine at Indiana, felt one of the most important lessons I taught her was the value of taking care of the people around you—assistant coaches, academic advisers, athletic trainers, strength coaches, managers, custodial staff, secretaries, facilities crew, and equipment managers. We should treat all people with respect. The way we interact with the people we see daily provides us with a perfect opportunity to demonstrate this. By never feeling greater or more important than anyone else, we build a powerful relationship of respect, trust, and appreciation for one another.

Teach

It was not so much a person as it was a statement that started my vocational search. Going to college as a first generation child is always a major undertaking, and the idea for me was sparked by two of my elementary teachers, who both told me I needed to go to college. How became the next issue, and a high school teacher showed me a path by helping me find a necessary scholarship opportunity.

Teachers affect our lives forever. The following are but a few examples. My high school English teacher opened my eyes to public speaking as she coached me through my high school graduation speech. What a powerful experience that was, one that made me, a painfully shy kid, aware that I could in fact speak comfortably in front of an audience. I have never forgotten the empowering feeling I experienced standing in front of that audience, and this confidence propelled me further on my search for my vocation.

My student teaching supervisor taught me the joy of teaching. She loved her students and their enthusiasm for life. She gave me my first lesson in not taking myself too seriously, a lesson I continue to work on today. Not only were her classes fun and her teams excellent, she possessed great passion for her work, and her passion became a model for me in my coaching career.

Encourage Excellence

Many of my colleagues may disagree with me on the next point, but I feel very strongly about it. We have all recruited students who are perfectionists. The perfectionist always struggles to perform at the level she expects of herself and, as a result, is unable to fully enjoy her accomplishments. If that were the only issue, maybe perfection would be a worthwhile goal. Unfortunately, I see perfectionists destroy their performance. They try so hard to be perfect, they underachieve.

Having coached many such women, I have worked on changing their focus from perfection to excellence. Excellence demands a great effort from us, but it allows for the understanding that there is failure along the way. Excellence encourages us to let it all hang out. Failure need not be fatal or consume us.

Our staff works on redirecting students, and even one another, toward excellence. Achieving excellence is something we strive for every day. Excellence involves being able to duplicate the skill, strategy, performance, or task again and again. It is not a one-time goal; it is a standard for which we strive. Once we move an athlete's focus away from perfection and toward excellence, we see greater confidence, belief, and ultimately success.

Prepare Assistants to Become Head Coaches

Granted, some assistants are better suited to be career assistants, and that is fine. However, the vast majority of assistants aspire to be head coaches. Part of our responsibility to them is to help prepare them for this move. Of course, there is no preparation quite like becoming a head coach and having the responsibility fall squarely on your shoulders. But by involving assistants in all aspects of the job, we better prepare them to become competent, successful head coaches.

Seek Mentors

There are numerous opportunities to mentor and be mentored. As I start my 24th year of college coaching, I can honestly say I learn new and interesting things every year.

A first step in finding a mentor is to become active in groups that offer potential mentors. This could include our coaches association (NFCA), coaching clinics and camps across the country, or someone as close as a colleague in another sport at your school. Many softball programs around the country would welcome you at their practices and games, as would clubs and organizations within your own community. Seek out the people you respect, admire, and would like to learn from, then interact with them.

Look for opportunities within the game. Offer to volunteer, manage, or assist with home game management. Jump in and get your hands dirty. You rarely get to start at the top. Ask any coach with at least a decade of experience, and you'll likely find they did not begin where they are now. Be willing and eager to find your own opportunities.

Consider who you may already be guiding by your knowledge, expertise, enthusiasm, and passion for the game. You might learn that the best way to find a mentor is to be one. Frequently we gain personal control by giving what we want to receive. Sinetar (1998) shares a story from "The Wisdom of the Desert Fathers" about a monk whose secular brother always wanted a handout. It seemed the more the monk helped his brother, the more destitute his brother became. When the monk talked with his spiritual leader and explained the problem, the adviser suggested that the monk ask his brother for help. Upon the monk's plea, the brother started providing help to the monk and the destitute brother began to prosper.

Observe

Observing our team and staff as they train and play allows us to determine how best to work with each of them. Mike Krzyzewski in his book *Leading With the Heart* (2000) talks about the importance of knowing each member of your team, where they might be on a given day by their body language, eyes, or speech and determining how best to work with them at that time.

Three stories come to mind, two from a former player and one from a former assistant coach. Deb Bilbao, an All-American pitcher at Iowa and now head coach at Utah State, said she recalled an experience during her senior year when we were getting ready to play at the Sacramento State Tournament. Deb had been struggling with her hitting and was frustrated as she tried to figure out what she was doing wrong. Shortly before the game, I put my arm around her and assured her she was fine, that she would play well, to have confidence in her abilities. Deb said this vote of confidence made a world of difference in how she felt going into the game. Deb hit a grand slam in her first at bat. I suppose I should have said this to her sooner.

Deb shared another story that occurred later in her senior year, a particularly challenging year for her. We had made three consecutive World Series appearances in Deb's previous three years, so she wanted in the worst way to get back to the big dance in her senior year. However, our team was young and Deb and the other two seniors were trying to lead a young team to a new experience. As is often the case, Deb was pushing too hard, trying to be everything for the team. After observing her frustration and disappointment, I took her aside. Our conversation was about allowing herself to enjoy playing the game versus trying to take the weight of the world on her shoulders. Deb told me she has remembered both of these experiences and now, as a coach, works to try to incorporate them in her own interactions with her athletes.

Diane Stephenson recalled a situation in 1986 when I was head coach at Indiana. We were headed to Minnesota for a chance to win the Big Ten title and qualify for the NCAA tournament. Diane said she remembered the pressure that we felt and knew that ultimately the team could have experienced this as well. What she most appreciated was the way in which we stepped back and turned the reins over to the team—took the pressure off of them, thereby enhancing their chances of playing well. She said we knew what they could do; all we needed to do, as coaches, was not get in the way. Diane said she knows many coaches would not know how to handle this situation. They would have choked their teams with the pressure. Instead, we lightened the load, allowing them to play relaxed, confident, and assertive ball.

Listening is one of the simplest skills at our disposal, yet it is one of the most difficult things for us to do. Too often we think we must solve our assistant's or student athlete's dilemma when all they want and need is for us to listen. Each year I make it a personal goal to become an even better active listener.

Risk

A favorite lesson I have learned and have shared with coaches and team members involves taking risks. The wonderful thing about sport is having the opportunity to succeed or fail on a daily basis, coming back day after day to try it all again. A great lesson we can pass along to others is that we can fall short, make a mistake, even fail, but still survive and enjoy life. Too many withdraw or quit, rather than risk failure.

Encourage others to take risks. Many young women are hesitant to take a coaching job until they have experienced every task and responsibility associated with it and have succeeded at each. Often they feel they must have everything in perfect order. Men, it seems, are more readily willing to jump into a situation and gain the experience while on the job. Women, on the other hand, seem to need to be encouraged, maybe even pushed into opportunities.

Women need mentors. Rarely do we know everything we are expected to handle. A former player of mine, who is very talented and has a great personality and love for life, is someone I think would make a great coach. Several years after she finished her degree at Iowa, I talked with her about one of our coaching vacancies. Unfortunately, she did not feel prepared; in her mind, not all of her ducks were in a row. Eventually, she found her way into the coaching profession and proved to be an excellent coach.

David McNally's *Even Eagles Need a Push* (1991) demonstrates our need to provide the direction even when it appears it is not wanted by others. He describes a mother eagle gently pushing her eaglets out of the nest, so they will learn to fly. As they struggle to stay in the nest, she thinks, "Why does the thrill of soaring have to begin with the fear of falling?" She fears that perhaps this time it won't work, that the air won't catch the wings of the small birds as they fall, but despite her fears, she pushes them from the nest. He finishes the story: "Until her children discovered their wings, there was no purpose for their lives. Until they learned how to soar, they would fail to understand the privilege it was to have been born an eagle. The push was the greatest gift she had to offer. It was her supreme act of love. And so one by one she pushed them . . . and they flew."

Final Thoughts

Mentoring gives us the opportunity to experience a special relationship with those with whom we closely work. It is one thing to pass along the Xs and Os of our game; it is something else to share life's lessons, passions, values, struggles, and triumphs. My hope is to make the following the greatest gift I pass along in our profession, one that remains long after I have relinquished my coaching to another generation: to be a model for those who will follow; to empower others to make responsible decisions; to nurture and care for those who ultimately care for all young people; to teach and encourage others to be passionate about their work; to observe others in their efforts to become good coaches; and to encourage others to risk in order to grow. What greater opportunity can any of us be given?

References

Belasco, James A., and Ralph C. Stayer. 1993. *The flight of the buffalo.* New York: Warner Books.

Huang, Chunglian Al, and Jerry Lynch. 1995. *Mentoring: The Tao of giving and receiving wisdom.* New York: HarperCollins.

Krzyzewski, Mike, with Donald T. Phillips. 2000. *Leading with the heart.* New York: Warner Books.

McNally, David. 1991. *Even eagles need a push.* New York: Delacorte Press.

Sinetar, Marsha. 1998. *The mentor's spirit.* New York: St. Martin's Griffin.

CHAPTER EIGHT

Building a Recruiting Network

Brian Kolze

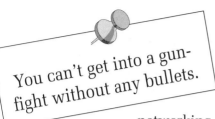

You can't get into a gunfight without any bullets.

Recruiting is the backbone component to any program and any sport. The plain and simple truth is good players make good coaches.

When developing parameters for you and your staff, there are many topics to be addressed, including philosophy, responsibilities, networking, and current and future needs. We will look at all of these areas and more as we establish a plan and approach for recruiting the talent to make our programs better.

Developing a Philosophy and Game Plan

With the growth of softball programs and the success rate of those programs, I've learned by coaching at different types of institutions that the framework and approach on how you recruit are very important. Whether you coach at a large school, small school, commuter school, private school, or public school, you must develop a philosophy and approach that works within the framework of your school and program. The framework and approach may change from school to school, but how you develop the philosophy and implement it remains the same.

Every staff must have someone who is not only able to recruit but wants to spend the time recruiting. Someone must be prepared to spend the hours at the ballpark. Each program is different in regards to who does the recruiting; it may be the head coach or an assistant. Just remember that to be successful, recruiting must receive the same dedication, attention, and hard work as the playing season. Programs that settle or give minimal effort most likely stagnate and remain mediocre.

To have a successful and efficient network within your own program, you must have everyone understand and accept what each individual's responsibilities are in the recruiting process. It must be decided who writes the letters, who makes the phone calls and sends the e-mails, who is going to spend the time out in the field identifying the talent, and who is going to make contact with the prospects and their parents.

In reality, recruiting creates a small window of opportunity for future improvement each year. But to take advantage of this you and your staff must be organized in your approach, so you don't waste your time, your team's time, and the time of the prospect.

Deciding What and Whom to Recruit

Once you get a philosophy and approach scripted for you and the staff, a more important question must be answered: Who and what positions do we recruit? To get this answer you must analyze many things.

Look for Recruits

First, what type of athlete do you need? Is the program going to recruit a specific position or the overall, versatile athlete? When you are limited in scholarships and team depth, versatility takes a higher priority. I think especially when recruiting pitchers, we don't judge their possibilities at other positions or their possible offensive capabilities. Don't limit your options; you may end up with an empty cupboard.

Second, are you going to focus on high school prospects or junior college prospects? This decision is probably the singular, most individual choice made in the recruiting process regarding prospects. High school prospects are obviously long term and they provide more stability. The thought of having someone for four years instead of two years adds a lot of consistency to a program. Junior college players can fill a specific need. A junior college prospect needs to be someone who can make a major contribution immediately. If you have to spend a year developing a player to do something she wasn't capable of doing originally, then you may not have made a smart investment. Academically you find that it's easier to find out where the high school person stands versus the junior college person. You need to investigate why the prospect was at junior college to begin with; you may find out it was an academic reason.

Third, are you going to recruit nationally, regionally, or statewide? Your decision on where to recruit is determined by how well-known your school is, the costs of out-of-state tuition, budget constraints, and how many positions you need to fill for a particular year. We rarely, if ever, recruit players from the East Coast here at Pacific. First, the prospect probably hasn't heard of us (unless she was the one who made the intial contact); second, if we spend all our time trying to educate someone that much about our program, we lose out on the recruits we could have signed. Since Pacific is a private university, everybody pays the same, so there isn't any out-of-state tuition. But when I first got here, I spent just as much time recruiting out of the West as in the West. As it turned out, I wasted a lot of money in places I didn't need to be. I invested too much time introducing our program to people who didn't have any interest and who had plenty of options already. So, I adjusted; I spent more efficient time and money in the regions of the country where we could be successful.

Other items you need to consider when deciding where to recruit are walk-on potential, number of recruiting staff, and budget constraints. If you are a relatively inexpensive school, you may have four to six prospects try out each year. If you are adding depth by keeping some of these individuals, it may change your needs. You also don't want to spread your staff so thin that they don't get to see what they need to see consistently—your top prospects in continuous competition. Finally, there are always budget concerns. You should have your plan in place so that you are efficient with your money and time invested. One thing we have learned here at Pacific is that we never cut from the recruiting budget. If needed, we cut from other areas and allocate more to recruiting.

Size Up the Competition

Know who else is recruiting the prospect. This gives you an idea of what you are up against. Part of your job is to know your competition, what you have over them, and what they have over you. This knowledge helps you know what the chances of signing may be. You are probably going to have to recruit three or four players for every slot that needs to be filled, and it is very important that you don't lose whom you could have signed by spending all your time chasing someone you probably couldn't have gotten anyway. The more experienced you get with the balancing act of recruiting, the more you understand where your true chances lie.

Know Yourself

Know what you have to offer the prospect in regards to playing time, role in the program, finances, and academic plans and strengths. This area is where you need constant updates from prospects, and you should be expected to give the same information. As you get deeper in the recruiting process, always be prepared to let them know where they stand. This is the same question you want answered as well. Always be honest with the recruit, even if it means you may not get her. If you lead her in any particular direction just to sign her, you will regret it—as will she—once she is in the program. Be honest when a financial offer comes about. When you have to make an offer, be honest and tell the recruit all the parameters—for example, only so much the first year, then so much after the first year. Document all the details; never assume anything! Don't be held hostage by the prospect, her parents, or her coaches in regards to a scholarship offer. If you have only so much to offer, whatever the parameters, and you change because of the pressure from coaches, prospects, or parents, you will regret it. If a person signs with your institution only because you offer the most money, it's not the right reason, anyway.

Be prepared with all of these scenarios when it comes to the monetary talks. Prepare yourself for the questions regarding finance and always be honest. For example, if you offer 75 percent for the first year and say you will increase it after the first year, be prepared to document and answer how much the increase will be, even if it's minor. The recruit and her family deserve to know the truth if they have been honest with you. Finally, realize that the higher-level Division I program has the advantage in the recruiting process, even if it has been less successful than a Division II or III program.

Finding Recruits

There are many ways to start out when trying to find talent, but there are no secrets; it takes lots of time and effort. This investment is why you want a plan and the responsibilities in place so that you are efficient with your time.

Before you observe the athlete, start networking by phone. Get as much information from her coach, either school or club, up front. This homework allows you to spend less time talking at tournaments and more time watching. We have a difficult sport to recruit because we can watch a player for a long time without her being involved in any action to evaluate. It helps when you form a consistent network with your top high school or club team coaches. Do this under the premise that you will regularly recruit more than one player from their programs. There are times when my dealings with particular club teams are between three and four years, but this doesn't mean I quit communicating with them. You have to continue to build these relationships. Never burn a bridge! Be honest with recruits and coaches, even if it turns out you were wrong. Recruiting is tough enough, even without someone who doesn't trust you.

Obviously travel ball tournaments are the best site to evaluate talent. This is due to the level of competition and the number of athletes involved. You can also attend high school games and exposure camps like those sponsored by the National Fastpitch Coaches Association. These camps are usually held in conjunction with major tournaments. They allow you to see the prospects perform skills in repetition, and they let you follow them throughout their tournament games. Practice is another great source for evaluation. At the high school level, I like practice more because game competition can be inconsistent.

The more years you recruit, the better contacts you make, the more successful you are in evaluating and identifying talent. Remember to never overlook your own local players who can potentially help your program. The grass isn't always greener elsewhere.

Evaluating Talent

Once you have identified where to find the talent, you now need to evaluate it. Evaluating the prospect isn't just how she plays; there are other areas of consideration as well.

One area to consider is her background. Have the prospect fill out a questionnaire so that you know where she is academically. A sample questionnaire is shown in figure 8.1. Also request a copy of transcripts and test scores so that you know where she formally stands. Evaluate her academic status as soon as possible to determine whether you are wasting each other's time and to prepare for any potential questions.

Softball Questionnaire

Name _____ Birth date _____

Address _____ City/state _____

Zip code _____ Telephone _____ Height _____ Weight _____

E-mail _____ Social Security number _____

Father's name and occupation _____

Mother's name and occupation _____

Planned major _____

Position(s) _____ Bat _____ Throw _____

Video available _____

High school _____ Graduation date _____

High school address _____

SAT or ACT score _____ High school GPA _____

Coach's name _____ Telephone _____

Junior college _____ Graduation date _____

Junior college address _____

Dates attended _____ Units completed _____

Junior college GPA _____ Major _____ AA degree? Yes ___ No ___

Coach's name _____ Telephone _____

Summer league team _____ ASA level _____

Coach's name _____ Telephone _____

Special honors and other sports:

Figure 8.1 A sample recruiting questionnaire.

Another area to look at is her interaction skills and her character. When evaluating, pay attention to how she interacts with coaches, parents, and teammates. It's important to observe how she treats others to evaluate whether it meets the expectations of your program. If at all possible, try to get character information from someone who doesn't have a vested interest in the individual. This assessment is probably the hardest item to attain in the recruiting process because everybody indirectly wants to feel a part of the process and thus may not give you the entire truth. Your source may want to be your buddy instead of telling you what you need to hear. When someone is a problem off the field or is tough to coach, we want to know. Now is when your network of relationships comes into play because you know whom you can trust. Far too often we find out more information about recruits after we sign them than beforehand.

The final area to evaluate is talent. Everybody can find the great athlete, but most of us need to find the athlete who with an investment of time can become a major component of your softball program. There are far more viable athletes who we can make better than there are great athletes to begin with.

When evaluating prospects, take into account the level of their competition and evaluate how they compete against the highest level. Pay careful attention to how they react and interact when they are doing poorly. Everybody is happy when they are doing well; we want to see how they are when they are struggling. Do they throw equipment, pout, or talk back to teammates and coaches? These are questions to be answered. The answers to these questions probably indicate if it's more important for them to win as a team or as individuals.

Interaction and attitude are so important within the team framework. This is why we want as much information regarding these areas at the beginning of the recruiting process, not at the end. The best way to do this is to make sure you observe prospects more than once. When you are about to pursue a major investment for your program, you can never have enough information.

Pursuing Recruits

After you have decided whom to pursue, you need to figure out how you are going to land the recruit. At this time, your approach comes into play.

We start out by sending letters and literature to introduce the recruit and her family to the university and what it has to offer. The literature you send is extremely important because it may be the majority of information looked at by the prospect's parents. At times you find that communication between the prospect and her parents isn't very good, so you have to provide the most complete information for both. This challenge is really evident when the parents are divorced. You are then educating two households. Take advantage of the Internet, your team Web page, and e-mail.

Once you have sent the literature, you may follow up with phone calls and e-mails. The two most important things for you to do in all communications: One, promote the strengths of your program and university, and two, always solicit any questions that need to be answered.

It's arbitrary how often to correspond with the prospect. Some coaches send out information or write every week; others do it biweekly or monthly. Your success rate and experience make this decision for you. Just remember that there is far more competition than there used to be. As a seller of your program, you must be more dedicated to your recruits than your recruits are to you.

Regarding phone calls, we know we only have one per week. Be organized before you get on the phone; it may be your only opportunity to sell yourself and the program that week. Be efficient with your call; don't waste the opportunity to sell and always ask if the parents have any questions. Your program makes a greater impact if the initial phone call is made by the head coach.

At this juncture of the recruiting process you need to start trying to find out where your program stands in the equation and whom you are competing against. You need to find out if you are spinning your wheels or if you have a legitimate shot at the recruit. Your ability to communicate and sell yourself, the program, and the university is the key to the entire process.

Before you get more deeply involved with the prospect, the parents, and the process, find out if your school is in her top four or five choices. There comes a time—and you learn this through experience—when a recruit is either leading you on or can't tell you *no* because she doesn't want to hurt your feelings. Let her know that you need to know so that everyone can move on.

You have already invested time and effort in the recruiting process. If a prospect at this time tells you she isn't interested in your program, wish her luck and move on. Don't take it personally. You are always more committed to them than they are to you. If they are interested, then you need to go to the next step of the process.

Arranging Home and Campus Visits

The home and campus visits can be done in any order. Sometimes it's best to let the recruit and her parents decide because the parents may not accompany their daughter on the trip.

Home Visits

Home visits are where you can learn about the family environment. You can observe how the recruit treats her parents and family. Your home visit tests your ability to sell and promote your program and university since this may be the first real impression you make on the parents. The home visit has many objectives. The most important are to make sure you get a feel for the home environment, answer each parent's questions, and get a better feel for where you stand in regards to your competition. It is also possibly the one time you address recruits with parents in the same room, so information regarding finances, playing time, and team rules and policies won't get lost in the translation. If there is any item you want to emphasize to a recruit and her parents, the home visit is usually the best place to do it.

Campus Visits

Whether a recruit takes an official or unofficial visit, you need to treat the recruit the same and show her what needs to be seen. If she decides to take an unofficial visit, try to encourage her to spend a little money and spend a night on campus so that she gets a better feel for the campus. It is more important for balance on a recruiting trip. She needs to spend plenty of time with the team instead of the coach. Because of this, I recommend that the recruit stays with team members and not in a hotel. I also recommend your team plan at least one activity where everyone on the team attends, but the coaching staff doesn't. This opportunity allows the recruit to interact naturally with her peers and ask questions she or her parents may not have asked the coaches. After all, at the end of the trip, you are going to ask for your team's input, so they might as well have plenty of time to get to know the recruit.

When the recruit is on campus, you must show her everything your program has to offer, both academically and athletically. She needs to see the housing, the study hall, classrooms, admissions, the weight room, and all other facilities. If it is important for her to see your team practice, you must keep this in mind when scheduling trips during early signing. If she requests to meet with advisers or a professor or to attend a class, then adjust the schedule to adhere to her requests. When she attends these meetings, it is important for the head coach to have some involvement. This way, she knows your commitment to her and what you expect in return.

Remember that your current team is part of the process. Don't overburden them with too many recruits at one time. Make sure whom you designate as a host is someone who has some familiarity with the school and the program. Make sure you and the team present a true picture of the program and only promote your program. Our players are instructed to talk to recruits only about Pacific. When a recruit asks our team about other programs, they let the recruit know that they can't comment on other programs. I believe some negative recruiting comes from our athletes who are unaware they are doing it. If a recruit doesn't get a true picture and promotion of your program, when she attends, she may not stay.

Post-Visit Follow-Up and Evaluation

Once a recruit leaves campus, sit down with your staff and evaluate the recruit. Talk to your team and get feedback on their perceptions and ask if the recruit will fit in. Here at Pacific we always tell our players that they can come to the coaches in private if there is something they want to tell us about a recruit. Remember, a recruit may already have friends in your program or may have made new friendships that could be damaged by speaking in front of others. Your team must know that their input is critical to the decision-making process. Every program in the country, no matter how successful, has had players come to the coaching staff to tell the coaches things they didn't want to hear about recruits.

If everything goes well, the next step is getting the recruit to commit. You hope her visit to your campus was her highest moment. However, when you follow up with her and you don't get good feedback, start preparing yourself to move on. You need to know where you stand, just as she needs to know where she stands. Remember, you have been more committed to the recruit than she has to you. She is making a decision that at the time is the most difficult of her life. In most cases, we as coaches are asking unselfish young ladies to make a selfish decision that they feel benefits them the most. All you can do as a coach is provide the information, answer the questions, and sell the program. Too many of us take it personally if a recruit turns down our school. There are still coaches in this profession who slam the phone or yell at the recruit when she denies them; to you I say, "Grow up!" I also believe we must be careful in our profession because we are slowly and collectively starting to use pressure tactics on these young ladies to make them cave in and sign with our school. I also don't believe that consistently telling recruits that offers are only on the table for a short time frame is the way to keep the recruits from visiting or signing with other schools.

After you have players commit to your program and they are signed, sit down and evaluate the process you used to get them. Talk about any changes or adjustments you and the staff might need to make. Talk to other successful coaches in your own department to see what they have tried.

Final Thoughts

Recruiting is a long and tedious process that provides the backbone of any program. Continue to evaluate and adjust your approach as you would anything else.

Remember: Good recruits make good players; good players make good coaches. Be as dedicated and work as hard at recruiting as you expect your athletes to work at their skills. If you cut corners and become lazy in recruiting, you get the same results when your team cuts corners in their duties. Nobody gets the job done.

CHAPTER NINE

Marketing and Promoting Your Program

Yvette Girouard

Photo by Steve Franz, courtesy of the Louisiana State University Athletic Department

I long came to the realization that controlling one's own destiny is a task that can only be undertaken with a rolling-up-the-sleeves attitude. Simply accepting the quote "It's a female sport; no one would be interested" was not an option for me. So with that attitude in mind, my staff and I set out to market and promote what we honestly felt was great family entertainment: college fastpitch softball. The excuse of a tight budget—or worse yet, no budget at all—and a lack of a marketing and promotion department was not an obstacle for us in our effort to raise funds for the program and put fans in the stands. A strong belief in what you do, a ton of hard work, and a never-say-no attitude ultimately win you many fans. I have always believed that when people see you sacrifice your own time, effort, money, and heart, they tend to give you a shot. When done right, that one shot at the ballpark convinces the fans that the entertainment and enjoyment of our great collegiate game are worthy of their time, and they ultimately brings them back for other games on your schedule.

How many times have we heard from first-time fans "Wow! I did not know that girls could play that well or that intense"? Well, I believe that this phenomenon is occurring every night, all over the country during our season. However, to keep our fans returning and investing in our programs, we must realize that we are in the entertainment business, and sometimes the game itself is not enough to make them full-time fans—especially with the attraction of movies, malls, the Internet, 500 channels on TV, beaches, and other sports and recreation. Therefore, we must do more than simply present the game; we must relax our attitudes and beliefs and allow our games and environment to become more like a minor league atmosphere. A realistic, achievable goal is making sure that the fan is having fun and leaving the ballpark smiling and upbeat, even if the home team lost the game.

Build It and They Will Come

Comfort, aesthetics, and easy accessibility to and from the ballpark must be addressed first. When your fans are not comfortable, you lose them before the first pitch is thrown.

If they cannot see through the backstop—many of which are constructed of pipes and fence material that make it hard to see through—correct the problem. We were one of the first programs in the country to have a backstop made of netting and cables that eliminated pipes and fencing. The backstop cost a total of $5,000 and created instant appreciation from fans and players alike.

If your bathrooms are not clean or worse yet, if you have none, get this resolved quickly. Dirty bathrooms destroy your attendance quicker than anything else.

A fan-friendly environment in and around the ballpark must be a priority. Shade, if at all possible, needs to be provided for elderly fans. These fans are usually the staunchest of ballpark regulars. When feasible, plant trees, provide umbrellas with benches and tables, or construct awnings of some sort so that fans can escape the heat of the sun.

You can create a cozy environment without a monument made of steel that costs millions of dollars. Local nurseries can and do donate plants and containers to soften up the facility.

If at all possible, your facility must have lights. Night games are a must for fan attendance. How many fans are able to attend a two o'clock double-header on a Tuesday afternoon? Most people I know work at this time.

Try to use the school colors and logos as much as possible to foster team pride and tradition. Before you know it, your fans begin to attend your games in these very same colors.

Build, construct, or manufacture some sort of gift shop to market and promote your program with unique and saleable items. This building does not need to be an expensive facility. We created a metal building, with a donation from a local community service organization, and it instantly began turning a nice profit.

Create a playground area for the younger children if space is available. It is very hard for the younger kids to remain seated for an entire double-header. And keeping your crowd for both games should be a priority.

Seating your fans as close as possible to the field itself definitely creates a home field advantage. Constructing stadiums where fans are seated in the nosebleed section never gives you the advantage of the intimate ballpark where your fans can and do make a difference in those close games.

Ticket takers, concession workers, game management staff, and gift shop employees must realize that the fans are the number-one priority at the games. Fans must feel as if they are the most special people in the facility. Our concession stand workers are among the friendliest people in the world. They take special pride in creating good, southern Louisiana food for the locals and visiting fans alike. Our special food is the talk of the country, so we try to make sure that visitors are given the authentic Cajun taste.

Make the Game an Event

With our decision to aggressively market and promote our program, we came to the conclusion that we had to make the game the thing to do in town. Yes, we did have a built-in advantage, as our team was a consistent top 10 program with three appearances in the College World Series. The fact that our program had achieved the highest national ranking of any collegiate sport at the institution was certainly a plus. After all, everyone loves a winner.

We made a conscious effort to know and target our audience, which consisted mainly of families, sports followers, youth, older single women, and senior citizens. By offering a unique season ticket option, many families found attending our games to be a reasonable entertainment purchase. A $50 season ticket consisted of a 30-hole punch card that could be used in many ways. If a family wanted to bring 30 people to one doubleheader, then that season ticket would have been completely used. However, if one person attended a doubleheader, then only one hole in the card would be punched. Many could not attend afternoon doubleheaders during the weekday, which we tried to keep to a minimum, so a family possibly could not use a complete season ticket. They could also bring other family and friends with this unique option, take a client to a game, or simply give the ticket to the client. We always felt that once we got them to the ballpark, they would return again not only for the terrific play on the field but for the fun they would have at the park. Also, the more fans in the stands, the more dollars spent at concessions and the gift shop.

We loosened up our attitude and made the atmosphere like a minor league environment, introducing what is likely the most creative and entertaining announcer in the country. This local entrepreneur, who could be classified as a comedian, artist, and general cutup, created a truly festive atmosphere. His job was to make sure that fans had a great time in the stands and left the park smiling, regardless if the home team won or not. He would ask fans to contribute their own jokes between innings; he performed a definitely signature rendition of "Take Me Out to the Ball Game," and he good-naturedly picked on people in the ballpark. For two years, he promised fans that Elvis would show up at the park—and Elvis (in costume) did in fact make a one-time appearance! He proposed to our catcher at home plate—and she said yes! Capitalizing on our unique Cajun music and lingo was a given. Fans came back just to hear what he would add from game to game and year to year.

I know that some fans and foes alike considered our announcer bush-league, but I also know that he captivated the audience and created an atmosphere unlike any other in college softball. For those who did not appreciate the humor, or worse yet, turned it into something it was not, I say to them, "Loosen up." Forget the stuffy attitude and allow fans and players alike to enjoy themselves. For the teams who accepted it as it was intended, they often commented that the excitement in the air made them actually play better and considered it the game on the schedule that fired them up. We must relax and embrace the attitude that the word *fun* needs to be in our vocabulary when we are considering our fans. Too often we get hung up on our ridiculous standards of acceptable, sanitized behavior.

Along with our unique announcer, we also implemented different events and promotions throughout the years. The following are just some of the ideas used in our program.

Game Night Sponsors

We promoted and sold each home game at a cost of $250. This covered our cost of officials and balls for the doubleheader. The business involved was given logo recognition on schedule cards, on posters in the stadium, and in ads in the newspaper. The business was encouraged to provide promotional giveaways for that game. The giveaways could include distribution of product, flyers, or some form of promotion like balloons or pom-poms. Giveaway items are tangible and can be taken home by our fans. Free tickets were included in the sponsorship, which were good for the day of the event. These tickets could be used for employees or clients or donated to a local charity.

An example of business interaction with events was Circus Nights, sponsored by Shoney's Restaurant. Our concessionaires dressed as clowns; balloons were given out; the Shoney's Bear threw out the first pitch; and our own unique clown was behind the microphone announcing the game. Our night had everything except the big tent representing a circus atmosphere.

Best Seat in the House

Two recliners that had been donated to the program were raffled off each home game. Tickets were sold for the privilege of sitting in these chairs. Not only were the seats truly the best seats since they were placed on a raised platform directly behind home plate, but the lucky winners were served food every inning from the concession stand. Between doubleheaders, a hot pizza, donated by a local pizza joint, was delivered. That restaurant would be given plenty of publicity from our announcer as the delivery was made. The fans selected to sit in the chairs were the object of constant attention from the fans in the stands and our announcer.

Horse Races

Three wooden horses placed on sticks painted in the different school colors "raced" behind our outfield fence. Raffle tickets were sold for this event, with one lucky winner sharing half the pot with the softball program. Usually it was a photo finish at the line to keep everyone guessing in the stands. The race took place between innings of a game.

50/50 Giveaways

Because we are also in the business of raising money for the program, we sold 50/50 tickets. The winner shares the pot with the program. More often than not, the winner would donate the money back to the program, thus gaining instant appreciation and recognition from our loyal fans.

Professor Night

Every athlete was represented by her favorite teacher of the semester on a designated night on the schedule. This night was promoted in the newspaper and on schedule cards and posters. Usually our athletes would pick the teacher whose class might be presenting a problem for them. The professors were usually very touched and appreciative of their selection. Being escorted onto the field by our athlete and being recognized for the course they taught and their professional background won over many teachers. It always served more than one purpose: It provided our program with new fans, thanked our professionals on campus for the jobs they do, and introduced them into our world of athletics.

Hometown Days

With our local athletes, we solicited a game day sponsorship from a local bank in their cities. Along with the recognition of their business on schedule cards and posters, the local bank was given a certain amount of free tickets to distribute to the town folk. They could say they were sponsoring a free night at the park to the citizenry while supporting one of their own. The town mayor was invited to throw out the first pitch, and the athlete's family and former coaches were invited on the field for the national anthem.

Girl Scout Day

Trying to promote girls and women in particular, we featured one doubleheader every year to honor this group. The girls attended the game in uniform and joined the team out on the field for the national anthem.

Diamond Dash

Selling raffle tickets for the chance to win valuable prizes was a fun event for the participant and the fans in the stands. One ball placed on the infield among many other balls had a $100 sign written on it. The lucky fan was given so many seconds to scoop up as many balls as possible. The "Jeopardy" theme song would play over the public address system, getting contestant and fans alike into the excitement.

Pocket Litter

Our announcer would think of an item that fans would have to produce that they would have in their possession, like a 1999 nickel. With our announcer it was always something more bizarre—usually something to do with Cajun country. It was a whole lot of fun watching people trying to search their pockets and purses. It then became a race to the press box to be the first to produce the item and claim the prize.

Other Fund-Raising

Because our program was not supported financially, besides coaches' salaries and scholarships, we were responsible for generating up to $80,000 a year to sustain our operating needs. This included team travel, recruiting, the second assistant's salary, umpire fees, equipment, uniforms, fifth-year financial assistance, and summer school scholarships. Never was a player asked to raise money, but players were asked to be present for major fund-raising events. Two of these major events were a car raffle, which generated more than $20,000, and a boat raffle. Tickets were sold at $100, allowing a couple to attend a party with music, hot dogs and apple pie, and a chance to drive home in a new car. Preceding the drawing, a live auction was conducted by our unique announcer, who warmed everyone up for the drawing for the vehicle. Ten numbers were selected from the tickets sold. Those ten individuals each chose a key, which they used one by one to try to start the vehicle. The suspense and excitment of each attempt was a ton of fun. The winner was actually allowed to drive the vehicle home that night. These events were tremendous fun and a huge financial success.

Promote the Athletes and Coaches

We have a never-say-no attitude when asked for anything in the community. We rely on the community so heavily for our fund-raising needs and fans in the stands that we created an ownership mentality with our program. Because they contributed financially, their concern for our success became important. They wanted to make sure that these student athletes received the necessary tools for success. Therefore, we became very active and present in their environment. We read in the schools, gave free clinics, visited patients in hospitals and the elderly in nursing homes, and we informed anyone who would listen to "just say no to drugs." We also worked Special Olympics every year, and we aided the United Way, helping clean up yards after a hurricane had hit and caused major damage in the town. I also spoke to every organization that asked, promoting our program and athletes at every turn. We gave demonstrations at halftime of our basketball games, where the different pitches were explained and thrown. While our pitchers and catchers were wowing the audience, the rest of the team was in uniform passing out pocket schedules to the crowd.

Softball players and female student athletes are wonderful role models and representatives in general. They are often highly motivated and intelligent and do a wonderful job with kids and adults alike. We made sure that our athletes attended a booster meeting and thanked our supporters in person for everything they did for our program. Anytime we had a season ticket drive or a drive to sell tickets for the car and boat raffles, we had our student athletes telephone our committee people and volunteers to say that they appreciated what these wonderful people did to help our program. Do not be afraid to utilize their wonderful natural instincts. Your athletes are really interested in promoting their sport: They sell themselves on and off the field beautifully, and they will take the time to accomplish these goals when you set the example and lead them.

Make Friends With the Media

The concept of media coverage may be the most difficult part of the equation. Trying to compete with the men's teams in terms of coverage by simply demanding it and bullying the editor is not an approach that is usually successful. Sometimes you have to genuinely earn their respect before decent media coverage is obtained. Being open, honest, and accessible to local newspapers and television personnel is crucial. Make sure that you make time for these people if they do indeed call for you. I have found that taking them out to lunch, asking their opinion, then truly listening to their comments do make a lasting impression. I have actually developed lifelong friends with some of them using this approach.

One young man was considered my good luck charm, and we always managed to eat a certain meal at the same restaurant before every big NCAA event. He took special pride and ownership in the team and in our relationship.

Also, remember that if you ask for an opinion and help, you must try in some sort of way to incorporate their views. Nothing is more frustrating than a person reaching out to extend a helping hand, then being ignored. Remember, these people are usually very articulate, passionate people who are obsessed with the sports world. Other ideas include involving their medium in a contest of some sort. If you have a fireball pitcher who is racking up Ks, devise a contest to nickname your ace. They could advertise this in the local paper and solicit opinions from their viewers. If you have the opportunity, allow television sportscasters or personalities to try to hit off your pitchers. They like to challenge themselves, and they love to try an untested skill. Everyone thinks they can hit at least one, and they usually jump at the chance—especially the men.

Try New Ideas

There are few new ideas on marketing and promotions. Usually everything is a variation of something already established and tried. However, the greatest form of flattery is copying what is successful. Pay attention at any and all venues you attend, and pay attention to what's on television and radio. Read as many articles as you can on marketing and promotions. You will be surprised at what you can invent and incorporate into your program. Keep trying new ideas in your sport, even if they have been borrowed from another arena. Your own passion and willingness to excite and entertain the fans in the stands will be noticed by all. Do not be discouraged by failure or by a no to a solicitation for money or help. There is always someone else you can ask or something else you can try. Remember that you and your team are your best ambassadors, so keep trying. Take the game of softball on the field dead serious, but remember to lighten up about every other facet of the production.

CHAPTER TEN

Establishing a Successful High School Program

Denny Throneburg

To establish a successful softball program at the high school level, you must first understand the requirements of such an endeavor. After coaching high school softball for 22 years, I am a firm believer that there is no right way to do it, but there are a few guidelines that make the process smoother.

Remember that one of the most important characteristics of a successful person or program is the ability to adjust. As the years go by and a program becomes more successful, certain concrete principles become the basis of your program. But a coach must also be flexible enough to adjust with the times and be in touch with the present athlete.

The author Tolstoy once said, "The strongest of all warriors are time and patience." Establishing a successful high school program requires a tremendous amount of both.

The Program

At Casey-Westfield, we have always played under the premise that the program comes first. We do what is best for the team before what is best for the individual. This standard sometimes means that each player does not always play at her best position. Simply put, the best team is always on the field. Everyone has to buy into this theory, which is one of the first steps in building a program.

Another key in building a program is that the best players play. This philosophy simply means that regardless of class (freshman, sophomore, junior, or senior) or any other factor, the nine best players, as determined by the coaching staff, play. This guideline does not mean that we are not loyal to our upperclassmen; we certainly are. We give returning players every opportunity to keep or inherit a position from the previous year. They are fully aware that their performance dictates whether they get it or not. This theory motivates the younger players in the program because they know that if they are good enough, they get to play. Just remember, the program comes first, and always do what is best for the team.

As the program develops, adjustments are always necessary. As the program becomes more successful, expectations become greater. At times, they may even become unrealistic. Remember to stick to the basic theories of the program so that the pressure and expectations do not become overwhelming. Keep in mind that the individuals change, but the program always remains the same.

One of the first times I implemented the play-the-best-team philosophy, I had a young lady who as a junior pitcher led us to the state finals and was named the most valuable player of the state tournament, allowing only one run in three games. During her senior year, I had a junior pitcher who was developing quickly. By the middle of the season, we were on a straight two-pitcher rotation, with the senior playing shortstop when she was not pitching. As the state tournament approached, I had a difficult decision to make. I could stay with the rotation and weaken the team when my senior pitcher was not playing shortstop, or I could go strictly with my junior pitcher and play the last year's most valuable pitcher at shortstop. I chose to go with the play-the-best-team theory and pitch my junior all three games in the state finals. Fortunately, she threw three consecutive shutouts. We won the state championship; she was named the most valuable player; and my senior made the all-state tournament team at shortstop. I was able to keep my job and once again experience a full night of sleep! Our program, with one of our basic philosophies now in tact, was off and running.

What is not tried never works. Do not be afraid to be a little unconventional in running a program. A coach who tries something and finds out it doesn't work is still better off than the coach who tries nothing and succeeds.

Our practices normally run two and a half hours from beginning to end. A problem was that on home game days, the game took approximately one and a half hours, and we lost one hour of valuable practice time. So we began to practice after each home game so that we could complete a normal practice schedule. Imagine what some of the other teams thought when they saw us practicing as they were getting on their bus! I hope opposing coaches used that as a motivation for their teams. It took a little while for the parents to understand, but before long, they actually enjoyed watching the kids practice and seeing the drills we were doing.

We believe we get an advantage on our opponents when we practice because we feel we get more done at practice than most teams. An effective coach who is well-organized does not confuse activity with accomplishment. We practice by the following motto: It is not the hours you put in; it is what you put into the hours that makes the difference.

The System

To establish a successful program, you must establish a learning system. Develop a system or method of teaching basic softball skills that can be implemented at all levels of the program. We have a method of hitting and a method of pitching that we teach throughout our program. Right or wrong, we are not confusing our kids by subjecting them to 20 different ways to hit or pitch, as suggested by 20 different people. Remember, kids are easily influenced and the more suggestions they hear, the more confused they become. We want our players to learn to think on their own and have the knowledge to make the proper adjustments. No brain, no gain!

Not everyone is going to buy into the system immediately, which is where commitment to the program becomes vital. Through clinics, camps, and coaching seminars, we have been able to get all of our coaches to follow the same system. It is imperative that a high school coach building a successful program be visible at the elementary, junior high, and summer league levels. This show of support for the teams builds cohesiveness and unity among coaches, which is so important in developing a learning system that can be implemented at all levels.

The successful high school coach must make all the other coaches in the program feel important. Listen to all of them—from the T-ball coach to the top assistant at the high school level. This does not necessarily mean that suggestions immediately become implemented; however, their suggestions are acknowledged, and that's what is important. The head coach can do likewise and suggest—not tell—other coaches what to do. Telling other coaches what and how to do it quickly dissolves a program.

Goals and Format

To build a successful program, coaches have to be goal-oriented. What separates the successful program from the searching program is the ability to establish a realistic goal. The coach of a successful program can recognize obtainable goals for the program and the individuals in the program. No goals, no glory.

At Casey-Westfield, we use what we call a contract for success. It is simply a form the coach completes, outlining a player's strengths and weaknesses and finishing with a short list of goals. The coach discusses it with the player until both are in agreement as to the evaluation and goal setting. The player signs it, agreeing to make every effort to fulfill the contract for success.

As a coach, always remember that, if the goals set are unrealistically high, the athlete becomes frustrated. If the goals are too low, the athlete never realizes the work ethic necessary to be successful and thus always settles for less. Unsuccessful teams almost always lack focus. The easiest way to maintain focus is to constantly strive to achieve higher goals.

One of my first goals was to establish a learning system within a step-by-step format. I chose to begin the learning system at the elementary level. Since the elementary school did not have softball, that meant I needed to work closely with the summer program. For two summers, I ran daily practices for all the teams in the 9- to 12-year-old league, spending 8 to 10 hours per day at the diamond. This gave me a chance to implement the system at the earliest level. I also coached the junior high team (seventh and eighth graders) for 15 years during the fall season, another great opportunity to implement the system. By coordinating the summer program, junior high program, and high school program, the efficiency and continuity of the total program multiply.

The Coach

After coaching well over 1,000 softball games and numerous players from T-ball to Olympic level, I've come to the conclusion that two of the most important attributes of a coach are the ability to teach fundamentals and the ability to motivate.

Although there are many great players, not every great player is a great coach. On the other hand, I know some very good coaches who were not exceptionally good players. Why is this? I believe it is simply the ability to teach fundamentals. Being able to break a skill down into learning parts and then transferring that knowledge to players through a series of progressive drills is an ability that all successful coaches have. Coaches gain that knowledge through a variety of ways. Some coaches were very good players and were taught by good coaches. Others use resources such as videos, camps, clinics, and seminars. I believe any coach who is willing to learn can learn. Coaches should check their egos at the door. No matter how many games or state championships a coach has won, every coach can still learn. Coaches who attend clinics, read books, or watch videos have admitted a great thing in coaching: They want to get better.

I guess the coaches who bother me the most are those who don't ask for help. Asking for help is a strength, not a weakness. I suspect that some coaches never attempt to get better because they don't want to admit how little they actually know. Some coaches seem to be more afraid of success than they are failure. With success, expectations become greater, and some people don't want that kind of pressure. A coach actually told me once he just wanted to be .500 every year, then the expectations would never be too high. I've never been able to rationalize that statement.

There is no magic formula to motivation. A successful coach simply has to do it his or her own way. If you try to be someone you are not, your players will see through you in a heartbeat. If you're emotional, be emotional; if not, don't. Players adjust once they realize you are being you.

A coach has to be able to challenge, inspire, and discipline. There is nothing wrong with demanding excellence. You do not always get it, but there is nothing wrong with striving for it. I always tell our players the two easiest things in life to do are to lose and to quit, and we're not real fond of anyone who enjoys either of them. We want to be contenders, not pretenders.

There are no shortcuts to success. Any coach or team can have the occasional exceptional season, but to win year after year requires the three Ps: patience, persistence, and practice.

Persistence leads to perfection. We don't do anything fancy in our practices. We believe in teaching a skill correctly and then repeating it over and over until muscle memory of the correct skill becomes an immediate reaction. Nothing takes the place of repetition. Another important lesson we instill in our players is "If it is done in a game, do it in practice." Usually this lesson relates to fundamental skills such as diving for a line drive or a grounder. If done in practice, it will succeed in a game. What some people attribute to luck, we attribute to the desire to practice.

Teach only one skill at a time. Whether it is a pitching workout, swings in the batting cage, or fielding a ball, don't confuse the player with constant adjustments. Give the player time to work out some flaws on her own. Let her think for herself. As we sometimes say, "Flex your brain."

In certain situations, overcoaching can be as dangerous as no coaching. When a player becomes robotic and stops to think about each move, there is no fluidity in her play. This goes back to repetition. Think before the play; react during the play.

All successful coaches love to teach. To me, the softball diamond is just another classroom. As long as you believe in what you are doing and you can pass that knowledge to the players, they will have the confidence to succeed. As a coach looking to establish a successful program, courage to succeed is a must. Don't be afraid of taking risks. It is easy to be average, which is perhaps why some people tend to be, but to excel and to be different from the rest takes a lot more courage. A coach has to be able to endure criticism and the occasional setback. We do not like to use the word *failure*. In fact, one of the more common slogans we use in our program is "Failure is not an option, just a nagging possibility that helps us stay focused."

It is easy for a coach to ask for respect, but it is much harder to earn it. The coaches who usually make the biggest difference are not necessarily the ones with the best credentials but the ones who show the greatest concern. Successful coaches have to be resilient. They have to be able to bounce back from adversity if they expect their teams to. To measure the character of a team, watch how they react after a loss. If they accept the loss as a learning experience, if they evaluate why they lost, and if they then correct those mistakes and make their adjustment, then they are on the right path. If a losing team immediately begins the excuse trip, then there is still a long way to go in building the successful program.

To me, teaching and coaching are synonymous. A coach feels a tremendous sense of pride and accomplishment when a player truly begins to excel. A coach who wants to establish a successful program never hides from the challenge but seeks it out and conquers it. The biggest obstacles to conquer are often the easiest because there is so little competition at that level.

Remember that whatever is demanded of others, you must demand of yourself. Good coaches, like good players, are made, not born. Success in coaching is a direct result of preparation. All good coaches are well-prepared. They are able to think ahead, and nothing that happens in a game surprises them. They know their players. They know who reacts best in a given situation, and they try to place players in situations where they are likely to experience that success. A coach cannot be afraid to take a risk, but it has to be a calculated risk. Your strength is in your belief, so give it your best and cope with the rest.

The best example I can give of believing in our system was the championship game of the state tournament in 1999. Entering the bottom of the seventh inning, we trailed 3-0 and did not have a hit off the opposing pitcher. As we huddled for our at bats, I told the kids, "We got 'em right where we want 'em. This is exactly where we want to be. Let's see if all this discipline is really what it is supposed to be." Down to our final out, we loaded the bases on an error and a pair of walks by using the discipline not to swing at a marginal pitch. I chose to sub for our runner at first, believing that if we managed a hit, we would have to score all three runners since the opposing pitcher was so outstanding. True to script, our batter hit a ball into the gap for our first hit, and all three runners scored. We held the opponents scoreless in the eighth inning, then we scored one run in the bottom of the eighth to capture the state championship.

There is no limit to what can be accomplished if you truly believe in what you are doing. If you can dream it, you can do it.

The Players

In a high school program, players come and go. A coach must adjust to the type of players participating that year but still adhere to the basic principles of the program. Some years a team may have more speed, so one can utilize the bunt and the hit and run more effectively. In the years lacking speed, a coach doesn't quit bunting, he or she just uses it more efficiently.

The one word that best describes a player in a successful program is *aggressiveness.* Make your players aggressive both offensively and defensively. We tell our players on offense, once they have mastered the location of the strike zone—which can be difficult for many players—attack the ball. We want to be aggressive with the bat and on the bases. Many times an extra base hit can be gained for no other reason than surprise. Force the opposing team to execute. Once a team has developed the reputation for being successful, they can usually take complete control by scoring a couple of runs early in the game.

Defensively, we want players who go after everything, especially in the outfield. Outfielders need to trust their teammates. They tend to go after every ball because they know and trust that a teammate is there to back them up if they miss it. Trust is important to a team and to the athletes who make up the team. They must trust each other to be successful and, if they make a mistake or an error, move on. We have eyes in the front of our head, not the back, so look forward, not backward.

Any successful program demands the four Ds from players: desire, dedication, discipline, and determination. Without the desire to excel, a player cannot contribute to building or maintaining a successful program. We often tell players, "Desire is the great equalizer." Desire is often the difference between the good and the great player. A player has to be dedicated to improvement. But before she can improve, she must first know her deficiencies and work to eliminate them.

In a high school program, especially at a smaller school, both players and coaches may have all the desire in the world but may have to share that desire with another sport or sports. We have never seen this as a major problem and have had many duel-sport and triple-sport athletes. This situation does require cooperation of the coaches. I think it is important that the coaches devise a schedule compatible to the athlete's best interests, not their own. This coordination is especially important in the summer when athletes may have so many demands on them that they are forced to give up a sport before the school year even begins.

When discussing discipline, we like to use the phrase *attention to detail*. Teams that pay attention to detail are always well-disciplined and always seem to win the close games. Isn't it ironic that the good team is also usually the lucky team? They put themselves in position to win by paying attention to detail, then they take advantage of the opportunity.

Our players pride themselves on never being late. We do not like to use lack of time as an excuse because we all have exactly the same amount of time—24 hours per day. It is not a matter of how much time there is but what is done with that time. One common phrase used in our program is "If you are early, you are on time; if you are on time, you are late; and if you are late, we are gone." We do not wait for anybody! Usually when a player is unsuccessful, it is not due to a lack of time; it is due to a lack of correct priorities.

We take great pride in having competitive players. We fully expect to win every game. It is not imperative that we always win, but it is imperative that we always compete. Coaches can teach players to be competitive if players are given enough opportunities. Almost every drill we run in practice is competitive. We want our players to feel the intensity, concentration, and poise required to be successful under fire. We do not want them to experience fear at any time. I believe fear is what keeps a lot of players from being successful. It is also a major reason many players and coaches do not like to set goals. They have the fear of not meeting those goals.

Every player must be aware of her role for the team to be successful. Be fair and honest in the evaluation of players. There must be a purpose for each player on the team, and each player must understand her purpose. It is not always easy to bench a player or play a freshman ahead of a senior, but if the players believe the coach is being fair and honest and is doing what is best for the team, they are much more likely to understand. Some players have tremendous potential, but potential does not always equal performance.

Players in a successful program will not be outhustled. They are determined to play hard all the time. We sell this to our kids by convincing them that they never know who might be watching: a college coach, a future opponent, or a younger future player. In fact, we encourage all of our younger players to come to as many games as possible and watch how hard we play. As long as they believe everybody plays that hard, the coach has won half the battle before those players ever get to high school.

The Support Group

No discussion of a successful high school program would be complete without addressing parental and community involvement. We have been blessed with tremendous support from parents in our program. Oh, don't get me wrong. I am sure parents have disagreed with me numerous times, but we have worked hard to get our parents to understand the system.

One of the first steps parents must take to help the program is to eliminate their egos. It is tough for some parents to realize that they are not the ones playing. Parents need to remember three points:

1. The best role for a parent is to be a fan, not an extra coach.
2. Parents must keep in mind whose desire they are encouraging.
3. Parents must make sure their daughter's goal is her goal, not their goal.

If parents stick to these rules, they simply enjoy the game more. We often refer to *parental eyes.* I think some parents are so intent on watching their own children that they lose sight of the whole game. This vision can be positive or negative. Some parents see only the good things their children do, and they blank out the negative, while some parents see the opposite.

The more knowledgeable parents are about the game, the more they appreciate it. We invite parents to observe practice. I like for parents to observe practice simply because I have nothing to hide. I want them to see how hard we work and the intensity level of our practices. I want them to realize what their daughter does for two and a half hours. This also helps parents evaluate their daughter's ability. If they sit in the bleachers and watch their daughter make errors during infield practice, drop numerous fly balls, or miss pitches in batting practice, they may have more understanding of why their daughter's name is not in the lineup at game time.

Notice I used the word *observe* when referring to parents. The more knowledgeable parents become, the more supportive they are of the whole progam. One can always count on people to support something that they feel they have helped to create, which is why we like to get our parents involved, but the coach has to guard against interference. There is a fine line between involvement and interference, and it is up to coaches and parents to realize the difference.

We give our players a written test on various aspects of softball such as rules, strategy, signs, and techniques. I tell the players to ask their parents to help if they do not know an answer. Of course, there is a humorous downside to this knowledge. I never changed my signs in 22 years of coaching, so almost everyone in our bleachers (and most of my opponents) knew my signs. Occasionally, when I would give the bunt sign I would hear from the bleachers "Get it down," or I would give the steal sign and hear "Get a good jump." Involvement or interference?

We are a small community but one rich in softball tradition. We have tried to make softball a community affair. We open every spring with a 100-inning fund-raiser. It is a great way to get the whole community involved. We have a facility of which we are very proud. It has a great playing surface, covered bleachers, large press box, sprinkling system for the infield and outfield, a large inning-by-inning electric scoreboard, practice diamonds, concession stand, and tarp. Almost all of the work done has been volunteer. If coaches can sell the concept of tradition, atmosphere, and pride, they are certainly on the road to establishing the successful high school program.

Final Thoughts

There is one word I have purposely left out because I wanted to finish with it. That word is *enthusiasm*. Ralph Waldo Emerson once said that "Nothing great was ever accomplished without enthusiasm." It is the coach's job to approach the game with enthusiasm. The coach's attitude toward practice organization, off-season improvement, game preparation, and parent and community involvement eventually determines the direction of the program. I have been fortunate to be surrounded by enthusiastic and dedicated people. Our success has come primarily from the enthusiasm of the people surrounding it rather than anything drastically new and innovative that we have implemented.

As a program becomes more successful, the coach must learn how to deal with winning. This may sound strange, but it is true. Never compromise the principles of the program for the temptation to take a shortcut to success. There is no shortcut. Winning takes care of itself as long as the program maintains stability. Quality is always in style. We all want to be respected for what we have accomplished, but we should also realize that everyone is pursuing what we have; therefore, we cannot allow our drive to diminish. No coach makes it alone. No matter how remotely involved in the program a player may be, continue to emphasize the team concept and the importance of each individual.

Establishing and maintaining a successful high school program is a fascinating and rewarding journey. Enjoy the journey and always maintain the courage to succeed.

PART III

Creative and Effective Practice Sessions

CHAPTER ELEVEN

Organizing Indoor and Outdoor Practices

Bill Edwards

Photo by Brian Ballweg

No matter what level of softball you coach, if you coach in a cold weather climate, you have had to at least think about planning indoor practices. The planning of a softball practice in a cold weather climate takes time, energy, imagination, and creative thinking. Every softball coach should experience at least one season of indoor practice planning. It is difficult enough to plan an effective outdoor softball practice. In cold weather environments, we must learn to prepare a team indoors for the upcoming outdoor season.

During my tenure at Hofstra University, we have always opened our season in warm weather settings. We step off a plane and find ourselves competing against top 20, Division I softball teams. Overnight, we go from the gym floor to the dirt. We don't consider this a problem. Even though the teams we compete against practice outside, play many more games, and never take a ground ball off a gym floor, we honestly believe we are at a minimal disadvantage and thus relish the challenge. In a perfect softball world, it would always be sunny and 80 degrees. Unfortunately, this is not always the case. The key to the success of any softball team is practice planning and organization, whether practice is indoors or outdoors.

To successfully prepare our teams for the upcoming season, we must create a positive teaching environment. The coaching staff must author this attitude. When school administrators create those rules and regulations that make it difficult to practice indoors, do not become discouraged. Answer all their concerns and memos with your own philosophy: "Please do not tell me what I can't do; just tell me what I can do!" Never allow your team to sense the negative feelings or frustrations that are sometimes associated with an indoor practice session.

Never complain about the weather, facilities, equipment, time allocated for practice, or other distractions. We should not consume ourselves with the issues we cannot control. Dwelling on these issues prevents us from taking charge of the things we can control. Indoor or outdoor practice planning is not easy, but then again, anything in life that is worthwhile is not easy.

Our practice philosophy has always been to find a way to get it done. Remember that practicing indoors is temporary. A softball season is a marathon, not a sprint. Eventually, we do get outside. No obstacle has ever prevented me from preparing a team for its opening game (unless, of course, there were two feet of snow on the field at game time).

Practicing Indoors

We honestly enjoy practicing indoors. Practicing indoors under the proper structure and atmosphere sets a tone for outdoor practices. There are many advantages to practicing indoors.

Our coaching staff has a captive audience. The four walls of a gymnasium, classroom, hallway, or cafeteria permit our coaching staff visual contact with the entire team at all times. Nothing a student athlete does goes unsupervised. Our athletes are in the ideal teaching environment where player-coach communication and feedback are immediate and focused. This atmosphere increases the player-coach line of communication that is the cornerstone of any successful team. Because of the facility limitations, we concentrate on individual fundamentals that can be practiced easily in the tighter space. The emphasis the coach is able to place on details becomes more poignant and dramatic. This in turn instills team discipline and, more importantly, self-discipline.

Developing a Practice Philosophy

It has taken nearly 33 years of teaching and coaching for me to develop a coaching philosophy that works for me. Practice organizational schemes and the team's practice habits are a direct reflection of the coaching staff's practice philosophies.

We want to make our athletes softball players and make our softball players athletes. From T-ball to Division I, our responsibility is to teach and improve athletic performance. Our primary priority is to increase the softball skill level of each athlete. We also want to make our skilled softball players more athletic. Essentially, our goal is to coach each individual athlete to her highest potential.

We make every attempt to practice as much as possible every day. Over the course of the season, this philosophy allows a great deal of practice time for each area of the game, thus establishing the complete player. It also allows all players to practice not only their strengths but also their weaknesses. Athletes, if given their choice, practice only what they excel in. Power hitters hit until their hands bleed; slick-fielding infielders take grounders until the bell rings.

Every player receives an equal amount of practice repetitions. Players develop at different stages. A player who is slow to develop at the beginning of the year may gain insight and confidence later that same year. This slow-developing player adds needed depth and competitive spirit to your team when it is needed at the end of the year. Give each player an equal opportunity to succeed. This fair treatment helps create team attitude and chemistry. If a player does not contribute this year, she always has the potential to be an asset in the seasons to follow.

Our practices include drills and teaching stations that allow our athletes as many repetitions as possible. Repetitions become paramount, as you can see in the sample practice sequence shown in figure 11.1. We create the proper muscle memory in our athletes by steady repetitions and immediate feedback from the coaching staff. This constant feedback assures that every repetition is practiced at 100 percent with the proper effort and mechanics.

Short Game Practice Sequence	
#1	Catcher/2nd baseman/1st baseman: throws to 1st, 2nd covers Pitcher/shortstop/3rd baseman: throws to 3rd, shortstop covers Outfielders: drop steps going back on fly balls, routine catch
#2	Pitcher/2nd baseman/1st baseman: throws to 1st, 2nd covers Catcher/3rd baseman/shortstop: throws to 3rd, shortstop covers Outfielders: drop steps, running over-the-shoulder catches
#3	Pitcher/catcher/shortstop: throws to 2nd, shortstop covers 3rd baseman/1st baseman/2nd baseman: throws to 1st, 2nd covers, return throw to 3rd Outfielders: running in for fly balls, sliding catches
#4	Pitcher/2nd baseman/1st baseman: triangle work at 1st, communication and coverage Catcher/3rd baseman/shortstop: throws to 2nd, shortstop covers Outfielders: perfect fly ball catching technique
#5	Pitcher/3rd baseman/shortstop: triangle work at 3rd, communication and coverage Catcher/1st baseman/2nd baseman: throws to 2nd, 2nd covers (certain slap defense situations) Outfielders: drop steps, back to infield, running over-the-shoulder catches
#6	Pitcher/catcher/1st baseman/2nd baseman/shortstop/3rd baseman: right-handed slap coverage Outfielders: fence work
#7	Pitcher/catcher/1st baseman/2nd baseman/shortstop/3rd baseman: left-handed slap coverage Outfielders: sun work (shield with glove)

Figure 11.1 A sample practice sequence.

We break the skill down to its simplest common denominator. Even at the elite level of Division I, we start defensive progressions at the remedial stages. With elementary skill progressions, one can adapt the skill to the level of player and the facility available. We never begin any softball season using drills that incorporate the teaching of an entire skill. We always begin our teaching skill progression with the parts of the skill. After the athlete becomes proficient with one part of the skill, we progress to the next part until we eventually get to the whole.

We introduce new material early in the practice sessions when the team is alert and fresh. This strategy enables our team to have total focus. At other times during the practice, tired legs can mean tired minds.

We change drills frequently. This keeps practices moving at a high level of intensity and prevents boredom. One only has to watch MTV to notice how long the attention span of our youth is.

We post our practice plan daily to let our players know what to expect. This communication gives them the opportunity to get ready for practice mentally as well as physically. Athletes tend to concentrate on the task at hand, instead of wondering what will be next.

We like to finish practice with a snappy, positive drill. This finale creates confidence and camaraderie among the team. Everyone leaves practice feeling good about herself.

It is important to establish a practice routine. Athletes need routine in every aspect of their lives. As mentors, it is our responsibility to teach this routine.

Team members dress in practice attire. They look sharp, even in practice. A team that looks good on the outside feels good on the inside. This also includes proper care of equipment. Look the part, act the part, and someday you will be the part.

We name each drill for quick and efficient practice transition. Nothing is more time-consuming then having the team stand around while the coach explains a drill. Naming drills helps make practice transitions smooth and efficient. It also helps keep practices at three hours.

We establish a ready area for players. A ready area is an area of the practice facility set aside for athletes. We want our athletes to step between the lines for practice focused and ready. Softball players often run to practice from a class or school activity, rarely having the time to refocus. Personal problems can distract an athlete from top performance. Athletes sometimes need space and distance to get ready for practice. The ready area gives the student a place to prepare herself for practice with no questions asked by the coaching staff. We allow the athlete as much time as she needs to be able to step on the field in the correct frame of mind.

When the practice field is in sight, the players are on the hop, which means jogging or running. This creates a practice attitude for the team even before we start practicing. Players arriving late to practice are usually in full view of those already practicing. As they jog to the practice area in full view of the team, the team sees them hustling to practice. We use another term, *get here* (or *get there*), which means sprint. This keeps our sessions intense and exciting.

We always start practice on time. Being prompt is paramount to practice and the structure you establish. It sends a message to your team about discipline and punctuality. As a coach, you cannot expect it from your team if you do not follow it yourself.

Challenge your players every day with intense gamelike situations. You cannot expect your team to play well under pressure situations unless you create them in practice. Players need to be challenged daily. These situations also show you which players are clutch players.

Limit practices to three hours, no longer. When players are hustling and practice transitions are smooth and efficient, this sometimes impossible task becomes a reality.

Organizing Practices

It is important to integrate your philosophy into your practice organization. The creation of an effective practice session is a combination of planning and philosophy. You must be consistent in both areas if you expect to conduct an efficient and effective practice. We have always tried to keep our practice planning very simple. It is the old KISS philosophy: Keep it simple, stupid.

The two systems we use to organize our indoor and outdoor practices are checklists and sequences (see figure 11.1, page 112, for a sample sequence). Checklists and sequences provide you with the vehicle needed to create a practice. They tell you what you must practice. We carefully plan our indoor practices so that the only things not covered or practiced inside are those few items that must be practiced outside.

We also use our indoor practice format for outdoors. When the weather permits us to practice outside, we just change venues, keeping our athletes in the same routine so that we do not lose valuable time teaching new drills or sequences. We feel this is a very simple and comprehensive practice philosophy. Figure 11.2 is a list of the fundamental drills we use every day.

The first thing we need to do as coaches is to make sure we teach the entire softball curriculum. Having checklists for every position and aspect of our game assures us that our team is totally prepared when the season begins. Figure 11.3 is a team defensive checklist I have developed over the years, and figure 11.4 is a position-specific checklist for the shortstop.

It takes many years to compile your checklists. These lists are never complete. They are an ongoing resource that you add to as your knowledge of the game expands. As you become a student of the game, you should create your personal softball encyclopedia. My bible is a compilation of check-lists, sequences, skill teaching techniques, and motivational material that I have accumulated over many years of coaching. I contribute to my bible regularly. I update my bible after every article I read or clinic I attend. I always have new information available at my disposal anytime I need to retrieve it. I never stop learning.

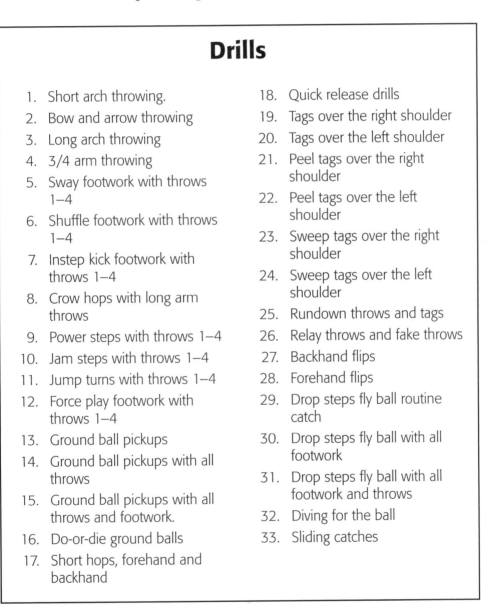

Drills

1. Short arch throwing.
2. Bow and arrow throwing
3. Long arch throwing
4. 3/4 arm throwing
5. Sway footwork with throws 1–4
6. Shuffle footwork with throws 1–4
7. Instep kick footwork with throws 1–4
8. Crow hops with long arm throws
9. Power steps with throws 1–4
10. Jam steps with throws 1–4
11. Jump turns with throws 1–4
12. Force play footwork with throws 1–4
13. Ground ball pickups
14. Ground ball pickups with all throws
15. Ground ball pickups with all throws and footwork.
16. Do-or-die ground balls
17. Short hops, forehand and backhand
18. Quick release drills
19. Tags over the right shoulder
20. Tags over the left shoulder
21. Peel tags over the right shoulder
22. Peel tags over the left shoulder
23. Sweep tags over the right shoulder
24. Sweep tags over the left shoulder
25. Rundown throws and tags
26. Relay throws and fake throws
27. Backhand flips
28. Forehand flips
29. Drop steps fly ball routine catch
30. Drop steps fly ball with all footwork
31. Drop steps fly ball with all footwork and throws
32. Diving for the ball
33. Sliding catches

Figure 11.2 Fundamental everyday drills.

Team Defensive Checklist

_____ Throwing
_____ Receiving
_____ Footwork
_____ Fielding ground balls
_____ Fielding fly balls
_____ Covering bases
_____ Double play (footwork and feeds)
_____ Force play footwork
_____ Backing up
_____ Bunt defense (sacrifice, squeeze, surprise, slap)
_____ Steal defense (regular, delay, double)
_____ First-and-third defense
_____ Tagging runners
_____ Sprinting to positions
_____ Hit-and-run defense
_____ Cutoffs
_____ Relays
_____ Communication (who is in charge?)
_____ On-field positioning (pull, away, squeeze)
_____ Infield in defense
_____ Pitcher, first triangle
_____ Pitcher, third triangle
_____ Shortstop, 2nd baseman screen plays
_____ Locating to pitch and count
_____ Diving for balls
_____ Dugout decorum
_____ Equipment organization
_____ Ready for a play after a play
_____ Every play a critical play
_____ Pickoffs
_____ Shielding the sun
_____ Appeal plays
_____ Decoys
_____ Rundowns

Figure 11.3 A sample team checklist.

Positional Checklist: Shortstops

_____ Defensive set position	_____ Cover 3rd on steal and bunts
_____ Ground ball fundamentals (forehand, backhand, charge, routine, short hop)	_____ Bunt responsibilities
_____ Ground ball footwork	_____ Throw to 3rd on force plays
_____ Double play feeds	_____ Fire play
_____ Double play pivots	_____ Option defense
_____ Force plays	_____ Running through the runner for ground ball
_____ Tag plays	_____ Rundowns
_____ Pickoffs 3rd	_____ Making sure runners touch the bases
_____ Pickoffs 2nd	
_____ Cutoffs	_____ Decoys
_____ Relays	_____ Relays signs
_____ Popups	_____ Slap defense (LHS, RHS)
_____ Fence work	_____ Hit and run defense
_____ Cover 2nd on steals and bunts	_____ Calling the ball
	_____ Diving for the ball

Figure 11.4   Position-specific checklist for shortstops.

Once we know what to practice, we can create our daily practice plan. I use a form (figure 11.5) to keep track of what I want to cover in practice. A sample completed form is shown in figure 11.6. Our practice sessions are broken into segments according to the fundamental skill drills:

- Individual offensive
- Individual defensive
- Positional
- Team offensive
- Team defensive
- Conditioning and agility
- Everyday skill drills
- Evaluation skill drills (sometimes needed for tryouts)
- Teaching skill drills (introduction of new material)

Prioritize your sequences and checklists into what your team needs to practice that day and list those items on your practice form. Designate the

Practice Plan

Date _____ Place _____ Time _____

Warm-ups/stretching   **Individual defense**

Conditioning   **Positional defense**

Baserunning   **Team defense**

Weight training   **Special situations**

Hitting   **Short game**

Team reminders   **Equipment needed**

Figure 11.5 A blank practice plan form.

Practice Plan

Date _____ **Place** ___Gym_____ **Time** _____

Warm-ups/stretching
1 (20) Indian relay 5 min
Stretch routine (led by seniors)

Conditioning
5 (20) 5-1-1-1 running drill
3 sets agilities
3 sets plyometrics
Day at the races (fun)

Baserunning
2 (20) Run each base drill
Sliding drill
  • bent leg (1st)
  • head first (2nd)
  • pop up (3rd)
  • back door (home)

Weight training

Hitting

Cage 1	Cage 2
OF 3 (60) 5 IS, 5 OS, 5 M	Count hitting
IF 4 (60) 3 bunts each	Bunts (same
(sac, surprise,	as cage 1)
slap, double)	

Team reminders
Team dinner Wednesday

Individual defense
Throw progressions   OF 4 (60)
Footwork drills
Ground ball fundamentals   IF 3 (60)
Sequences 1-6 (IF & OF)

Positional defense
Sequences 1-6

Team defense

Special situations

Short game

Station 1	Station 2	Station 3
No-ball drill	Stationary ball	Side toss
1/4, 1/2 swings	IS/OS tee	Self hitting
Load drill	10 each	2 ball hi/lo
	standing/	
	kneeling	

Equipment needed
3 screens, Wiffle balls, softies, regular balls, bases set up, infield measured, IS/OS tee

Figure 11.6 A completed practice plan form.

amount of practice time for each of these items with a circled number. The noncircled number indicates the practice sequence. This is the most critical part of practice planning. It really tests your organizational skills. You never want to waste time moving from one checklist item, skill, drill, or sequence to another. Creating a practice that flows with no delays or wasted time is the most difficult and time-consuming process in organizing a practice.

The skill level of your athletes dictates your practice needs. Remember the most important practice philosophy is to improve each player every day and make every attempt to practice everything every day.

During the early stages of a softball player's development, the skills of throwing and receiving secure the highest priority. Never compromise these two skills. When softball players cannot throw and receive properly, the game becomes horrifying.

We try to accelerate our athletes' growth by continually challenging them during practice. Athletes respond when we set ambitious goals for them. Only when we need to teach something new or when the individual players are weak in certain areas do we modify our teaching pace and progressions. Athletes never learn to raise their personal expectations unless we motivate them to the higher standards and goals once perceived to be unattainable.

You must create your own timetable. Usually there are two timetables coaches are most concerned about: the preseason practice schedule (the amount of practice time preceding your first game) and the in-season practice schedule (the practice time available between games). I have prepared teams for the opening game in as little as five days and as long as four weeks.

I have a general formula for practice preparation, and I usually exercise these formulas in two ways—daily and weekly. Generally, I allocate one-quarter of practice time to individual offensive and defensive skill work, one-quarter to positional skill work, and one-half to team offensive and defensive execution. The offensive segment of your practice (hitting and short game) may be structured under both individual and team timetables.

A typical two-week period allows 14 days of practice. We all need days off and many of us are now mandated to take days off, so let us assume we have 12 days of actual practice. Our weekly formula allows three days of concentrated individual skill work, teaching, and tryouts; three days of intense positional skill work; and six days of extensive team system. Each daily session under this type of practice is an intense concentration of softball skill and personal development.

Assuming a three-hour practice is the norm, our daily formula divides 180 minutes into the appropriate segments: 45 minutes for individual skill work, 45 minutes for positional play, and 90 minutes for the team's system.

As the softball season progresses, we try to maintain our formula. We may tweak it a little, based on our needs at the time, but usually this is one of my uncompromising issues. Whether we choose the daily plan or the weekly plan, our team has to improve simply because the individual athlete is improving.

Efficiently Using the Facilities Available

The facility dictates what items on the checklist you can practice and the equipment needed to accomplish the practice goals. Equipment setup and breakdown usually occur between the offensive to defensive segment of practice and must be completed quickly and efficiently. If needed, one 10-minute time period should be allotted for the team to make this transition.

Many colleges now have state-of-the-art indoor facilities that provide conditions that closely simulate an outdoor field. However, many schools still struggle with facilities that are shared with other school teams, clubs, and activities. It is not uncommon for the softball team to return during the evening hours to hold their practices.

All one needs to prepare a softball team indoors is an average-size junior high school gymnasium. If you are fortunate to have a larger facility, then you can incorporate more into your practice plan. If your facility is smaller, then you must be more creative. It is not uncommon for softball teams to practice in classrooms, hallways, wrestling rooms, or dance studios. That is why the checklist becomes so valuable. I have learned to modify my daily practice schedule based on the facility available and the equipment that can be used in that facility. Figure 11.7 shows a sample setup for an indoor facility with no batting cages.

Our sport does not need the same area that a baseball team needs. Although there are many similarities within the practice structure of baseball and softball, the differences are profound.

There are times, however, when it becomes impossible for the entire team to practice in the facility available. Then the team must practice by position. Infielders, outfielders, pitchers, and catchers practice at separate times. It also may work to practice just the middle infielders or corners until a larger indoor facility becomes available. During this time, concentrate on the part, then move on to the whole.

Creating daily lesson plans for your team ensures total preparation for the season. It is also important to highlight practices that were exceptional and reevaluate the practices that did not accomplish your goals for the day. Keep all of your practices on file. This resource proves invaluable when you are in need of a refresher course.

Organizing the Hitting Phase of Practice

We hit every day. Whether we are inside or outside, we always create hitting stations as part of our practice plan. We select the stations needed from our hitting drill checklist, set up our rotation, then allocate the appropriate time. Every station is set up in full view of the coaching staff so that every swing is monitored and evaluated with continuous feedback.

121

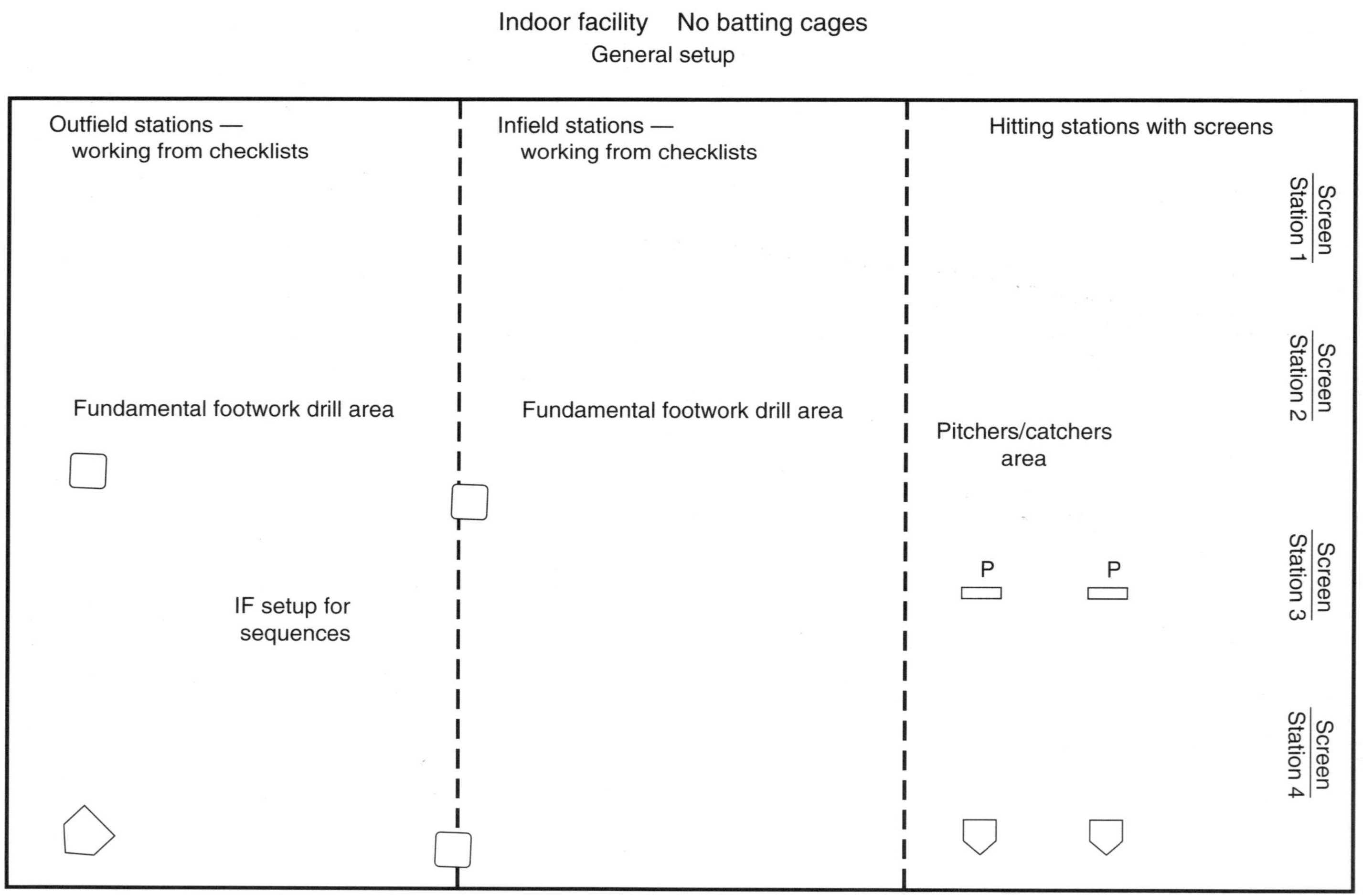

Indoor facility   No batting cages
General setup

Outfield stations —
working from checklists

Infield stations —
working from checklists

Hitting stations with screens

| Screen | Screen | Screen | Screen |
| Station 1 | Station 2 | Station 3 | Station 4 |

Pitchers/catchers
area

P   P

Fundamental footwork drill area

Fundamental footwork drill area

IF setup for
sequences

Figure 11.7 Setup for an indoor practice in a facility with no batting cages. Checklists like the one in figure 11.4 can be used in the infield and outfield stations. The fundamental drills listed in figure 11.2 are used in the fundamental footwork drill area.

Our hitting stations always include at least one competitive, gamelike station. It may be ball tracking, count hitting, situational hitting, live pitching, or short game. Other stations include a no-ball station, a stationary ball station, a side-toss station, and a front-toss ball station.

If we do not have a cage, we use our no-ball drills, stationary ball drills, or side- and front-toss drills. We substitute real balls with Wiffle balls, softies, rag balls, and even rolled-up socks.

We use machines early in the year. If we do not have a cage, we use machines with Wiffles and softies; however, we do always try to create as many live pitching drills as possible. Machines serve their purpose, but there is nothing like a ball being thrown by a real person.

Each station is designed to break down the swing components, making it easier for players to groove their swing. We believe in developing the swing before we hit a ball. Your hitting checklist provides you with the drills that can be adapted to any indoor facility.

Organizing Pitchers

Remember how important pitching is to the success of the team. Creating the perfect pitching environment and practice routine is critical. Making sure that our pitching staff is ready for the first game is sometimes a most difficult task. We know that our team performance is directly related to the effectiveness of our pitching staff. Therefore, we must create indoor, gamelike situations for our pitchers.

Our pitchers throw before or after team practice. Throwing before or after practice gives the coach an opportunity to stress and reinforce fundamentals and techniques. New pitches are taught during this time. Spin drills, targets, ladders, and pitcher conditioning drills are also practiced during this time. Figure 11.8 shows the form we use to plan practice for pitchers and catchers. Figure 11.9 is a sample completed plan.

Our pitchers also throw competitive batting practice, tracking drills, short game, or scrimmage situations during team practices. If needed, we can simulate live game conditions in an indoor batting cage. We protect our pitchers with a pitching screen, floor mats, and gymnastic padding. This creates the indoor, competitive gamelike atmosphere needed to prepare our staff. Our pitchers never throw batting practice for the hitters. They always try to ring up the K.

The skill level of your pitchers dictates the type of pitching checklist you are able to develop. You may have to modify drills to suit the skill level of your pitchers. They usually are the franchise players. Many teams only have one, so it is important that you organize this part of practice with great prudence.

Practice Plan

Date _____ **Place** _____ **Time** _____

Pitchers **Catchers**

Figure 11.8 A blank practice plan form for pitchers and catchers.

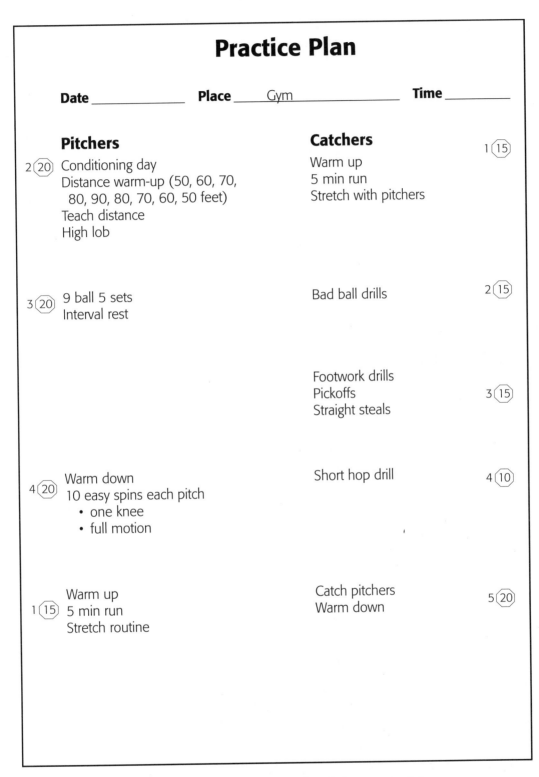

Practice Plan

Date _____ **Place** ___Gym_____ **Time** _____

Pitchers

2 (20) Conditioning day
Distance warm-up (50, 60, 70,
   80, 90, 80, 70, 60, 50 feet)
Teach distance
High lob

3 (20) 9 ball 5 sets
Interval rest

4 (20) Warm down
10 easy spins each pitch
   • one knee
   • full motion

1 (15) Warm up
5 min run
Stretch routine

Catchers

1 (15) Warm up
5 min run
Stretch with pitchers

2 (15) Bad ball drills

3 (15) Footwork drills
Pickoffs
Straight steals

4 (10) Short hop drill

5 (20) Catch pitchers
Warm down

Figure 11.9 A completed practice plan form for pitchers and catchers.

Always incorporate your pitchers as part of your master daily practice plan. Do not forget that pitchers must condition, hit, field, and learn your offensive and defensive systems. We need to develop the pitcher into a complete softball player, allowing her every opportunity to compete at the highest level. This philosophy gives your pitcher a better knowledge of the game while adding depth to your team.

Final Thoughts

When I first started teaching and coaching at the junior high school level 33 years ago, it was such a distinctive feeling to have my athletes call me *Coach*. *Coach* made that student-teacher relationship very special. No administrator, classroom teacher, or, in some cases, parent could affect a child's life more than his or her coach. It was a responsibility that I have valued and tried to honor during my teaching and coaching career.

Now that I have retired from teaching and am coaching full-time, I have come to appreciate the finer intricacies this profession provides all of us. Now more than ever, I appreciate my student athletes complimenting me on my teaching abilities. Having that special player-coach relationship developed and refined by effective teaching creates the ideal learning environment for our athletes. As mentors, we have an obligation to organize and provide our athletes with an exciting and safe learning environment. The organization of indoor or outdoor practices becomes the launching pad for the athlete's development, much in the same way a teacher's daily lesson plan affects the learning in the classroom. We must never compromise the most important part of our coaching responsibilities, the organization of practice.

CHAPTER TWELVE

Conducting Innovative Practices

Deb Pallozzi

Photo by Tim McKinney, courtesy of Ithaca College

The ability to conduct practices in a creative and interesting way lays the groundwork for a finely tuned team. One of the main responsibilities of a coach is to have your team work hard, stay focused, and maintain enthusiasm during practice and, ultimately, the game. You can enhance the development of the quality of your program through effective and creative practices.

Before you sit down and plan practices, you need to have a starting point, your belief in the way your program should be run. This is your coaching philosophy, the foundation on which all your coaching decisions are made. It is important to have a solid, consistent philosophy that works both for you and the team. By being consistent, you make certain that your players understand exactly what is expected of them.

Once you have established your philosophy, your attitude sets the tone for the team. A consistent mood and attitude are critical for the success of your team. If you want an upbeat, fast-paced practice, you need to be upbeat and organized with a well-thought-out practice plan in front of you. If you want players to work hard, you need to demonstrate a greater work ethic than they do. You constantly challenge your players to make a total commitment to reach their full potential, but if you do not make that same commitment, the players recognize the inconsistency. You as a coach must set the proper tone.

Defining Expectations

Define for your players the foundation of a good practice, and be explicit about what you expect of them. I call these expectations the player's responsibilities. These responsibilities must be done in every practice and become as routine as tying shoes:

- Always hustle, station to station, drill to drill.
- Always move your feet to the ball; do not get lazy.
- Keep your eyes active for complete concentration.
- Chest is in front of every ball, whether it is a grounder or a thrown ball.
- Use two hands for quick and efficient execution.
- Always move to the ball, preparing to throw ahead of receiving the ball.
- Work with the player you will be working with in a game.
- The way you practice equals the way you play.

Once these responsibilities are stated, the athletes are responsible for monitoring each other. This encourages players to be responsible for each other as well as themselves. Once you have shifted the burden of responsibility from you as a coach to the players, the players begin to take on more responsibility and the team gradually becomes theirs. The players begin to develop a sense of pride and start to demand a higher level of execution in practice.

The coach's responsibilities are in essence the blueprint by which you run your practices. These responsibilities come from the beliefs that formulated your coaching philosophy:

- Always be prepared for practice. (Can you set up early?)
- Everything that is done has a purpose.
- Quality not quantity. Proper execution is what is important, not just finishing a drill.
- Athletes have short attention spans. Have short periods of time with intense work.
- Keep practice moving. Watch out for fatigue.
- Make practices competitive and fun; create challenges.
- All coaches need to have a timing device.

These responsibilities are for all the coaches on your staff. Every practice you plan should have the same expectations for the staff. All these principles contribute to a creative, fast-paced workout that your players will respond to positively.

Conducting Practices

To conduct practices efficiently and effectively, organize your plans on all aspects of the game. Take into account the space available and the time allotted for practice. In our program, we have developed a structure for starting practice, teaching hitting, teaching defense, and honing individual skills. Remember, always incorporate some sort of competitive element, as well. We have also become very creative with the facility usage, as you will see a little later.

Starting Practices

In our program, players begin practice 15 minutes before the posted starting time with a five-minute warm-up run and a stretching routine outside the practice facility. Players use the stretching time to prepare mentally and physically for the upcoming practice. This is the time players actively dismiss any outside distractions and begin centering their focus and energies on softball and, specifically, the practice planned.

Once we enter the practice facility (for preseason we are indoors), the players are assigned equipment duties and are responsible for setting up the entire facility according to the practice planned. We make the captains responsible for making sure the finer details of setup are done such as plates at every hitting station, boxes taped down to the floor, infields measured and set up, and screens placed where they belong. This takes five to seven minutes.

After setup, we meet in the middle of the floor and go over practice and the general focus of the workout planned. The tone is set for the type of attitude and focus we want from the athletes. To help players develop the proper focus, we have each player set one defensive and one offensive goal, based on the practice agenda. Once practice begins, all focus is on the activity at hand.

Using Facilities Creatively

The size of your facility and the time allotted to you are significant factors in your practice design. Facilities and time are a premium. We actually have two different practice designs. Each design is based on how much of the main facility we are given and the amount of time we have. Figure 12.1 shows the size of the facility we have to use. We either have a one-gym workout (gym 3), or we have all three gyms.

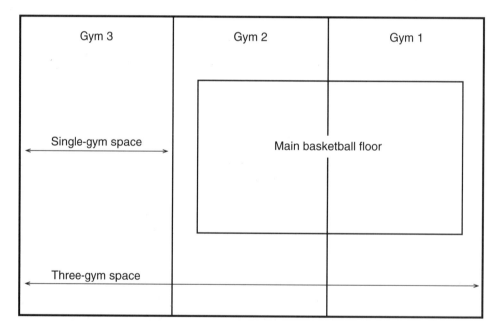

Figure 12.1 The gymnasium setup. The gyms are divided by folding doors.

Our single-gym workouts take place in gym 3. Gym 3 is a little smaller than the average high school gymnasium. Our focus for a single-gym workout is hitting, conditioning, and individual fundamentals. We divide the team into three groups: pitchers/catchers, infielders, and outfielders. I strive for relatively even numbers in each group. If I am short on catchers, then I bring some players from one of the other groups to work out in the pitcher/catcher group.

Generally a one-gym practice is all station work timed by an assistant coach. For example, for an hour and a half practice slot, after setup and explanations, each group would get 25 minutes in stations of hitting, conditioning, and individual fundamentals. A coach or manager is with each group.

A general design for a single-gym workout might go like this. We have two cages, one that is 70 feet long and one that is a 12 × 12 foot square, located at the end of the long cage. The cages run along the folding door that divides gyms 2 and 3 (figure 12.2).

The number of hitting stations we set up depends on where we are in the season, but in setting them up, some items are a constant, regardless of the season. Screens and dividing nets are tremendously important for safety and maintaining order in the stations. Additionally, all kinds of

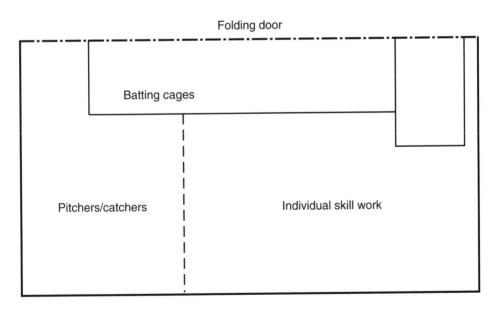

Figure 12.2   Gym 3 setup.

balls are useful—from softballs to Wiffles to taped balls. The objective to hitting stations is quality swings. You can get swings using a lot of different things. I will share more specific ideas on the hitting stations later in the chapter.

I usually begin with the pitcher/catcher group at the hitting stations. This allows the outfield group to have use of the entire length of the gym to work on their individual fundamentals for outfield play. The infielders condition just outside our gym, with the trainer overseeing their progress. The stations are timed to make maximum use of the 25 minutes. When 25 minutes are up, we have a big switch. Now the pitchers and catchers set up the correct mound distance, then the infielders hit and the outfielders condition. It is done in this order so that the pitchers can do their warm-ups and the catchers have space to work on fundamentals. On the third big switch, the infielders move to the gym for individual fundamental work, but the space is shared with the pitchers/catchers. The conditioning station for the battery is skipped, so they have to condition on their own. This is their time to work on specific pitching and catching workouts. This gives the pitchers/catchers a 50-minute throwing and receiving time slot.

For the conditioning segment of the workout, we do several different things. We do agility circuits, rotator series with tubing, forearm work for bat speed, medicine ball work, stair work, and abdominal/back series to strengthen the core region. This segment is timed and monitored by a trainer or injured athlete. Pitchers and catchers do conditioning on their own. They are responsible for interval StairMaster workouts and the shoulder, abdominal, and low-back series. Some of the wrist work is done in their part of the pitching/catching workout.

When we have all three gyms for practice, practice generally runs one and a half to two hours. This is the time we work on team offenses and defenses, combination defensive drills, and scrimmage situations. In addition to the team aspects of the game, we always have our hitting stations, so the pitchers and catchers can still get their workout in.

We have a couple of different ways to organize these practices. If there is no live throwing planned for the practice, we separate the team into three groups: infielders, outfielders, and the battery. We have three 20-minute segments. Pitchers/catchers begin their workout for the day in gym 3. This opens gyms 1 and 2 for more extensive teamwork. One group goes to the hitting stations, located primarily in the cages and netting. The other group in gyms 1 and 2 works on individual and combination skills needed for the team defenses that we are going to review that day. For example, if the outfielders are hitting, the infielders go over individual skills from their positions: different types of throws, correct steps and angles to a batted ball, footwork for receiving and throwing the ball, and lots of quality reps. Combination drills include feeds and pivots around second with the middle infielders; the corners working together on bunt coverage; 'tweeners with the third baseman and shortstop, then the first and second basemen; and feeds from the adjacent players on the field.

After the 20 minutes are up, the infielders and outfielders switch stations. Now the outfielders get to work on individual skills specific to outfield play: pursuit of a ball at different angles, cutting balls off, hitting relays, one-hop throws to bags and home, wrong-way turns, and fence balls. Some of the combination drills for the outfielders are pursuing balls and backing up, and pursuing and calling for balls.

For the third 20-minute segment, the pitchers/catchers go through the hitting circuit while the infielders and outfielders do combination drills with each other: relays with the middles and outfielders; right fielder and second baseman going for the out at first; one-hop throws to the baseman covering the bag; pursuing the Texas leaguers just behind the infield and in front of the outfield; and hitting all the different cuts. Again, what is rehearsed is contingent on what defenses are rehearsed during the second segment of the workout.

Remember, this format is one I use for a full-facility practice. I sometimes have everyone go through the hitting portion of the practice together. For this setup, the pitchers are probably going to throw live. While the pitchers and catchers get warmed up, the infielders and outfielders have the other two gyms. There are number of things that can be done. We can do combination drills or work individual skills. Sometimes I call for clinic time. Clinic time is a portion of practice set aside for the players to work on any skill of their choice that is considered a weakness. The amount of time set aside for clinic time ranges from 10 to 20 minutes. All coaches are available to help in whatever way the player wants. This availability allows for the athlete to work on some of her personal goals set early in the season.

Approaches to Hitting Workouts

If we have a live hitting day and everyone is participating in the hitting stations, the time allotted is about 50 minutes. The group is split into the live group and the station group.

When we work on hitting, the players warm up their swings just like they warm up their arms for throwing. Once players are good and loose, they have a set routine for every hitting workout and every pregame. We call the routine the hitting progressions. First they do a set of 15 to 20 dry cuts, then focus on hitting off a tee. After a set number of cuts off the tee, the players focus their eyes on an area 20 feet in front of the tee and then move their eyes to the tee and pick up the ball and swing. The next progression is to a soft toss, with the tosser placing the ball in specific areas to work on specific types of swings. The next step is to work on tracking a ball coming from the front. The players call where the ball is located by yelling either *Strike!* or *Ball!* The last progression before the hitting stations is to hit the ball from a front toss. We always use Wiffle balls during these progressions and for our pregame warm-up.

Each hitting station has a specific purpose. Live hitting stations are not for reps; they are for quality at bats. We set up scenarios in advance. One example of a live hitting station is having the batter start with an 0-2 count. The pitcher and catcher work together to get the batter out, and the batter tries to work out of the jam, learning how to protect the plate until the pitcher makes a mistake. We start with 0-0 counts, 3-1 counts, and 3-0 counts when the batter gets the green light to swing. This particular station is valuable because you learn if the batter recognizes her pitch. We do the same for bunt work, making the players get the bunt down with two strikes.

Before I go on, I would like to add how we explain at bats to our players. We explain to players that there are me-swings and team-swings. A me-swing is when the count is in the batter's favor and the batter takes a swing to rip the ball hard up the middle with a pitch she can handle. A team-swing is when the batter is behind in the count and she is battling the pitcher and protecting the plate. A team-swing also takes place on a hit-and-run play and with runners in scoring position. The batter looks for a different pitch to optimize the chances of getting the type of hit the team needs to be successful.

In station work, we often have two machines in the same cage. We try to simulate the fast/change pitch sequence, the inside/outside sequence, or the high/low sequence. During these stations, we have cue cards for the players with specific things to do. For example, we may have hit-and-run, surprise-base-hit bunt, squeeze, or a two-strike cut. There are a lot of skills you can have your players work on. I also have a station where the players just groove their cut. I know everyone teaches not to have players just hit the pitch that is grooved, but I do believe that a batter needs to stay confident and maintain that feel of driving a ball hard. So I always make sure we do one station of grooving that cut.

Motivating Players

Motivated players are interested players. The one place that is very easy to motivate players is in the practice session. The best compliment I hear from my players is when practice is nearing the end, and they say they can't believe practice is almost over. The trick is to keep players interested so that they practice at a highly intense level. This is where planning and organization on your part are extremely important.

The skills in softball are such that repetition is what makes the player solid and confident. But remember to keep practice moving, to have short periods of practice rehearsal for each skill, and to make practice competitive and fun. The players want to play ball, they want to compete, and above all, they want to have fun doing it. A player used to say to me, "Coach, let's skip the skills and drills and just play ball!"

We do a few different things to try to incorporate competition in a workout. For example, I divide the squad in half and have blue versus white. This actually starts in the fall program with our intersquad scrimmage. In this scrimmage, they play for all the marbles. The losing team has to cook and serve dinner to the winning team. I have an umpire, and they suit up in their real uniforms. It has become quite a competitive game. I carry over the blue/white teams to the preseason. We keep a running total of points for the entire preseason until our spring trip. Points can be earned for different achievements, from everyone on one team dressing alike and looking like a team to winning different types of games incorporated throughout practice.

One hitting competition that we always do is a production rating. This production rating is taken straight from Ron Polk's *Baseball-Softball Playbook* (1983). The basic premise behind the production rating is the determination of how hard the batter is hitting the ball. You are basically awarding the batter with a higher score when she hits a ball that generally enables her to achieve success as a hitter, such as the home run ball, the line drive, the hard ground ball, and so on. At the same time, she receives a lower score when a swing of the bat does not produce a productive ball in play, such as the swing and miss, the foul ball, the pop-up, the routine fly ball, the weakly hit grounder, and so on. In table 12.1, you can find the numerical rating used.

TABLE 12.1

Production Ratings for Hitters

Rating	Productivity
0	Batter swings and misses; takes a called third strike; foul tips the ball directly back to the catcher
1	Batter swings and fouls the ball straight back to the backstop or the area from dugout to dugout, on the ground or in the air
2	Batter swings and fouls the ball off weakly beyond the area of the dugouts on the ground or in the air; hits a pop fly anywhere in the infield area, fair or foul
3	Batter swings and fouls the ball off sharply away from the foul line; hits a routine fly ball in the outfield that is fair
4	Batter swings and hits a fair ground ball weakly; hits a humpback line drive anywhere in fair territory in front of the outfielders
5	Batter swings and hits a ground ball fairly hard; hits a long fly ball fairly hard; hits a line drive foul ball that is close to the foul line
6	Batter swings and hits a line drive either on the ground or in the air; hits a home run

We make a few adjustments so that the rating can be used in the cage. We also try to have the same person do it for the entire hitting round. For the team competition part, I tally up the scores for each player and the team they represent and take the average. The highest average for the round gets the points for the day of hitting. It is amazing how competitive the players become.

When we work on certain defenses—for example, squeezes—I may call out *Competition!* after doing the drilling phase; this earns team points. The two teams compete head-to-head in a squeeze competition. You can use live pitching or a machine, depending on what you need to accomplish. We set up a cone to the left of the catcher. The runner must break from third on the pitch and touch the cone before the catcher touches it with her glove. Points are rewarded to the team that touches the cone. If the batter misses the ball, the defensive team earns double for the rundown play, or the offensive team scores a point for returning safely. This type of competition can be done for any defensive set. We have done competitions with sac flys and runners on third, steals of second, and the double steal for the first and third plays. These little competitions create the competitiveness in your athletes and have them perform both offensively and defensively under a little more pressure than just drill work. The players love it.

Another little offshoot from competitions or competition day is bust-a-gut day. We have bust-a-gut day once or twice a preseason. This is an all-out, high-intensity level activity. You could divide the team in two or have each player get with a partner or into groups of three. Maybe have your middles buddy up, then your pitchers/catchers, corners, and so forth. For 45 minutes, your players compete in various drills, conditioning segments, do-or-die plays, or anything else you can think of. One of our bust-a-gut days looked like this:

- Competition 1: Two pairs join. Players exchange partners and compete against this person. From 25 feet away, both players face the wall, one in front of the other. The person behind has a tennis ball. She throws the ball against the wall and tries to throw it past the opponent. There are boundaries. Have each pair go through two rounds of 10.

- Competition 2: Terrible 10. Partner groups compete against each other. Partners stand 30 feet apart. The defensive pair stands between two cones 20 feet apart. The offensive pair hits grounders, trying to get the ball past the two defenders. Two rounds of 10. Both people must fungo the ball.

- Competition 3: Sac bunts in the arc. The object is to get the ball to die within a specified arc.

- Competition 4: Calisthenics. Any kind of push-ups, sit-ups, or touching lines—all done in a specified amount of time.

- Competition 5: Pursuing a ball. A ball shoots out of a machine, and the player starts from a specified point. This should be challenging. It should take a great pursuit to get to the ball. Have players start from a seated position or on their stomachs.

I have coaches keep track of the scores. The whole idea is to go from one activity right to the next with no pause (hence the bust-a-gut name). The activities you can choose are endless. Any activity you want to work or movement you want to rehearse you can do in the bust-a-gut competitions. Players have fun competing, and you truly see who your fierce competitors are.

Scrimmage play is another great motivator. You can set up scrimmages in many different ways. You can play a regular game, play six outs, short game only scrimmage, off a flip toss that works on location hitting, and just as many as you can come up with. We scrimmage whenever we get a full facility. I also have had scrimmage Saturdays that lead into clinic Sundays. Whatever situation gave us the most trouble during Saturday's scrimmage would set up Sunday's practice format. But the more they play and the more they feel pressure while performing, the more confident the players will feel in real game play.

Final Thoughts

Remember, a motivated player is an interested player. What better environment is there but the practice setting to motivate your athletes. You may not be in control of the facility you have to practice in or the time allotted to you for practice, but you are in control of the practice you plan. With just a little effort and imagination, you can plan a workout that players will be excited to participate in. Remember, one of your main responsibilities as a coach is to have your team work hard, stay focused, and maintain enthusiasm for the game of softball.

CHAPTER THIRTEEN

Using Practice Drills Effectively

Betty Hoff and Jacki Wright

Photo courtesy of Luther College

Softball coaches can find many examples of useful softball drills in a variety of publications. It is not the intent of this chapter to provide an endless supply of drills, but rather to present some principles and guidelines for the coach to think about. Application of these principles should help the coach select and conduct drills to better advantage. In addition, consideration is given to developing a sense of drill progression for the advancing ability level of players.

A smart starting point is for the coach to be certain that the goals of the drill meet the needs of the players. Rather than searching for a drill to fill 15 minutes of practice time, wise coaches begin by thinking about what aspect of the game their players need to improve. Many published drills include objectives or purposes for the drill. If a match for the team's needs cannot be found, a little creative thinking is needed to design one that fits the situation.

Another early consideration in planning the use of a practice drill is to eliminate as much risk of injury as possible. The practice facility itself must be inspected for possible hazards. All softball playing equipment should be kept off the practice space until it is needed. When the practice is held in a gymnasium, players near the wall must be taught how to avoid injury on an overthrown ball that bounces off the wall. If they turn to face the wall, the ball is likely to hit them in the face. Instead of turning to look for the ball, they should simply wait for it to bounce off the wall, perhaps even putting the glove over the back of the head to avoid receiving a hard impact there.

Visualize the traffic pattern of players in the drill before the players are asked to run the drill. Make sure there is enough space between groups so that players do not collide with each other. The path of the thrown ball must be open, and other players must not be permitted to move into that path. Consider what dangerous play might happen, and develop a plan to limit the risk. It may be necessary to establish one or two safety rules for each drill used. For example, players should be taught to make eye contact with the person to whom they are throwing or hitting. This is the best assurance one can make that the fielder is indeed ready to make the play. If an overthrown ball rolls behind another group of players, the player who charges after it may be hit by an overthrow from the other group. Set that territory off limits until the drill is stopped. When players have bats in their hands, they must be surrounded by safety space. It is the responsibility of the coach, rather than the players, to establish rules of conduct that will ensure safety.

Conduct all drills so as to promote correct performance of skills. It is easy to make the mistake of rushing the beginning player. Keeping the pace slow at first allows players to utilize self-talk (cue words such as *see the ball*) to help guide them in producing correct technique. It is also helpful for beginners to be able to perform fundamental skills before progressing to more complex situation play. A very competitive drill or a complex game situation interferes with the beginner's ability to focus on correct performance of the technique. Similarly, with batting skills, beginners need to show command of the skill using shadow swings and hitting a stationary ball off a tee before attempting live hitting. A novice player's beautiful swing during a shadow drill may be totally lost the first time a live pitcher is used.

Drills should allow very little standing around. In the early learning stages, players may benefit from watching teammates long enough to understand the technique and the design of the drill. Once that is understood, players have little chance to improve by standing in line for 8 minutes of a 10-minute drill. They need to have adequate rehearsal time to improve performance. The amount of equipment available or the nature of the facility might provide some restrictions, but the most effective drills are those that maximize active participation.

In a similar vein, it is important for the coach to continue the drill long enough so that the repetitions of the skill allow for learning and improvement. It is helpful for players to complete 5, 8, even 10 successive attempts at the desired skill, as opposed to trying the skill once before giving way to the next player. At the other extreme, when beginners have been working at a skill for 20 minutes, it is probably good to discontinue that drill. Players benefit from a change of focus.

Whenever possible, drills should provide immediate feedback. Result-oriented drills heighten player interest, motivation, and enjoyment. In addition, feedback allows players to note their improvement and progress toward success. Simply setting a goal provides immediate feedback—for example, have players try to field cleanly and throw accurately 9 out of 10 opportunities. Another example: use towels or hula hoops as targets to measure the success on the placement of bunts. When a drill design is result-oriented, it is important that correct technique is not sacrificed.

As the performance level of players increases, it is important for the coach to select and design drills that help players progress to more gamelike play. Once a beginner attains competency at throwing and fielding, add target throws to bases after fielding grounders and catching fly balls. Another useful idea is to coordinate small units of position players for gamelike play, such as a pair of infielders or outfielders, or dividing the field in half and using the catcher, third base player, shortstop, left fielder, and center fielder. In this unit, players learn to cover their territories and to back up plays their teammates are responsible for making. Adding imaginary runners teaches players to make correct throwing decisions for game situations.

So that the team may perform successfully in games, drills should be designed to rehearse the desired performance in game situations. One example of using practice time effectively is to begin scrimmage play with a runner on first base. By repeating this single situation, the pitcher and catcher work at pitch selection and desired location for a variety of hitters. The defense has to adapt to the bunt situation along with the possibilities of an attempted steal or a hit-and-run. The batter may practice either taking signals or selecting an appropriate pitch location while also attempting a designated bat skill. The base runner practices timing her leadoff and works on her acceleration and slide. One modification that may help to increase the amount of action is to allow each batter only three pitches. If the batter does not put the ball in play on one of the first two pitches, the third pitch becomes a suicide bunt or a hit-and-run. Any defensive situation may be substituted.

Select conditioning drills and activities that are specific to softball. Since a minimal level of aerobic fitness is important, continuous running for 20 minutes (or about two miles) would be reasonable. Running distances beyond three miles would probably fall into the overkill category, increasing the chance of injury and taking up time better spent on softball specific drills. Remember, the maximum running distance for a player in a game is 240 feet. To condition players to accelerate around the bases or to run and catch a challenging outfield fly, focus on conditioning drills that utilize the fast-twitch fibers of the leg muscles, all-out sprinting from 20 to 100 meters, for example.

The conduct of a practice must reflect the following principle: Players tend to perform during a game as they perform in practice. Encourage players to hustle in practice, just like they are expected to hustle during the game. When players work hard during practice, they put themselves in a better position for success during a game. On the other hand, if practice becomes a time to go through the motions, they are not preparing themselves for the game atmosphere. Hustle, excitement, and a positive attitude are qualities that are paramount for a practice setting to help the player be prepared for the game setting.

The offensive and defensive drills in the following sections progress through different levels. Coaches should select the level that best fits their teams. To jump in at a level too advanced and too early in the progression does not allow athletes to develop correct habits in their skill work.

Progression of Drills for Offense

Level one is designed as a starting point and is appropriate for either novice players or for advanced players who may let it serve as a warm-up. The offensive drill progression begins with hitting and is followed by the short game and baserunning. Each level of drills promotes correct learning of fundamental skills and guides players through increasingly more advanced and gamelike drills. Table 13.1 summarizes the progression of offensive drills.

TABLE 13.1

Progression of Drills for Offense

HITTING

Level	Focus	Progression
1	Swing fundamentals	Shadow swings Tee swings Soft-toss drill
2	See the pitch	Pitching machine pitches from pitcher's position Cage games Live pitching
3	Decision making	Situational hitting off live pitching or pitching machine Simulated inning with groups of 3 or 4 hitters
4	Game situations	Controlled scrimmage

THE SHORT GAME

Level	Focus	Progression
1	Swing fundamentals	Shadow swings
2	Precision	Target bunts using hula hoops or towels Cage games Target pokes and slaps
3	Flexibility	Mix short game skills with full swings Pattern hitting using a pitching machine Pattern hitting off live pitching
4	Game situations	Result-oriented scrimmages

BASERUNNING

Level	Focus	Progression
1	Fundamentals	Line drills to teach basic footwork Slides Small-group running drills to teach rounding bases
2	Application	Combination drill

Hitting

Hitting involves more than making contact. Beginning players learn the proper swing technique, then practice seeing the ball, and finally move to making decisions during game situations. The hitting progression begins with shadow swings in level one and progresses to gamelike situations in level four. Reinforce proper technique at each level.

Level One

A good place to begin the development of hitting skills is with shadow swings. In the shadow swing drill, the player swings without a ball present. Since the player doesn't have to see the ball, this drill allows her to concentrate on correct hitting technique. Instruct players to swing the bat at levels that range from the top to the bottom of the strike zone. When first learning, players may want to swing in slow motion in order to permit the use of cue words (self-talk). The speed of the swing is gradually increased as the drill proceeds. For more experienced players, shadow swings are an excellent warm-up drill before proceeding to other hitting drills. Coaches need to keep safety in mind when positioning players for this drill so that no one is hit by a swinging bat.

The next step in level one is to hit tee swings. Players apply correct hitting technique to a stationary ball sitting on top of a tee, which eliminates having to focus on a moving ball. Swings can be done at the player's own pace, giving her time to use self-talk to correct her technique. Hitting off a tee also gives players immediate feedback regarding contact on the ball. Players see that hitting the ball too far under the center creates a pop-up. The tee also allows the hitter to work on getting her hands and bat through at different heights. Tee swings can be set up in many places. Wiffle balls can be hit into the sides of a batting cage or net screens, or players can hit softballs into an open and safe area. Tee swings are also useful for more advanced players as a warm-up drill or for working out technique challenges.

The soft-toss drill is the next logical step in the offensive drill progression for hitting. Hitters focus on applying proper technique to a ball that is tossed softly a short distance from the side (see figure 13.1). The hitter works on making a level swing with the ball tossed at different heights. Hitters can easily execute several swings within a short time. Organization for soft toss can be varied. It can be set up so that batters are hitting into screens or nets or hitting to receivers in the field. Safety is always a concern in this drill. Even if there is only one group hitting to receivers, ball feeders must be sure that the receivers are looking at the hitter and ready to field. If the drill is organized with more than one hitting station in a small area, feeders must alternate tosses and be certain that receivers are looking.

Figure 13.1 Setup for soft-toss drill.

Level Two

In level two, the ball comes at hitters from the direction of the pitcher's position. Use a pitching machine with novice players, so they grow accustomed to seeing the ball at a controlled speed and location. Adjusting the machine to pitch at a certain speed and location eliminates some of the hitter's decision-making, allowing hitters to focus on seeing the ball and timing the swing to make good contact. Eventually, move pitches around the strike zone so that hitters must adjust their swings to meet the ball at different locations. For example, at the first practice of the week, the target can be low-inside pitches and at the next practice low-outside pitches. Safety is important when using pitching machines. Use slower pitching speeds at first, then graduallly increase speed as the hitters become more experienced. All hitters and machine feeders need to wear helmets, and a protective screen is needed for the machine feeder.

When players are ready to be more challenged, proceed to cage games, drills that give immediate feedback and reward good technique. Cage games break up the monotony of repetition after repetition and add excitement and fun to practice. Creativity is necessary when inventing cage games. For example, create a contest among players where points are awarded for solid hits off the pitching machine. Hitters score five points for smacking a line drive to the back of the cage, three points for other line drives, and one point for a hard-hit ground ball. Players tally their scores and are rewarded through recognition and cheers from the team and, if time permits, another round in the cage. Or, players can be rewarded with additional pitches for each line drive hit. Designating 10 successive machine pitches in which players count and record solid contacts is another way to add some zip to batting practice. Each time a player steps in to hit, she challenges herself to increase her number of solid contacts. With a little creativity, coaches can create many types of cage games to provide immediate feedback and make hitting drills more fun.

Hitting against live pitching is the final step in level two. The emphasis shifts from proper technique only to making good decisions in the selection of pitches to hit. Hitters must learn to judge which pitches are balls and strikes and when to initiate their swings. It might be helpful for hitters to receive a predetermined number of pitches in which they focus on seeing the ball well, deciding which pitches to swing at, and making solid contact using proper technique.

Level Three

Decision-making at the plate is a crucial skill that hitters must develop and improve. Choosing the right pitch to swing at becomes vital in game situations. Level three drills emphasize placing the hitter in a decision-making setting where she must consider a particular game situation, select a good pitch to swing at, and execute properly to get on base or advance teammates. These drills are more gamelike and serve to prepare players for competition.

One way coaches can help players become better decision makers in game situations is to practice situation hitting off pitching machines or live pitching (either in the cage or on the diamond). Place an imaginary runner on base or predetermine the count and number of outs to encourage players to think about pitch selection and the type of swing needed for the situation. Coaches can set up numerous situations for hitters.

While using the cages, it may also be useful to organize hitters into pairs or into groups of three or four hitters who play an inning. For example, if the first hitter gets a base hit (coaches can define what constitutes a base hit for cage play), then the next hitters play the situation until there are three outs. Strikeouts, pop flies, or weak hits are outs. Practicing situations such as these provide hitters with decision-making experience and place them in a better position to be successful in game situations.

Level Four

Controlled scrimmage play on the diamond is the final step in the offensive drill sequence for hitting. In a controlled scrimmage, the coach designates the situations—such as no runners on base and the batter is the leadoff hitter—and the team plays them out. These situations provide excellent opportunities to work on decision-making skills and correct execution.

The Short Game

Practice of the short game is an absolute necessity if a team is going to be able to execute in competition. The sacrifice bunt, bunt for a hit, suicide bunt, fake bunt and poke, and the running slap are short game skills to incorporate into drill progressions. Start slowly with correct technique for each of these skills.

Level One

Shadow drills for short game skills are just as valuable as they are for full swings. Hitters can work on timing, upper- and lower-body position, and bat position and movement without having to focus on a ball. The coach should mimic a pitcher's motion so that hitters can work on timing their movement. More advanced players can also use this drill as a warm-up exercise.

Level Two

Once the basic technique is learned for bunts, place towels or hula hoops on the floor or ground as targets. The goal is to place bunts into the hula hoops or onto the towels. Result-oriented drills like these heighten the player's interest and motivation. Coaches can initiate cage games with a scoring system to make it more interesting and fun. Do not let players sacrifice correct technique in cage games. Use similar drills to practice pokes and slaps by presenting players with an image of where the ball should travel, such as the hole at second base or shortstop.

Level Three

In competition, hitters may be called upon to execute a short game skill at any time. To help prepare for this moment, vary the pattern of practice to mix a short game skill with full swings. Beginning with the pitching machine, hitters follow a pattern, such as three full swings, three bunts, two swings, two bunts, one swing, one bunt. Switching skills forces a change of focus and goal for the hitter. Once other short game skills are learned, more skills can be worked into the pattern. Coaches must not overwhelm novice players with too many skills early in the learning process.

After players are successful working off a pitching machine, move them to practice off live pitching. Live pitching challenges players to use decision-making skills and proper execution. Examples of drills to utilize off live pitching may include giving hitters a designated number of pitches in which they attempt to execute two or three different short game skills.

Level Four

Result-oriented scrimmage play challenges hitters to make good decisions and execute correctly. Allow several opportunities for players to execute short game skills off live pitching and against a full defense. One idea is to place a runner on first and give the hitter only three pitches to advance the runner using a short game skill. If the hitter is not successful after two pitches, she must perform a suicide bunt or poke. This keeps the drill moving and sharpens the player's focus. Other examples may include practicing the suicide bunt with a runner on third base or performing a running slap with a runner on second base.

Baserunning

Since baserunning is the only way to advance and score, technique and judgment are critical to offensive success. Break baserunning into basic components, such as getting out of the batter's box, running through first base, leading off, rounding bases, and sliding.

Level One

Line drills in the gym or on the diamond are a good starting point for learning baserunning. Basic footwork for getting out of the batter's box, the lead-off, and tagging up can be taught by organizing players into short lines that are spaced out on the baseline or in the gym. For example, players can straddle the baseline and assume a hitter's stance in an imaginary batter's box. Players swing at an imaginary pitch and sprint out of the box using correct footwork.

Safety precautions are a must when teaching the basic slide. Before practicing slides at full speed, have players lie down on the floor or ground and assume a correct sliding position. Check for correct and safe body position. After players learn position fundamentals, use a line drill outside to work on technique and timing. For safety reasons, have players slide into unattached bases before proceeding to anchored bases. A favorite drill of ours is setting up a line drill outside where players slide into orange plastic bases in the snow. Another idea is to hose down a grassy area and practice sliding on a slippery surface.

To practice rounding bases on the diamond, use small-group running drills in which players are divided into three groups (at home, first, and second base, for example). Each player practices approaching the base and rounding it correctly. The next step could include working on getting out of the batter's box and sprinting toward first base (in foul territory) where a coach tells players to either run through the base or to round it.

Level Two

At this point, incorporate a combination drill that applies all the baserunning skills on the diamond. Divide players into three groups and place them at home plate, first base, and third base. On a pitching motion made by a coach or manager, the player at home executes a shadow swing and sprints through first base. Simultaneously, the runner at first base leads off, rounds second base, and sprints to third. The runner at third base leads off, tags up (as if a fly ball were hit), and waits for the third base coach to say *go* before sprinting and sliding into home plate. This drill utilizes baserunning skills well and keeps players moving.

Progression of Drills for Defense

Defensive drills progress in much the same way offensive drills do. Beginning drills focus on fundamentals and repetitions, then as players advance, they move on to gamelike situations and scrimmages. Table 13.2 lists the progression of defensive drills for pitching, infield play, and outfield play.

Pitching

At all levels, emphasis is placed on correct performance of pitching techniques. Pitchers moving through the drills get many repetitions and have multiple opportunities to fine-tune their techniques. When analyzing a pitcher's progress, a video camera provides excellent feedback about the pitcher's execution.

Level One

Beginning pitchers need many repetitions to learn good pitching mechanics. Early on, they may complete some of their throws into a wall or screen, so they can work independently. Sometimes pitchers can throw back and forth to one another, and at other times, a catcher is needed. Some of the drills focus on a single part of the pitching motion since the primary goal is to establish good pitching mechanics. Some of the beginner drills may become a part of the advanced pitcher's daily warm-up routine. Once young pitchers have learned to throw a fastball, a pull-up (or straight) drop, and a change-up, they have the tools to be highly successful.

Level Two

For pitchers, a variety of sources provide feedback during drills. Once the basic mechanics of the pitching motion have been established, pitch location becomes important. Completed pitch location charts provide valuable feedback for the pitcher and the coach.

To create the chart, the coach or another pitcher or player notes the location of a set of fastballs to a single target set by the catcher. The recorder stands behind a screen behind the catcher to get a good sight of the pitch location as the ball crosses the plate. (For the change-up, one might limit the chart work to just 10 pitches to the low-outside target since that pitch is harder on the arm.) The coach and pitcher can use this chart to identify any adjustments that need to be made. A scoring system could be developed to

TABLE 13.2

Progression of Drills for Defense

PITCHING

Level	Focus	Progression
1	Mechanics	Throws to wall or screen Throws to another pitcher Throws to a catcher
2	Location	Completion of pitching chart Recording of ball placement
3	Game situations	Catcher calls balls and strikes with imaginary hitter or stand in Game situations in the batting cage
4	Scrimmage	Repeated work on a particular situation Inning-by-inning scrimmage play

INFIELDERS: THROWING AND FIELDING

Level	Focus	Progression
1	Fundamentals	Line drill with throwers on one knee Throws in the box Infield line throws Fielding a thrown ground ball
2	Position play	Line drill, fielding a batted ball Positional drill, fielding a batted ball
3	Game situations	Fungo grounders and flies with imaginary runners Second to first double play with imaginary runners Second to first double play with real runners
4	Scrimmage	Live pitching and hitting Different situations can be staged

OUTFIELD PLAY

Level	Focus	Progression
1	Throwing/catching	Partner drills in gymnasium or outfield Fly ball catching Fielding ground balls (one knee) Fielding the ball on the run
2	Distance	Fielding fungo hits Long/short drill Gray mark drill
3	Team play	Partner drill to reinforce priority Texas leaguers with shortstop Fungo hits to the outfield, situational fielding
4	Scrimmage	Live pitching and full defense Game situations

reward the great locations with a +1 or +2 score but penalize the belt-high pitch or a location over the middle of the plate with a −1 or −2. Such a scoring system would enhance the effectiveness of goal setting for the pitcher's workout.

Pitch location charts are a valuable tool for the intermediate and advanced level pitcher as well. If a radar gun is available, record the speed of each type of pitch.

Level Three

Another good opportunity for feedback is to have the catcher call balls and strikes with either an imaginary hitter or an extra player (wearing a batting helmet, of course!) who stands in but does not swing. The catcher calls a mix of pitches and targets for a set of 30 throws, and the count progresses as in a game. A scoring system might be worked out such as +2 for each strikeout, −1 for a walk, and −1 for any pitch down the middle except with a 3-0 count.

The batting cage is a good place to include game-like situations such as the following:

- facing three hitters in a row in a leadoff batter situation;
- throwing five pitches to each of three hitters with a constant count such as 0-2 or 3-0; or
- facing the number-four hitter with a runner on second but first base open.

More situations could be added to this list, but each design calls for the pitcher and catcher to select and practice both mental and physical performance of skills in a gamelike situation.

Level Four

Depending on the number of pitchers on the squad and the concentration of games in the playing schedule, conducting scrimmages during practice time is another excellent preparation for competition. Opportunities for the pitcher may range from repeated work at a single situation to regular inning-by-inning play.

Infielders: Throwing and Fielding

Similar to the design for offense, level one for defense is targeted for the novice player but can be utilized as a review for the advanced player as well as for warm-up. For level two, fungo hitters put the ball into play, and player position work is introduced. At level three, game situations with imaginary runners are added, but the ball continues to be put in play by a fungo hitter. The use of live scrimmage play becomes the focus of level four.

Level One

For the novice player, an effective drill is to have the team in two lines about 15 feet apart, each player with a designated partner. Partners throw back and forth to each other while kneeling on their throwing-side knees (see figure 13.2). This exercise allows players to focus on proper shoulder rotation, elbow position, and release while eliminating concern for the lower body. The partner receiving the throw works at catching with the fingertips of the glove up for balls waist high and above (figure 13.3a) and fingertips down for balls below waist level (figure 13.3b). The throwing distance can be gradually increased within a practice and from one practice to the next.

Figure 13.2 The throwing position for the one-knee throwing drill.

a *b*

Figure 13.3 For the one-knee throwing drill, the receiver catches the ball with fingertips up for balls waist high and above *(a)* and fingertips down for balls below waist level *(b)*.

To emphasize accuracy of the throw, ask players to complete six to eight throws in the box from a given distance. For a throw to be considered in the box, it must be at or below the receiver's shoulders—but not below the waist—and between vertical lines from the left and right shoulders (see figure 13.4). The drill can be used indoors or outdoors. To increase difficulty, players may move farther apart, and the number of successful throws may be increased.

Another way to increase distance on the throw is to have partners throw to each other from just outside the infield foul lines. Use flat cones to identify six to eight throwing sites, starting about 20 feet from home plate and extending past the base to the edge of the outfield grass (see figure 13.5). Throwing sites need to be about 10 feet apart to provide a safe area. Half of the players progress down the third base line while their partners move down the first base line. The first

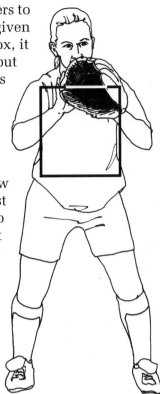

Figure 13.4   In the box.

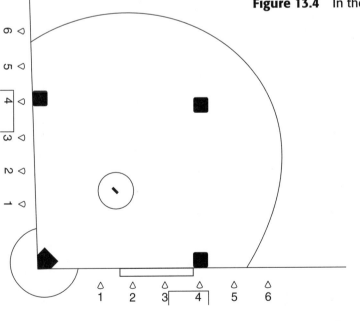

△ Cones

Figure 13.5   Setup for the progressive throwing drill.

set of partners begins at the throwing site nearest home plate and attempts to throw over and back successfully. If their throws are accurate and reach their partner without bouncing, they move to the next throwing site and the next set of partners begins at site one. If there is a bad throw, that pair of partners returns to the end of the line at the home plate area, provided there is a safe space through which they can move. The goal for each pair of players is to complete successful throws and catches at each successive throwing site. Since there are a limited number of participants, this drill is best used when part of the squad is doing another activity.

The fielding of ground balls may be initiated with players using an underhand throw to roll balls back and forth between partners. Young players are more accurate with a thrown ball than a fungo hit ball. Similarly, a thrown ball can be delivered with much less velocity, so young players can realize greater success at fielding. When players work in partners, everyone is active, and participation is maximized. Try having all players in one line throw about 10 successive grounders to their partners. Their partners field the ground balls and throw back to the initial player. For one set of 10, the thrower's target might be at shoulder level (for a force out), and for another set of 10, the target might be at knee level (for a tag out). Rather than allowing partners to change roles on their own after exactly 10 throws, have them switch on a whistle signal from the coach. This way, all overhand throws are made in the same direction, reducing the likelihood of a fielder moving into the path of another player's overhand throw. It is also easier for the coach to observe fielding technique when the active fielders are all in the same line.

Level Two

Next, add fielding a batted ball. Groups of three work nicely with a fungo hitter. The fungo hitter and a receiver stand on one side line of the gym, and the active fielder starts near the opposite side line. Since players have less control with fungo hits than when throwing, provide adequate space between groups. In a gym, spread out five groups down the length of one floor if the fielding is straight on. When the focus is on lateral movement, you may need to reduce to four groups to keep the practice area safe. Have each group practice fielding grounders to the left, then switch everyone to the right at the same time. Use a whistle signal to rotate players to new roles after a given period of time. Players crossing the gym at random are both distracting and dangerous.

Use a similar organization outdoors on the infield. The smaller space allows a safe practice space for two parallel groups. The direction of the layout of the field determines whether to have fungo hitters located outside the first or third base line. Avoid having the fungo hitter and receiver looking into the sun since they would have trouble seeing the thrown ball coming back in their direction. Emphasis should be placed on fielding with soft hands, making eye contact with the receiver, then making an accurate throw.

Next, place the players at their infield positions to field fungo grounders and infield flies hit by the coach from home plate. In addition to their practice at fielding and making an accurate throw to each base, players also learn who should cover each base when the ball is hit to the various positions on the infield. Depending on squad size, players may be two or three deep at each position, provided the backup players stay far enough behind the active fielder so that they have time to react to a batted or thrown ball that gets past the active fielder. Do not have extra players at the pitcher's position; this is dangerous when throws are made across the infield. Give each fielder three to five chances to field and throw to a particular position. When a round of throwing to first base has been completed for every player, the next person at each position may rotate in.

Level Three

At level three, select game situations and practice fungo-hit grounders and infield flies using imaginary runners. For example, while practicing with an imaginary runner on second base and fewer than two outs, players look at the runner on second base to hold her there, then play the ball to first base. The first base player follows with a throw to third base as though the runner advanced on the throw. When players have demonstrated that they understand the strategy of the play, extra players (in batting helmets) may be used as base runners. A good safety rule is to have the offensive player assume responsibility for avoiding a collision with the defensive player.

Any other game situation may be introduced this way. Once the middle infielders learn a couple of pivot plays at second, the double play from second to first can be done with imaginary runners, then with real runners. For a bases-loaded situation with less than two outs, the middle infielders are pulled in and the initial throw after fielding a fungo grounder goes to home plate. The catcher may follow with a throw to first base. Defensive sets for bunt coverage with runners at different bases can be practiced in this format as well.

Level Four

When the team has learned coverage for various situations, the team can work to improve performance using live pitching and hitting. Each inning might begin with a runner on first to ensure adequate practice rehearsals for that coverage. Another option would be to start each inning with a different situation.

Outfield Play

Outfielders need to develop fundamental throwing and fielding skills like infielders. As soon as possible, however, they need to work at lengthening their throws, fielding ground balls off a grass surface, and fielding fly balls and grounders from a greater distance. At all levels of play, it is important for each player to have completed adequate warm-up throws before working at her skills from the outfield depth.

Level One

Early practice for outfielders can begin with partner drills across a gymnasium floor or the outfield. Keep safety in mind if separate infield drills occur at the same time. One of the most basic drills is for partners to simply throw fly balls to each other. As catching skills improve, alter the drill so that the active fielders get in good position to make the catch and then make accurate throws back to their partners, who then toss another fly ball. On the diamond, have a player at third base throw fly balls to the left fielder, then one at second base throw to the center fielder, and finally, one at first base throw to the right fielder.

Fielding grounders may progress as for infielders with the addition of a couple of special skills. The outfielder must learn to drop to one knee while fielding a ground ball to ensure that the ball does not get under the glove. Outfielders also need to learn to field the ball outside the glove-side foot while on the run.

Level Two

At this level, thrown flies and grounders are replaced with fungo hits that lengthen the distance to the fielders. Depending on overhead construction barriers, it is usually possible to carefully fungo hit fly balls down the length of a gymnasium. The long/short drill is an efficient design for introducing fungo hit fly balls outside. A fungo hitter and receiver set up in foul territory outside the left field line (figure 13.6). The active fielder is in right center field facing the left field foul line, and the short fielder is halfway between. The active fielder has 5 to 10 chances to field fungo flies. The short fielder retrieves any grounders or short hits. The active fielder uses the short fielder as the relay person on the throw back to the receiver. The design is also beneficial in very cold weather when coaches want players to use shorter throws to prevent injury.

For more advanced players, remove the short fielder so that the active fielder is responsible for catching every batted ball. The fielder receives a gray mark for every failure to catch and for every errant throw within a set. The goal of each fielder is to finish the drill with a score of zero. A set of six chances would be a good starting point. To challenge the player's endurance, increase the number of hits in a set.

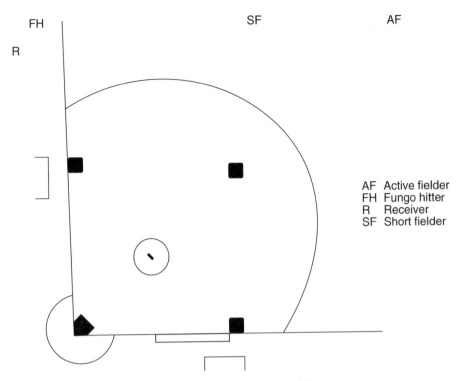

FH   SF   AF

R

AF   Active fielder
FH   Fungo hitter
R   Receiver
SF   Short fielder

Figure 13.6   Setup for long/short drill along left field line.

Level Three

Having players practice in small units helps them perform as a team. A simple partner drill can reinforce the rule that the center fielder has priority over the outside fielders. Two active outfielders stand ready to field, one designated the center fielder. Fly balls are hit to the space between them. The center fielder is given the right to catch each ball she can reach. When the center fielder knows she can make the catch, she is to call "mine, mine, mine" while the other fielder moves to backup position and responds with "yours, yours, yours." (These words, *mine* and *yours*, are very clear and leave no room for misunderstanding.) An easy modification of the drill is to place all three outfielders in their defensive positions and fungo hit to the gaps on either side of the center fielder.

Another example of an effective small unit drill would be to have the shortstop, left fielder, and center fielder chase down Texas leaguers. The outfielder has priority over the shortstop for all hits into the short outfield space. The shortstop listens for a call from the outfielder and moves out of her path to avoid a collision. The second baseplayer is used as an insurance person if no active fielder made a call since the view from the side of the play would be advantageous in deciding which player had the best chance to reach the fly ball.

Using a full defensive team and fungo hitting fly balls and grounders to the outfielders is another good way to practice fielding and decision making. A specific situation can be rehearsed several times. Outfielders work to apply general rules such as throwing two bases ahead of the lead runner on a base hit and one base ahead of the runner on a caught fly ball. Each infielder gets reinforcement about whether to cover a base or serve in a relay, cutoff, or backup role. Infielders also work at appropriate foot placement to receive throws at the base, as well as on making the tag of the imaginary runner after receiving the throw from the outfielder.

Level Four

With live pitching and a full defensive set, outfielders work at their various roles with each live batter in a scrimmage situation. For a given practice, the focus may be on defensive play with a runner on second base in game situations of no outs, one out, and two outs. Outfielders execute their backup roles for plays that stay in the infield. If the team at bat fails to get enough balls to the outfield, you can make a few adjustments. Rather than having the pitcher throw to the hitters, a coach might use the soft-toss technique. Or the pitcher may pitch to the catcher, but the coach fungo hits a second ball to the outfielders, so they can handle many fly balls and grounders.

Final Thoughts

Coaches should have a broad vision when selecting and conducting drills. The best softball drills are purpose-driven and are conducted with safety as a priority: They emphasize and reinforce correct technique; they provide immediate feedback; and they progress from fundamental skills to game-like settings.

PART
IV

Individual
Skills and
Team
Strategies

CHAPTER FOURTEEN

Developing Productive Hitters

Mike Candrea

Photo courtesy of the University of Arizona

I have had the opportunity to observe or coach many of the great hitters in college softball and to listen to many of the great teachers of the game. Whenever we talk about softball or baseball, the one thing that can be agreed on is the difficulty of teaching and performing the skill of hitting a round object with another round object.

This chapter covers the principles I feel are important in hitting. I do not include much about style, but more importantly I focus on preparation and the elements of the swing that all good hitters have in common. Every coach has his or her own opinion about the makeup of a great hitter. Opinion is what makes our game so special. The following information was formulated during 25 years of coaching the skill as well as borrowing from the thoughts of many great players and coaches. The common denominators are basic, but the ability to perform them quickly under pressure is what makes the great hitter in softball so special.

Approaching the At Bat

The physical and mental preparation of a hitter is critical to success. How a hitter approaches the plate and prepares herself determines whether or not she has a successful at bat. What is a successful at bat? My definition of a successful at bat is when a hitter swings on time, sees the ball well, hits the ball hard, and executes the skills of the game (sacrifice bunt, drag, slap-and-run, hit-and-run, and so). Too many young hitters have only one definition— getting a hit. Hitting is a process-oriented skill. Once hitters understand the process and learn to execute, they become successful more consistently.

Great hitters learn to make slight adjustments between each at bat and between each pitch. We want our hitters to approach the plate with a clear mind and a high level of trust in their hands and eyes. Proper preparation puts a hitter in a confident attack mode.

Mental Preparation

Once the physical aspects of a hitter's swing become consistent, mental preparation grows more important. An early skill to understand is how to deal with failure. Softball is a game of failure when you consider that the best hitters fail 7 out of 10 times. A hitter's ability to handle this aspect of the game often determines her ability to have a consistent, positive approach at the plate.

Mental preparation begins in the dugout. In the dugout, we identify the tendencies and physical cues of the opposition. These questions may come to mind:

- Does the pitcher show her pitches?
- What pitch does she use to get ahead?
- Does she have a good off-speed pitch? Is she consistent with it?

- Does she work in and out or up in the zone?
- Is the rise ball tempting to swing at, or is it always out of the zone?
- Does she have any pitch sequence that is consistent?

As you can see, the dugout is not a social club.

From the dugout, the hitter moves to being in the hole. At this time, she puts on her helmet, grabs her bat, and starts preparing to hit. Hopefully, she takes with her the small checklist of physical and mental cues she observed from the dugout or her previous at bat. She should control her breathing and use self-talk to become relaxed and confident. Then she is prepared for the on-deck circle, which is the perfect place for her to rehearse her timing and rhythm against the pitcher.

Every hitter prepares in her own way; the key is that she uses her time productively. Routines are a huge help in assuring the hitter that she is ready, confident, and relaxed. Every good hitter has a consistent routine as she approaches the plate. Controlling breathing is a huge part of a good routine. By the time the hitter gets to the plate, her focus should have narrowed so that she can see the ball as long as possible and as soon as possible.

Physical Preparation

Physical preparation is easier to understand and master. For a hitter to maximize her chance for success, her position in the batter's box must allow her to maximize her visual skills and provide a solid foundation from which she can achieve balance.

When deciding where to stand in the batter's box, the hitter should consider the pitcher, her own abilities, and her knowledge of the pitcher's tendencies. Pitchers are creatures of habit, and many times a hitter can set the pitcher by the position she takes in the batter's box. Keeping track of each pitcher's tendencies takes a genuine student of the game, but planning each at bat increases the hitter's chance of success.

The hitter's position in the batter's box should give her the best chance to take away the strength of the pitcher while allowing proper plate coverage. After discussing positioning in the batter's box with many great coaches and players, I have concluded that there is no black-and-white answer for every hitter and every at bat. The two essential factors to consider are movement and speed. The hitter's comfort zone also should be considered. A hitter must feel comfortable and confident no matter which position she chooses. Adjustments should be made from each at bat depending on movement, speed, and pitch sequence. In general:

- The hitter stands up in the box (toward the front) when the pitcher has average-to-below-average velocity, when the pitcher's dominant pitch is down in the zone or sideways (curve or screw), or when the pitch's movement shows a late break.

- The hitter stands back in the box (her pivot foot is on the back line of the batter's box) when the pitcher has above-average velocity, when the pitcher's dominant pitch is a rise ball, when the pitch's movement shows an early break (especially for a drop ball), or when the hitter needs a longer look at the pitch.

The closer a hitter stands to the plate, the quicker her hands must be. Most hitters who stand close to the plate are pull hitters who like the pitch in. Hitters who set up off the plate usually are looking for the pitch away and like to hit the ball where it is pitched.

Effective hitters are always observing and trying to find visual cues to increase their chances at the plate. Many pitchers give away certain pitches with changes in hand position or body position. A catcher who sets up early also may give away the pitch location or type. Great hitters note these clues when they are in the dugout or watching the game.

Stance

The stance, although cosmetic, can either help or hinder the hitter's ability to see the softball. I urge any serious player to have a thorough eye examination that includes testing for depth perception. No matter how well the hitter performs the mechanics, if her eyes are relaying bad information to her brain, her chance of success decreases.

The stance shows the greatest amount of variety from hitter to hitter. Great hitters have hit from every foot and hand position imaginable. The primary purpose of the stance is to allow the hitter to see the ball with both eyes and to allow her to arrive in a position that creates balance and proper plate coverage. I have found that whether the hitter's stance is open, closed, or square (see figure 14.1), successful hitters stride to square position to get maximum coverage. Depending on the hitter's dominant eye, the proper stance can enhance her ability to see the ball with the greatest amount of clarity.

Two other common characteristics that I have found in the stance of effective hitters are flexibility and rhythm. A key element to any athletic movement is balance. Without flexibility in the ankles and knees, it is impossible to create a balanced and powerful base from which to hit. It is important for the hitter to keep her weight on the balls of her feet and not have her weight falling to her heels. This flexibility explains why you see many hitters in their prepitch routines bend at the waist and touch the outside portion of the plate with the bat in their bottom hand only. This routine is helpful in creating a balanced base and also ensures that the hitter has proper plate coverage.

Rhythm is another key to hitters with high batting averages. The ability of a hitter to create rhythm in her stance helps her execute the stride. It allows the hitter to keep her body and hands tension-free. Tension is a hitter's worst enemy. The tighter she is, the slower her reaction is. The

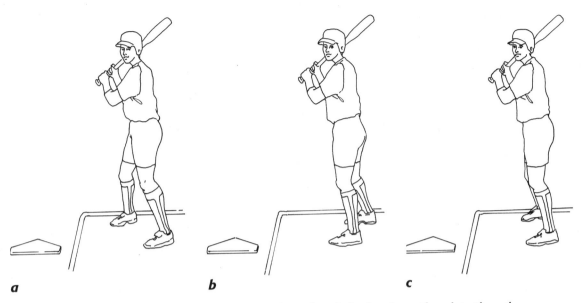

a   *b*   *c*

Figure 14.1   In the open stance *(a)*, the front foot is farther from the plate than the back foot. In the closed stance *(b)*, the front foot is closer to the plate than the back foot. In the square stance *(c)*, both feet are equal distance from the plate.

locking of any body parts before contact causes extreme problems in the execution of the swing.

Rhythm is much easier to demonstrate than to describe. Simply put, a hitter who has rhythm can control her movements in preparation and execution of the swing. The ability to control movement and allow proper sequencing is the key to maximizing power and efficiency. Rhythm is noticeable in great hitters. Any movements made with the lower body or hands must be minimal and controlled. The more movement a hitter has when preparing to swing, the easier it is for the pitcher to disrupt her timing. When I discuss rhythm with hitters, I stress that the hitter should match her movement with the pitcher's movement. As the pitcher moves toward the plate, the hitter must get into launch position and secure her base for the execution of the swing. This movement should be smooth and controlled. Many young hitters wait too late to execute the loading phase; therefore, they come in late and out of control.

The main purpose of effective pitchers is to throw off the timing and rhythm of a hitter. The rhythm displayed by hitters is slightly visible in the lower body and hands. The head, of course, should always stay as quiet (still) as possible during the initial stance.

As I mentioned earlier, the stance is purely cosmetic: Although a hitter does not hit from the stance, a solid stance makes a huge difference in how she sees the ball, the plate coverage she achieves, and the preparation of her body and hands to attack the pitch.

Stride

In my estimation, most of your coaching and teaching probably centers around the next phase of hitting, the stride. The stride is nothing more than a small movement that allows the hitter to achieve a strong, powerful position to initiate the swing. There are many terms used to describe this movement including stride, trigger, load, and so on. The important fact of this movement is that the hitter places her lower and upper body in a position that allows her to generate a swing on time and on the proper plane of the pitch, with maximum bat speed while managing some degree of balance.

Through my years of teaching this phase of hitting, I have found that many hitters make this move too late and create a base that inhibits their ability to use their legs properly. A hitter can never stride too early! The key to this movement is to understand the proper sequence and the foundation the hitter is trying to achieve.

1. As the heel lifts and the knee rolls slightly inward to initiate the stride, the hands slightly move into the position from which the batter launches the bat (figure 14.2). Contact with the ground is made with the inside of the foot.

2. The stride is completed by executing a short, soft step toward the pitcher, maintaining a degree of closure with the front foot (45 to 90 degrees in relationship to the plate). Contact with the ground is made with the inside of the foot.

3. The lower body has maintained flexibility, the head is perfectly still, and the hands are prepared to initiate the swing.

Figure 14.2 The stride.

Common flaws that exist in the stride occur when the hitter overstrides to a point that her weight must move forward, causing her head to have excess movement. When the hitter attempts to load her hands as she strides, it creates a separation of her power base (hands and weight, moving in opposite directions at the same time). Therefore, it is very important to load the hands before moving the stride foot.

The final point I would like to make regarding the stride foot is that the heel must get down to the ground to allow a firm base (front side) to hit against as the hitter begins the explosive movement of the swing. Many hitters do not actually move their stride foot forward but rather pick it up and put it down, or they just execute the loading phase and then hit. This type of hitter usually spreads her initial stance to achieve a balanced and powerful position. I have found that hitters move into a strong hitting position or start in that position.

Swing

After the hitter has achieved a good base from which to hit, it is time to execute the swing. The swing is initiated by a sequential unlocking of body parts. Powerful hitters unwind from the bottom up with a combination of linear and rotational movement. The back side rotates against a firm front side. The word *firm* is important: If the hitter locks the front side, her weight actually moves back as she executes the swing. This movement does not allow the hitter to create a positive weight shift that delivers her energy toward the contact point. When locking occurs, I like to use the term *negative movement* (hitter's weight is moving away from the contact point).

If we divide the body down the middle from the head through the belly button, the front side of the body supplies the direction while the back side provides power. This principle is the same when you are teaching proper throwing mechanics. Let the back side knock the front side out versus using the front side to pull the back side through.

A key element of generating the proper leg and hip action is the position of the back (pivot) foot. By watching the pivot foot on contact, you can tell what kind of weight shift occurred by the position of the heel of the pivot foot. Another key is the position of the back leg: L-shape versus straight leg. We like a hitter to have her heel up at contact (figure 14.3). This tells me that she has achieved a positive weight shift. The closer the heel is to the ground, the more weight remains on the back side and is not transferred to the contact point. Some hitters actually finish on the toe of the pivot foot. This habit is common for hitters who hit off their front foot—for example, Laura Espinoza. Front foot hitters need to be strong in the upper body and gifted with great hand-eye coordination. Obviously, Laura has both, as she is the NCAA leader in home runs. As long as the hitter can achieve a positive movement to the contact point, the pivot foot takes care of itself. I have found more young hit-

Figure 14.3   The swing. The hitter's back heel is up at contact.

ters who have worked so hard pivoting that they actually overrotate, forcing their front sides to fly open and create a long swing.

Now that we understand that the legs lead the swing (unwind from the bottom up), it is time to discuss some key elements of the hand action to the contact point.

Successful Slap Hitting

Larry Ray

Because fastpitch softball is a short, quick game, an offensive technique known as slapping has become very popular. This technique is nothing more than starting a left-handed batter in motion before she makes contact with the ball.

A lefty has a built-in advantage over a right-handed batter by being several feet closer to first base, plus the lefty can start in motion (run parallel to the flight of the pitch), whereas the right-handed batter cannot. One of the most important traits of this type of hitter is that she should possess good-to-excellent speed; otherwise, her success rate will be lower.

To break down the defense, one would like to hit a medium-to-weak ground ball to the farthest point in the infield away from first base (the shortstop area). The idea is to make the defense do several things quickly: Field a ground ball, throw it accurately, then catch it. When the defense has ample time, this is not difficult; but to execute this in less than three seconds, from contact with the ball to the slapper reaching base, makes this a very tough play.

With a slap hitter, extra pressure is applied to infielders, especially the first and third basemen. As the slapper runs in the box, the corners (first and third) react forward for a possible bunt, reducing their range and reaction time, making it easier to get a ground ball past them. If the ball is hit to the shortstop area, generally the first baseman is responsible for getting back to the base, which can cause problems for the defense.

The first step I use in teaching slappers is the inside-out swing (similar to baseball's hit-and-run). The swing starts with the hands high in the strike zone and relatively close to the body. The initial movement is of the knob of the bat being brought forward with the head of the bat lagging behind. The front shoulder remains closed. At this point, many players drop their hands. The slapper should allow the ball to get deeper into the hitting zone than normal, resulting in the ball going to the opposite field. As long as the head of the bat is neither parallel nor ahead of the handle, the ball should go where the batter wants it to.

The footwork is basic: The left foot crosses over the right foot, then the slapper pivots as if to run directly toward the pitcher. I like for my players to land their left feet as close to the front line of the batter's box as possible and for contact with the ball to be made as the left foot lands on the ground. Timing plays a big factor in this skill. My general guideline for a slapper is not to make the move forward until she sees the ball released from the pitcher's hand.

To teach a beginning slapper, especially a right-handed player, follow this progression:

1. Have the hitter catch balls from a pitching machine to get used to seeing the ball from the left-handed batter's box.
2. Have the hitter catch balls from a pitching machine while running. Make sure the hitter catches the ball behind her left foot, not in front, to ensure the ball going to the opposite field.

3. Ask the hitter to execute a drag bunt. I ask her to show me what handwork is comfortable for her (sliding either one or two hands up the bat, for example).

4. Ask the hitter to execute a slap hit. On the initial step, the handwork should look the same as on the drag bunt.

Here are a few coaching keys I share with my players:

- See the ball come out of the pitcher's hand before starting. Don't anticipate.
- The first step is a run—don't walk. (This is the most important step.)
- The first step is directly toward the pitcher with the front side closed.
- Don't get anxious to hit the ball. Allow it to get deep into your hitting zone.
- To hit a ground ball, look for a pitch below your waist, or keep your hands above the ball.

A well-placed slap hit can stymie the defense and inspire an offensive charge. Train hitters to execute the skill successfully, and your team always has a surprise waiting for the defense.

Larry Ray was the inaugural coach of the University of Florida's softball program. In four seasons with the Gators, Ray compiled a 169-106 record overall and a 65-42 Southeastern Conference (SEC) record. The 1998 SEC Coach of the Year, in 2000 Coach Ray led the Gators to a third place finish in their second NCAA regional appearance.

The bottom hand (the pull hand) sets the plane of the swing; the top hand (the throwing hand) finishes the swing. Both hands work together and have equal importance. Successful hitters keep their hands relatively close to their bodies and have a knack for controlling the barrel of the bat.

I use the phrase *Throw your hands inside the ball*. If the hitter is going to deliver the barrel to the ball, her hands must be inside the ball. Hitters who always try to hit the outside of the ball often have poor results. The only pitch hit on the back of the ball is the inside pitch. All other pitches are contacted on the inside half of the ball.

Some common attributes of the upper body in good hitters are:

- Hands are held in a strong position to throw the bat head (barrel).
- Hands are at the top of the strike zone. I like the bottom hand at the top of the strike zone.
- Bat is held at 45-degree angle. Stay away from extremes, like the bat positioned perpendicular, flat, or wrapped behind the head.
- Elbows are down.
- Lead arm forms an **L**.
- Both arms form an upside down **V**.
- Front side is soft.
- Front shoulder is slightly lower than back shoulder.
- Wrists are in an active or cocked position to allow a throwing motion.

One of the easiest ways I have found to describe the proper hand action that results in a short, compact swing is to isolate the bottom hand. When the batter holds her bottom hand in the hitting position, her lead arm has three joints: shoulder, elbow, and wrist. When the hitter unlocks in the proper sequence, the first joint to move is the shoulder, then the elbow, and finally the wrist. Another cue I use: I ask the hitter to imagine she is drawing a line through her chest with her bottom hand, then executing a karate chop to the contact point.

This skill is easier to demonstrate than to describe. If you watch a successful hitter from the pitcher's circle, you notice the first movement is her elbow, then the knob of the bat, and the last thing to arrive is the barrel. Proper sequencing of the lower and upper body produces a key ingredient of great hitters known as bat lag. The barrel of the bat stays very close to the hitter's back shoulder as the hands are delivered toward the contact point. If the bottom hand does its job properly, the top hand takes care of itself.

As the bat head arrives at the contact point, the arms maintain flexion, contact is made, and the hitter extends through the ball. A common flaw is when hitters reach extension before contact, therefore losing bat speed. A hitter's hand position at contact is usually from palm-up/palm-down in the lower position of the strike zone to backhand-of-the-bottom-hand/palm-of-the-top-hand in the upper portion of the strike zone. The rolling of the wrist is a follow-through motion and should not be overemphasized.

Contact points vary depending on the location of the pitch. I actually put three balls on the ground that signify the proper contact points for the inside, middle, and outside pitch. A key coaching point for proper contact is the following:

- For an inside pitch, the barrel is in front of the hands.
- For a middle pitch, the barrel is even with the hands.
- For an outside pitch, the barrel is behind the hands.

As the hitter completes the swing, her hands should finish somewhere around her front shoulder (figure 14.4). Hitters vary with the location of their follow-throughs, either above the shoulder or at the shoulder. The follow-through should allow the hitter to maintain balance and assure a quality head position.

Figure 14.4　The follow-through.

Final Thoughts

In conclusion, great hitters often have God-given talents that you cannot always teach—hand-eye coordination, bat speed, depth perception. I feel you can make any hitter better by understanding the principles of the swing. Develop a sound foundation that allows them to receive viable information and remain tension-free (stance). And finally, teach a short, compact swing that stresses a positive movement to and through the ball while maintaining a good head position and balance throughout the swing. Teach from the ground up, as a hitter must unwind from the bottom up to use her body effectively. Last but not least, softball is a quick, compact game that gives hitters little reaction time. My goal for them is to minimize negative movement and maximize efficiency.

CHAPTER FIFTEEN

Manufacturing Runs

Jay Miller

Offensive philosophy should be designed to accomplish one thing—score runs. To achieve this goal, instill in players the philosophy of never being satisfied with one base. Anytime a ball is hit, whether a player is a base runner or batter, her objective should be to reach home plate. Her mindset should be to go as far as she can until the defense prevents her from going any farther.

Teach your players that there is no such thing as one base. Every time a player is running bases, her goal is to advance two bases or more. This type of aggressiveness leads to mistakes on the defensive end and, more importantly, it allows your players to take advantage of any slight mistake, bobble, or misdirected throw the defense makes.

It can be difficult to get this philosophy across to young players. A big problem in the younger age groups is that players are not taught to play the game and to react to game situations. Rather, they are taught to rely on the coaches at first base, at third base, and in the dugout to let them know when to run, when to stay, and when to take an extra base. The majority of teaching, especially in the preseason, should emphasize gamelike situations in which the players must read the defense and react accordingly on the bases.

The philosophy of never being satisfied with a single, of always trying to stretch a single into a double, a double into a triple, and a triple into a home run, puts a great deal of pressure on the defense. When the defense knows you are going to be aggressive running the bases, they tend to look at your runners a little quicker, causing balls to be bobbled or missed. Players tend to hurry their throws, which causes more errant throws, and thus allows your team to take extra bases and manufacture runs.

Base coaches should stop runners only when they need to be stopped. For example, a runner at second base knows that on every hit ball, she is going home. When the defense fields the ball cleanly and is going to prevent the score, the base coach simply stops her. A batter's goal should be that every time she hits the ball, she is going to second base unless the defense prevents it.

Although this type of aggressiveness leads to more runners being thrown out, I feel it is a positive trade-off. More runs are going to score with an aggressive philosophy. If we get a few people thrown out along the way, that is fine. Remember, though, as the coach, if you ask your players to be aggressive and stretch singles into doubles and stretch doubles into triples, then you must accept the consequence that they will be thrown out more often. It's part of the game. If you get angry when they get thrown out, they become more tentative and less likely to take that extra base. Therefore, make sure you encourage aggressiveness, even though they may get thrown out at times. Make sure you differentiate between foolish baserunning and aggressive baserunning.

Along with an aggressive approach, players should follow a couple of rules. First, teach players to keep an eye on the ball. Knowing where the ball is at all times allows the runner to take advantage of extra-base opportunities. Second, teach players to keep an eye on the defense. Players can use their peripheral vision to have one eye on the ball and one eye on the defense. If the defense fails to cover a base, an aggressive runner can advance. Some defensive players are lazy; some shortstops do not cover second base with a runner at first; some catchers easily toss the ball back to the pitcher; and some pitchers don't pay attention to base runners (especially after a double or triple). Paying attention helps runners quickly take advantage of any mistakes the defense makes.

Baserunning

One thing I have noticed over the years is that many teams do a poor job of running the bases. From the little 12-and-under teams through some of the top collegiate teams in the nation, I am continually amazed at the lack of baserunning skills. If you want your team to score more runs, players first and foremost must run the bases aggressively. Start each season with a crash course in proper running form and spend practice time each day fine-tuning running form.

An in-depth look at proper running is beyond the scope of this chapter, and I am by no means an expert on running. I do know, however, some outstanding track coaches who make their living developing sprinters. I encourage you to visit the track coaches at your school, even invite them to practice once or twice to work with your players in developing proper running form. You will be amazed at the increased speed your players can generate by practicing correct running form.

The three key times we measure every week are home to first, second to home, and home to home. Home to first gets you on base, second to home scores runs, and home to home lets you know who your best base runners are. Take all times standing on home plate. Start the stopwatch when the runner's foot leaves home plate and stop it when her foot hits the base. Also time your players off a swing—start the stopwatch when the bat makes contact with the ball. It's helpful to compare the two times. Such data let you know who needs to work on getting out of the box a little quicker.

Running Through First Base

Teach players to accelerate through the base. They should not slow up until they are one step past first. The runner should always hit the front outside corner of the base with the ball of her foot (see figure 15.1)—it doesn't matter if it's the left or right foot. The front outside corner is the closest point to home plate.

A player who slightly leans forward with her chest and shoulders as she hits the base gets more calls from the umpire. Obviously, the runner shouldn't lean so much that she throws herself off balance, but a slight lean (see figure 15.2) leads to more safe calls. Remember also to teach players to never leap or jump at a base.

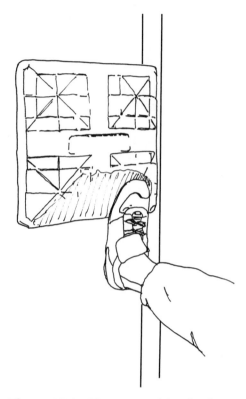

Figure 15.1 The runner hits the front outside corner of the base with the ball of her foot.

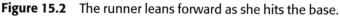

Figure 15.2 The runner leans forward as she hits the base.

After passing through first base, the runner squares her hips and shoulders so that she is facing second base. She stops before reaching the outfield grass. To slow herself, the runner squares up, widens her stride, and drops her seat to lower her center of gravity. This puts her in the perfect position to take advantage of an overthrown or bobbled ball. She is in position to take that extra base if the ball gets away; if it doesn't, she simply returns to first.

I have seen many runners continue past first base to the outfield grass or peel off at first base and head to the foul fence. They have no intention or opportunity to take an extra base if the ball gets away. They are simply satisfied with one base. Aggressiveness is more productive.

Rounding First Base

The key to rounding first or any base is to make sure that the player hits the front inside corner of the base and uses it as a starting block to accelerate toward the next base. The runner must not break stride while hitting the base (see figure 15.3).

Figure 15.3   The runner steps on the front inside corner of the bag as she rounds first.

Emphasize that runners must not break stride to hit the base with one foot or the other; whichever foot is there to hit the corner of the base is fine. Teach players to round out before reaching first so that the line to second is as straight as possible. The entire goal in running the bases, from home to home, is to make a circle (see figure 15.4). The smaller the circle (that is, the tighter the runner can turn on the base), the faster she gets home. Players must make as tight a turn as possible without breaking stride, making sure that all bases are hit correctly.

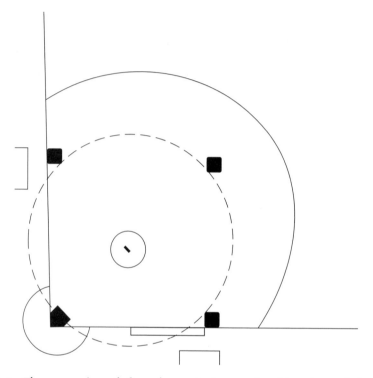

Figure 15.4 The runner's path from home to home should make a circle.

The arms play a vital role in the success of the base runner. Whether she is running straight down the line to beat out an infield hit or stretching a single into a double, she should pump both arms through the full range of motion and pump straight ahead so that her arms are not fighting her legs by going in a different direction. This is especially noticeable when a player rounds a base; she may tend to let her left arm hang limp rather than pumping throughout the turn.

Another method that helps a player make a tighter turn is for her to lean into the turn by dropping her left shoulder—really pulling it down with her left elbow and left arm. At the same time, if her right arm punches in front of her body toward the next base, it helps her make a tighter turn. The one-hundredths of a second that base runners save by turning correctly often leads to a safe call rather than an out.

Leading Off

Once on first base, the runner's goal is to get a good jump off the base with each pitch. A great drill to help you identify who is getting off base with proper timing is to set up a video camera and record each runner leading off. I would venture to guess that the first time you do this, 95 percent of your players are late leaving first base.

The rule states that the runner can't leave until the pitcher releases the ball. In actuality, most umpires let it go if she were to take off when the pitcher's arm is about halfway down her down swing. The key here is for the runner to push the envelope and try to get off more quickly until she finds the point where the umpire calls her out for leaving too soon. The base coach and players should pay close attention to the umpires to see which umpires are paying attention to the leadoffs and which ones are not.

Have your players practice three different types of leads and base starts, then time each player attempting each start to discover which start gives her the quickest move to the next base.

The first start is the baseball start. This start takes strong legs to execute properly. The baseball start brings the runner closer to second base with her first step than any other start (see figure 15.5). Players should use this start when tagging from third base on a fly ball because it allows the player to see the whole field. Whether the catch is made in right, center, or left field, the player can get a jump accordingly. Do not rely on the coach to tell the player when to leave.

Figure 15.5   The baseball start.

We always let our runners decide when to leave the base. Never do we have a runner rely on a cue from a coach as to when the player has caught the ball and when to take off. That split-second delay costs not only valuable time but often the opportunity to score. On a sacrifice fly, the baseball start gives the runner a clear view of the whole field no matter where the catch is made.

The second start is the sprinter start, where a base is used as a starting block. The runner should get low, drive, and accelerate toward the next base (see figure 15.6).

The third start, the rocker start, is probably the most common (figure 15.7). The player starts with one foot behind the bag and simply rocks forward as the pitcher goes into her motion. The runner times her stride so that she leaves the base just before the pitcher releasing the ball. The rocker start gives the runner the opportunity to build up momentum before she actually leaves the base. She also may be able to get a better jump. Be aware, though, that if the umpire sees movement before the pitch is released, your runner could be called for leaving the base too soon when actually her foot is still on the base. Now that most umpires are familiar with this technique, we don't see the problems we used to see with the rocker start.

It is important for players to practice all three starts, focusing on staying low to the ground, driving, and accelerating to the next base. The following baserunning drills are good for technique as well as conditioning.

Figure 15.6 The sprinter start.

Figure 15.7 The rocker start.

Leads and Returns

Divide the team into three groups. Position one group at each base, and assign a manager or coach on the pitching rubber to go through the pitching motion. The coach can throw a pitch or simply simulate the pitching motion so that base runners can work on getting a proper lead.

You can use many variations of this drill with each of the three base starts. For example, start with a sprinter start at first base, rocker start at second base, and baseball start at third base. At each pitch, the runners take their leads, square up to home plate, hustle back to the base, then simply advance to the next base and rotate. This is a great drill to use the first 5 to 10 minutes of practice to loosen up the team and focus on getting off the base correctly.

Four Corner Drill

Break the team into four groups, one group at each base (first, second, third, and home). Work on running one base at a time, accelerating through the base, hitting the front outside corner, and squaring up. This exercise is an excellent conditioning drill for the whole team. Start by having the first person in line sprint directly through the base. As soon as she passes the base, the next person takes off. In a short amount of time, each player runs numerous sprints and works on baserunning, too.

Line Drill

This drill works baserunning, accelerating through the base, making turns, observing and reading the coaches, and conditioning all at the same time. Place a manager or assistant coach on the pitcher's mound to simulate the pitching motion. Line up the team at home plate. With each pitch, two runners take off from home. The first runner runs through first base and squares up; the second runner rounds first base and heads into second with a double. Have your first base coach give both verbal and visual signals for each runner. Those runners then begin at first and second base for the next pitch to work on their timing leaving the base. With the next pitch, the runner at second scores, the runner at first goes to third, and the next two runners take off from home, one running through first, one going to second. The third base coach gives signals to the runners from second and first, and the runners work on reading the coach. You can create many variations of this drill such as having players slide into second base, adding a defensive player to make a tag, having players slide into third or home, and adding a third runner at third base to tag up on a fly ball.

Moving Runners

Once a runner reaches base, look for any possible way to score. Coaches have many options, depending on team personnel and the defense currently being played. First, try to assess the defense. What is the defense going to do now that there is a runner on base? How are they covering a bunt situation? A steal situation? How close are the corners playing in? How hard do the corners charge? Who's covering second, and how much of a hole is she leaving in the infield when she goes to cover? Evaluate all these defenses and choose an appropriate offensive strategy.

Sacrifice Bunt

In a sacrifice situation, the batter's goal is to give herself up to advance runners. It's important for your batter to remember the following key points in a sacrifice situation:

- Move up to the front of the batter's box.
- Only bunt pitches that are thrown for strikes.
- Bunt the first pitch thrown for a strike in fair territory.

Mechanically, the batter needs to pivot around, holding the bat parallel to the ground. This technique avoids the possibility of a rise ball glancing off the bat and into the batter's face, and it also gives the hitter some options to keep the defense a little more honest—like a slug or fake slug. Your runner may want to take a slightly delayed lead in a sacrifice situation, so she doesn't have to hesitate to see if the batter gets the ball down in fair territory. Baserunning should be continuous as much as possible. If a runner takes her normal jump in this situation, she gets off the base too soon and has to stop her momentum to see what the batter did before proceeding or returning to the base.

Runners should aspire to go two bases in a sacrifice situation. The runner's goal should be to advance from first to third unless the defense stops her. She should check who is covering third on a bunt and, if possible, take the extra base. If you have a good bunter at the plate, you may want to call the bunt-and-steal (the batter bunts the pitch no matter where it is and the runner is stealing). Do this with a slow base runner and a good bunter at the plate, or do it with a fast base runner who wants to take two bases.

Slugs

The slug play refers to a sacrifice bunt situation in which the batter shows bunt then pulls the bat back and slaps the ball past the charging first or third baseman. The batter wants to make a miniature swing so that when she squares around and the pitcher releases the ball, the batter simply pulls the bat back by sliding her bottom hand to her top hand, which gives her a choked-up grip on the bat. Then she slaps the ball on the ground past the charging infield. The goal here is not to hit a home run or drive the ball in the outfield; it's simply to knock the ball on the ground past the charging first or third baseman. Slugs are excellent offensive strategies against a defense that plays in too tight, tends to charge too fast in a sacrifice situation, or breaks its middle infielders too soon.

Drag Bunt

A drag bunt is also an excellent weapon for moving runners. If your batter is a fairly good drag bunter, allow her to drag in a sacrifice situation. The batter has a good opportunity to beat the throw to first base, and the defense has less time to react and throw out the lead runner. Variations can be tried such as the batter pulling back to fake a slug then laying down a drag bunt. The goal is to confuse the defense, preventing them from reacting until it is too late.

Steal

When you get a runner on base, look to steal the next base. Obviously, to steal or not to steal depends on the speed of your runner, the strength of the catcher's arm, and the pitcher's throwing speed. It also is easier to steal on a drop-ball pitcher versus a rise-ball pitcher because it is more difficult for the catcher to dig the ball out of the dirt and make a good accurate throw.

Look at who is covering the base—second baseman or shortstop. Assess whether or not your runner can beat that person to the bag. If you are able to obtain statistics for your opponents, check how many stolen bases they have allowed on the season and how many players they have thrown out. This information helps you assess the strength of the catcher's arm. Also, you can time the catcher's throws between innings when she throws to second base after the five-pitch warm-up.

Delayed Steals

Two types of delayed steals can be used. The first is a delay off the pitcher. The base runner takes a normal lead, then makes a break for the next base as soon as the catcher releases the ball back to the pitcher. Do this when the pitcher or the catcher is not paying attention to the base runner, or do it when the catcher throws a lazy lob to the pitcher, which gives the base runner an extra split-second of time to steal a base. A good time for a delayed steal is after a double or triple when the pitcher is mad and disgusted with herself.

The second is a delay off the catcher. Use this delay when the catcher likes to throw the ball around and pick off runners. The base runner takes a little larger lead than normal to draw the throw, then advances to the next base when the catcher throws behind her. The delay off the catcher is an excellent play to move a runner from second base to third but also can move a runner from first to second.

Hit and Run

The hit-and-run is an excellent way to advance runners without giving up an out on a sacrifice. By starting your runner with the pitch, you create numerous holes in the infield defense, allowing a batter with solid bat control to reach base with a base hit and advance runners at the same time. The key is to realize which defensive players are covering the bases so that the batter knows where to hit the ball. The hitter should not try to hit a home run, simply hit the ball on the ground in the open hole.

Situational Hitting

Players need to be prepared to hit in an assortment of situations during the game. Have players practice different situations in scrimmage games or during practices. Hitters need to be ready to step in and drive in base runners every time they come to the plate in a scoring situation.

Runner at Second

The easiest base to steal is third base. If the runner and the batter do their jobs correctly, third base is left uncovered the majority of the time. Here is how to do it. As the pitcher goes into her windup, the batter squares around to bunt. This move typically induces the third baseman to charge and the shortstop to move toward third base to cover a bunt situation or a runner stealing. The runner at second base steals with the pitch, and as the pitch comes home, the batter pulls back her bat, swings, and intentionally misses the ball. When the batter pulls back and misses, typically this fake freezes the shortstop and no one is there to cover third base.

However, the better teams and the better shortstops do not go for the fake. If the defense doesn't buy it, the strategy is simply to slug and steal. The runner steals third and the batter, rather than swinging and intentionally missing, simply slaps the ball to the shortstop hole. This play opens a lot of holes in the infield and allows your team to generate additional runs.

Some teams defend the third base steal by leaving the third baseman back to cover the base, keeping the shortstop in position, and having the pitcher cover bunts on the third base side. If this happens, the batter simply reads the situation when she squares around. If the third baseman does not charge, she simply bunts the ball down the third base line. This play is difficult for the pitcher to make. Often the pitcher fields the ball and throws it into right field, allowing the runner to score from second and the batter to advance past first base.

Runner at Third

We score many runs every year because we are a lot more aggressive in this situation than the majority of teams. With a runner at third and fewer than two outs, most teams tell their runners to wait until the ball is through the infield before scoring. Typically we have the runner break for home on any ground ball hit up the middle to the second baseman or shortstop. Anything up the middle we are going to try to score on. We teach our base runners to read the ball off the bat and read a ball that is angling down, rather than one that is a pop-up or a line drive.

A ground ball to the shortstop or second baseman is difficult for most middle infielders to field, especially if they have to move to the left or right, pick the ball up, and throw home. Even if the infielder fields and throws the ball cleanly, the catcher has to make a good catch and tag the sliding runner. We are able to generate a lot more runs than we would in a normal situation by being a little bit more aggressive with a runner at third.

Runners at Second and Third

With runners at second and third and fewer than two outs, we tell our players to run on any ground ball. Runners read the angle of the ball off the bat, get a good jump, and go. It doesn't matter if the grounder goes to the first baseman, pitcher, third baseman, second baseman, or shortstop. If the defense is going to get us out in this situation, I want them to get that out at home plate. The worst thing that can happen is the runner is thrown out at home. You can still have a runner at third base, and, if the batter hustles, she can get to second easily if the catcher is paying more attention to the runner sliding home than the batter. So you end up in the same situation, runners at second and third.

Suicide Squeeze

Most people are familiar with the suicide squeeze. The runner at third steals home with the pitch. The batter's job is to bunt the ball no matter where it is pitched. Again take a look at the defense; see what it is going to give you. Are the corners back where they can be susceptible to a squeeze play? Do you have a good bunter at the plate who can handle the bat? If so, the squeeze is an excellent call to generate some runs.

In this situation, many teams use what they call a safety squeeze in which the batter bunts the ball, but the runner at third does not break right away. She stays back to see if there is going to be a bad throw or breaks on the throw to first and tries to score. I have never felt that this option was very good. If I am going to give up an out, I sure want to score, too. If I feel that my batter can put the ball down effectively, we send the runner in a suicide situation.

Suicide Hit-and-Run

Another strategy is a suicide hit-and-run. For the base runner, this play is similar to a suicide squeeze. The runner at third takes off with the pitch. The batter hits a ground ball. The batter shouldn't square around, which gives the corners the signal to charge and make a play at home.

If the batter can simply hit the ball on the ground somewhere, the runner should score because of the jump she got at third base. The batter should have solid bat control. It's also helpful to have a drop-ball pitcher on the mound since it's easier to get the ball on the ground. A suicide hit-and-run can be an effective tool, especially if you're playing on a hard infield.

Runners at First and Third

With runners at first and third, you have many options. Which option you choose depends on your personnel, the speed of your runners at each base, and what the batter can do. It also is important to assess what the defense is going to give you. Will they let you steal second? If so, take advantage of it, and put two runners in scoring position by stealing.

A great play to utilize in this situation is a suicide squeeze. This seems to surprise most teams. If both your runners start with the pitch, it's easy for the runner at first to go to third. At worst, the defense gets you out at home, but you still have runners at first and third.

On a normal first and third situation, the first thing to look at is the speed of your runners. With a fast runner at first and a slow runner at third, typically you should try to steal second base to put two runners in scoring position. With a slow runner at first and a fast runner at third, start the runner at first and get her caught in a rundown, allowing your quick runner to score from third. If the defense throws the ball back to the pitcher or to the third baseman anywhere but second, the runner at first advances and takes second base. If the defense gives us two runners in scoring position, we take it. With slow runners at both first and third, try to assess what the defense is doing and if it concedes the base.

With a runner at third base only and a batter who draws a base on balls, you have an opportunity for a first and third play without a pitch being thrown. The batter simply continues past first base toward second, gets caught in a rundown (allowing the runner to score from third), or takes an extra base. Typically, we have our batter continue past if we have a fast third base runner who can make something happen.

Trick Plays

Trick plays can confuse the defense and generate runs. The element of surprise is key.

The fake walk-and-steal can be done with a runner at first or runners at first and second. It might work with bases loaded, although I haven't tried it in that situation. When your batter has a count of two balls and a pitcher throws the next pitch for a ball, the batter drops the bat as if it were ball four and trots down to first base. While this performance is happening, the runners on base trot to the next base as if they are being forced in a walk situation. Typically the catcher turns to the umpire and points out that there are only three balls not four. The umpire checks the counter, then checks with the rest of the umpiring crew to see what count they had. Once everything is straightened out, the batter is brought back to the plate. In the meantime, the runners have advanced. Warn your runners to be aware that if the catcher is sharp and isn't falling for the fake, they are going to have to hustle back to the bag if the catcher makes a play.

The Texas drag is so named because we first saw this play while playing ball in Texas and decided it was a fun thing to incorporate with our batters. Use this situation on a 3-0 count. Often on a 3-0 count, the batter takes the next pitch, hoping to draw a walk. For the Texas drag, have the batter relax at the plate, dropping the bat down to her side (figure 15.8a). This leads the first and third basemen to relax, assuming the batter is going to take the pitch. As the ball leaves the pitcher's hand, the batter brings the bat around her back (figure 15.8b) and is in position to lay down a drag bunt. If this is done correctly, it can catch the first and third basemen sleeping, enabling your batter to beat out the throw and reach base safely.

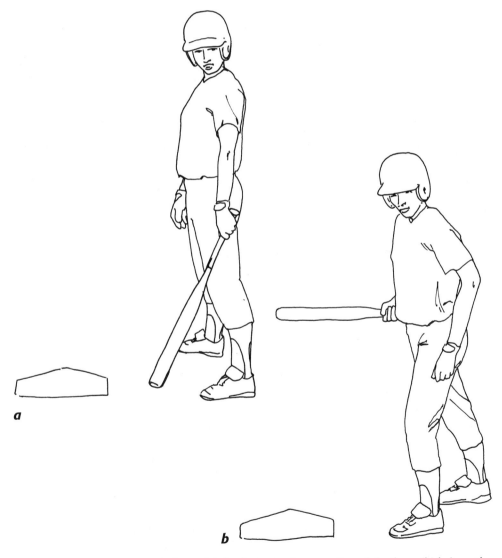

Figure 15.8   For the Texas drag, *(a)* the batter relaxes at the plate then *(b)* brings the bat around her back.

The China drag is so named because I first saw the play while watching the Chinese national team practice. It is done with a left-handed hitter, either a slapper or a regular left-handed batter. The batter tosses the bat in the air in a drag bunt situation and heads to first base. The ball strikes the bat as the bat hangs parallel to the ground. Meanwhile, the batter is on her way to first. Typically the play happens so quickly that the umpires and the defense do not know what happened, and the hitter can get to first without being called for being out of the batter's box.

Practice Situations

It's good to do a lot of offensive strategy work at practice with a pitching machine rather than against a live pitcher. The machine allows you to control the accuracy of the pitch, working on the runner's as well as the batter's execution. Advance to live pitching situations to assess who is going to be more successful than others in all areas. I recommend always using base runners during batting practice. This is an opportunity to work on taking the extra base, leading off, returning, jumps, and many other offensive strategy situations.

A great game for working on baserunning and defense of game situations is a game we call Toss Up. We put a full defense on the field with the remainder of the players on offense. The batter stands in the batter's box with bat and ball and tosses the ball to herself. Play regular innings and put specific limitations on the hitters—for example, opposite field hits, pulling the ball, no balls back to the pitcher, or whatever else you want to work on. At the younger age level, this game can be dangerous for pitchers because they are close to the batter. You might want to put a screen in front of the pitcher or simply remove the pitcher during this drill. In a short amount of time, the team practices a number of baserunning situations, and the infield and outfield get a lot of work on relays and cutoffs in a gamelike situation.

Final Thoughts

The main point I want to get across is to be aggressive and always look to take the extra base. This philosophy needs to be instilled in your players. It leads to many more runs for the ball club, but it also leads to more runners being thrown out. This sacrifice is something you, your players, and your fans and parents need to realize and accept. As the coach, sometimes you take the heat for your players getting thrown out; but we play an aggressive style of softball, and I feel that the reward is much greater than the risk. I can't get mad at my players when they are thrown out because it leads to hesitation, which results in fewer runs and more people being thrown out. We sell aggressiveness to our team as our style of play. Overall, it's been a fun way to play the game, and I encourage you to give it a try with your own ball club.

CHAPTER SIXTEEN

Producing Elite Pitchers

Cheri Kempf

Success in fastpitch softball relies heavily on the effectiveness of the pitcher. The pitcher commands the attention of players and spectators alike. The spotlight seems to focus on the pitcher, and many players at first glance think they want to pitch. Many parents as well desire the position for their young athletes.

But as you progress through softball, from youth leagues to travel ball and beyond, you start to see the complexity of the pitcher's position and what is required for success. One of the most commonly asked questions of pitching coaches is "Does my daughter have what it takes to be a successful pitcher?" The answer to that question lies within the athlete. To be great requires constant skill development. The greatest pitchers in the game today will tell you that they are still developing and polishing skills every time they pick up a ball. Athleticism plays a role in skill development in making a particular task easier or more difficult. Often though, talented pitchers hit a wall when it is time for them to perform tasks that do not come naturally—for example, pitchers who have natural speed at a young age.

Also, to become great, a pitcher must accept the immense responsibility that goes with the position. Many players do not want the responsibility of having a big impact on the outcome of the game. The impact could be positive, which is what everyone daydreams about, but the other possibility, a negative impact, is often too much for players to handle. Pitchers require self-confidence, a desire to lead, and the ability to focus and perform in pressure situations.

To be successful, the pitcher must be able to adjust. In practice and skill development, pitchers must be able to focus their attention on one particular area of their bodies for correct movements and techniques. They must be able to feel changes that occur or need to occur and make the necessary adjustments. In competition, pitchers must make adjustments immediately. Pitchers do not get the luxury of day to day, game to game, or even inning to inning to make adjustments. When the pressure is on, those adjustments sometimes must be made pitch to pitch. A pitcher succeeds when she develops the essential skills to pitch, when she possesses the mental toughness to remain in the circle win or lose, and when she can adjust her techniques and execution on command.

Coaching Pitchers: The Big Mystery

A common joke among coaches is "Pitchers: You can't live with 'em, and you can't live without 'em." Most coaches describe their pitchers as being quirky, cocky, stubborn, or difficult. Of course there are exceptions, but most pitchers fit one if not more of these descriptions, a truth most of them would aggressively deny.

In their defense, most pitchers put in thousands of hours of practice and have to deal with demanding parents and coaches. They have survived failure as much as they have relished success. They endure insults and harassment from opposing teams. They have grown up in an environment that demanded perfection of them, that had little tolerance for mistakes, and asked a high price in humility and embarrassment for failure. As a result, pitchers usually possess an extraordinary amount of confidence, which can be either admirable or ugly, but is always necessary.

Both the coach and the pitcher need to understand what is necessary for success. Communication is extremely important. The following tips help make the pitcher/coach relationship a healthy one.

- Familiarize yourself with the capabilities of your pitchers. Know which pitches are effective and which are not. Talk to pitchers about how to improve the pitches you feel are unsatisfactory.

- Discuss pitch calling and execution. Harmony and trust with selections is ideal. When pitcher, catcher, and coach understand the same strategies, they tend to agree on called pitches more often. This understanding leads to a more confident pitcher.

- Allow the pitcher to shake off a pitch she does not feel comfortable throwing. Of course, there must be boundaries and guidelines, but no coach should want a pitcher trying to execute a pitch in competition that she strongly feels is the wrong pitch for that particular situation.

- Eliminate the mystery of the starter. Let the staff know as soon as possible who starts a particular game and who relieves. This clear communication allows proper physical and mental preparation for all pitchers.

- Communicate choices and reasons with pitchers. If you have broken rotation or veered from what may be considered the norm, talk to your pitchers at least briefly. Chances are, the pitcher who is not in the lineup may be needed in relief or in a future game. Try to maintain their confidence in themselves.

- Structure pitching workouts. Let the pitchers know what the goals are and why they are important come game time.

- Establish and nurture the pitcher/catcher relationship. By and large, your pitcher has the ability to have the biggest impact on the outcome of the game. Her most important ally, the catcher, forms a union with her for the entire battle. The stronger the relationship between the two, the stronger the pitcher.

Teaching Fundamentals

Pitching is a violent action that requires pinpoint accuracy and execution. Often you will hear people say that there are a lot of different ways to pitch. The fact that there are many ways to pitch is true. You can look at snapshots or video of talented pitchers and see different methods. The idea that every method works should be clarified to say that every method works for someone, but certainly not for everyone.

Although there are many different ways to pitch, there *is* one correct way to pitch. "Correct" not according to old pictures of yourself, or "old Joe who pitched in the army," or "Sally who played college ball," but correct according to biomechanics and the laws of human movement. There is a correct way to deliver a ball in an underhand motion from point A to point B as quickly as possible.

We as teachers often make the mistake of basing the standard on the phenomenal. In other words, we want to teach every athlete to look like an elite pitcher who is exceptionally gifted and talented, which is a mistake. Gifted and extraordinarily talented athletes are few and far between. Athletes who make mistakes in the motion but still rise to the top and remain healthy are not whom we should base our standards on. The fundamentals that follow are not based on opinion but on the ideals of human movement. Fundamentals are also based on the fastball and form a solid foundation on which to build into advanced pitching.

The two basic goals of the fundamental pitching motion are efficiency and effectiveness. To achieve efficiency, the pitcher needs to use every bit of energy she has to throw the pitch. All her energy works toward the one goal of the ball going to the intended location. Energy going anywhere else but the intended location is wasted. Effectiveness occurs when the body works together—all parts positioned correctly—to accomplish the location or movement. If positioning is compromised, effectiveness is lost.

Pitching coaches are often asked, "Which should we be concerned with first, speed or control?" The answer is neither. The primary focus is fundamentals. If a pitcher has solid fundamentals, the rest falls into place. The pitcher should pitch as fast as possible while maintaining the integrity of the motion. With consistent speed and body movements, control is a matter of basic adjustments.

The Pitching Motion

The lower body—the feet and legs—forms the foundation of the motion. The pitcher should have a consistent stance on the pitching rubber with feet slightly separated widthwise and lengthwise. From the front foot through the target is an imaginary straight line (figure 16.1). This line is known as the power line, or line of force, and is the basis for efficiency. All the energy available should head down that line when the pitcher throws a fastball.

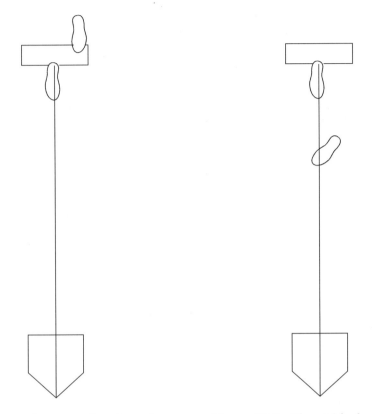

Figure 16.1   The power line, from the pitcher's front foot through the target.

Figure 16.2   The stride forward. The stride foot lands in a 45-degree angle with the toe on the power line.

The stride forward occurs with the back leg (hereafter referred to as the stride leg) and should result in the back foot landing at a 45-degree angle with the toe on the power line (figure 16.2). The stride foot should land flat with the knee flexed but firm (figure 16.3). During the stride, the heel of the front foot (the drive leg) should lift up, leaving the tip of the toe in the dirt. The length of the stride can vary, as long as the pitcher is able to land in this position.

The upper body—including the pitching arm; the glove hand; and the head, which is critical to balance—works off the foundation set by the lower body. As the stride begins, both arms should raise simultaneously. It is advantageous to keep the ball in the glove, as this habit not only conceals the ball and grip but also encourages both arms to work together.

The speed of the pitching motion itself relies on the whipping of the arm; therefore, we like the pitching arm to remain as loose as possible throughout the circle. On the front side of the circle, somewhere between the chest and head, the pitching hand and ball separate, leaving the glove out in front of the body and over the power line. Imagine a clock around the pitching arm. The glove should be located at least as high as three o'clock, as shown in figure 16.4. The head is crucial to balance and should be centered between the feet. If the head is off-center in any direction, the pitcher becomes off-balance. The body follows the lead of the head.

When the stride foot lands flat, the pitching arm should be located near the top and back half of the circle. At the setting of the stride foot, the ball should be located between 10 and 12 o'clock (figure 16.4). This gives the back side of the body and the drive leg ample time to deliver power to the pitch before release.

Figure 16.3 The stride foot lands with the knee flexed.

Figure 16.4 The glove is at least as high as 3 o'clock when the hands break apart. When the stride foot sets, the ball is between 10 and 12 o'clock.

194

As soon as the stride foot is set, the back-side of the body begins a continuous motion toward the target. The middle joints of the back side levers (arm and leg) lead the motion. The elbow leads the whip of the throwing arm as it comes down the circle, and the knee leads the drive of the back leg as it moves powerfully forward. The simultaneous movement of the leg with the arm provides efficiency of the total body and greatly reduces the chance of injury from pitching "all-arm." The back leg movement is often underestimated and overlooked in the motion.

At the release of the ball, the wrist snaps and the hand follows the path of the ball. In a perfectly natural follow-through, the hand turns over out in front of the body and dangles loosely at the wrist. In a more mechanical follow-through, the arm can finish upward in an L-shape with the elbow in front of the body and the hand straight up. With this type of follow-through, the arm should always remain loose at the joints. Snapping the elbow tight at the finish is unnecessary and may cause elbow soreness or injury. After release, the pitcher should be balanced and in control of her body, with glove in front and ready for defense.

Movement

Speed shortens the length of time a hitter has to decide whether or not to swing, but speed alone does not create a successful pitcher at the highest levels. In youth softball and situations in which the pitcher's ability overwhelms the hitter's ability, speed can dominate. However, it is a mistake to let a young pitcher believe that speed alone will dominate hitters throughout a career.

For elite pitchers, movement equals strikeouts, winning, and success. When athletes initially learn to pitch, their goal is to pitch the ball into the strike zone as much as possible. As they move into the upper levels of competition, however, the goal becomes to pitch the ball in the zone as little as possible or only when necessary. A pitcher must be able to locate the pitch to get strikes and strikeouts. Sometimes, a pitcher has to throw in the zone, but often we like to work on the edges or just off the edges and give the illusion that the pitch is much better than it really is.

The Fastball

Controlling the fastball is the basis of spot pitching and the beginning of pitching strategy. The fastball should be gripped loosely with the top crease of the fingers and the thumb resting on a seam of the ball. The basic grip of the ball can sometimes cause random movements to occur at release. Two common grips include the C-grip (figure 16.5) and the horseshoe grip (figure 16.6). Each of these grips could cause the softball to take a different path toward the target.

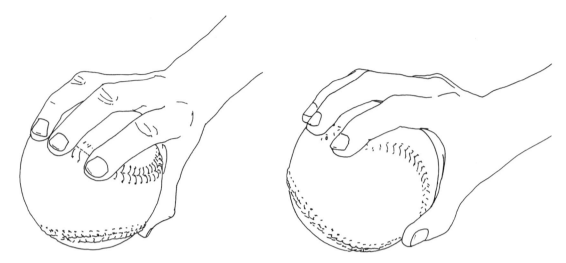

Figure 16.5   The C-grip of a fastball.   **Figure 16.6**   The horseshoe grip of a fastball.

The C-grip releases the ball in a four-seam rotation. When released correctly off the ends of the fingertips, the C-grip causes the ball to hold a straight line to the target. The horseshoe grip releases the ball in a two-seam rotation with the long seams of the ball rotating down. This long-seam, downward rotation often causes the ball to veer or break toward the throwing arm side of the hitter.

To be effective, a pitcher must be able to throw the ball to the weakness of the hitter—up in the zone, down in the zone, inside, or outside. Because a fastball has consistent location results and can be easily spotted to a target, many pitchers use it to get ahead in the count or when they need a strike. Locating the fastball in and out can be done by either of two methods.

First the pitcher can attempt to steer the ball with the arm and hand. This method can be effective for some, but it does not lend itself to advanced pitching. Movement pitches such as the rise and turnover drop require specific locations for the hand and wrist to impart the correct spin as quickly as possible. If the pitcher is also trying to steer the ball with the hand and arm, the sharpness of those pitches can be affected by the slight change in mechanics. Also steering with the hand and arm, although effective at times, is not as accurate as the second option.

The second option is to steer or guide the ball with the stride foot. This simple method allows pinpoint accuracy adjustments while maintaining the same mechanics above the waist no matter where the pitch is located. Locating the ball in and out with the stride foot relies on the basic premise of the power line. The power line goes from the drive foot to the target. In figure 16.1, the target was the middle of the plate, but wherever the target is located, the straight line goes from the drive foot to the target. In turn, the stride foot lands at a 45-degree angle with the toe on the power line, head balanced over the line, knee of the drive leg coming down the line, and throwing arm delivering the ball down the line. An easy way to remember this is that no matter where the pitch is located, there should always be a direct line up of the foot (drive foot), toe (stride foot), and target (figure 16.7).

Height location is equally important. It never fails that when a pitcher throws a ball 15 feet high into the backstop, at least one well-intentioned spectator or coach will yell, "Let go of it sooner!" The rationale behind the advice is correct: If the ball is too high, the pitcher released late; if the ball is too low, the pitcher released too soon. However, the practical application of letting the ball go a millisecond sooner or later is difficult at best and most likely impossible, especially since the pitcher does not know when she released the ball in the first place.

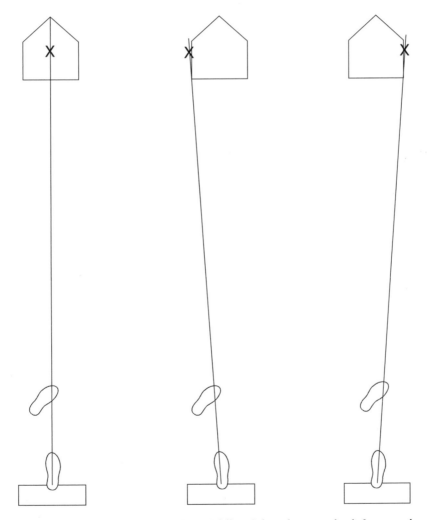

Figure 16.7 Whether the target is the middle of the plate, to the left, or to the right, the drive foot, stride foot, and target all line up.

To locate a ball high and low, use the dart method. If you focus on the bull's-eye when you throw darts and you miss high by two inches dart after dart, stop looking at the bull's-eye and start looking two inches below. In pitching, the pitcher must first choose a focus point, a spot about as big as a quarter. The focus point can be in the glove, on the catcher's equipment, on the plate, or even in the dirt. The pitcher starts with the focus point exactly on the desired location. If the pitch misses consistently high or low, she adjusts the focus point appropriately to gain the end result. Sometimes, even in advanced pitching, it is necessary to keep the focus point slightly higher or lower than the intended target throughout the game.

The Change-Up

The change-up is usually the first pitch developed after the fastball. This pitch is highly effective because it interrupts the timing of the hitter. In fastpitch softball, effective hitting is timing, and effective pitching is a disruption of that timing. When a pitcher has a solid change-up and can throw the pitch at will, the hitter's timing is disrupted, making all of the pitcher's repertoire more effective. Ideally, the change-up should be at least 15 miles per hour slower than the pitcher's fastest pitch. There are many ways to throw a change-up, but three primary goals should remain in place.

First the pitcher needs to maintain full arm speed past the hip. Many pitchers first learn a change-up by slowing the pitching arm down before release, thus slowing the speed of the pitch. This method only works when the pitcher's ability outweighs the hitters' ability overall. When the pitcher's and hitters' ability levels are more equal, this method is no longer effective. Experienced hitters notice the difference in arm speed and hit the ball solidly without being fooled.

To maintain full arm speed and slow the ball down at least 15 miles per hour, other speed factors must be limited or omitted completely. Two of these primary speed factors are wrist snap and follow-through. Most change-ups employ some type of grip adjustment such as tucking or digging knuckles, or rolling the ball deeper into the hand or palm. These grip techniques limit wrist snap, slowing the pitch. Follow-throughs are sometimes snuffed at the side by a heavier brush with the forearm at the hip or extended straight outward toward the hitter to simply pop the ball out of the hand, as opposed to snapping and finishing on through the release of the pitch.

The second goal of the change-up is to keep a flat appearance on the pitch. This does not mean the pitch cannot be angled up or down; it simply means that the path of the pitch should remain on a straight line as much as possible. Putting an arch or hump in the middle of the pitch often allows the hitter to read the pitch as being too high at the halfway decision point. This causes the hitter to hold up, thinking the pitch is not in the strike zone. As the ball comes back down, the hitter has plenty of time to load and swing. Coaches often believe the speed of the pitch to be the culprit in these cases, that the pitch is too slow, allowing the hitter to hold, reload, and swing. In most cases, however, if the pitch was flattened with the same speed, the hitter would commit to the swing before the ball's arrival.

The third goal for the change-up is for the pitcher to be able to throw the pitch in the strike zone. Why would a pitcher want to freeze a hitter with a baffling change-up only to have the umpire call it a ball, an inch or two out of the zone? Unless a pitcher proves consistency in the strike zone with any pitch, all a hitter has to do is be disciplined enough to read location and hold up for a taken ball. If hitters can hold up for a called ball, the change-up becomes useless. Figure 16.8 shows the grip for a knuckle ball change-up, and figure 16.9 shows the grip for a turnaround change-up.

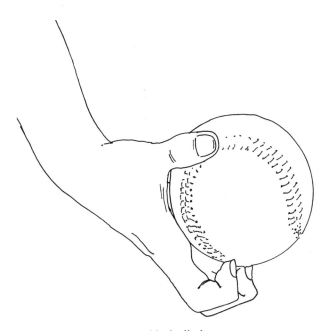

Figure 16.8 The knuckle ball change-up.

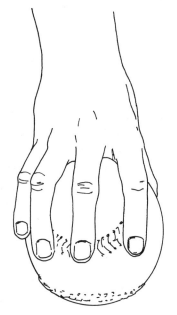

Figure 16.9 The turnaround change-up.

The next four pitches are directional movement pitches, meaning low, high, out, and in for the drop ball, rise ball, curve ball, and screw ball. The goal of these four pitches is to get the ball to jump or cut in a certain direction to elude the hitter. Each of these movement pitches contains four necessary elements, the CPRS of movement:

C correct spin

P posture and weight shift

R release point

S speed of spin

We'll look at these elements as we discuss each of the movement pitches below.

Drop Ball

The drop ball is often the first movement pitch added to a pitcher's repertoire. The drop is a popular pitch at any level because of its effectiveness not only in striking out the hitter but in controlling the hitter when she does make contact. A pitch in the lower half of the strike zone tends to be hit on the top side more often, creating more ground balls and hits that stay inside the park.

There are two common methods for spinning a pitch downward. Usually, the easiest drop for a pitcher to learn is the peel or pull-up drop. This drop can be taught from the fastball release directly off the fingertips. The pitcher's grip for the peel or pull-up (either C-grip or horseshoe works) places the fingertips over and across a seam. This technique allows for a fast snap at release, imparting tight downward spin as the ball leaves the fingertips.

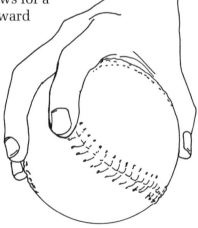

The second method of spinning a pitch downward is called the turnover drop. This drop is a little more difficult but at higher speeds maintains a steep cut downward. The pitcher's grip for the turnover places two fingers lengthwise on the seams (figure 16.10), either the index and middle fingers on the close seams or the index and ring fingers on the longer seams. At release, the pitcher's hand must move across the top of the ball in a straight line toward the catcher. This pitch is a wrist move only and when done incorrectly at full speed can cause injury to the

Figure 16.10 The two-seam turnover drop grip with two fingers on the close seams.

shoulder. Many pitchers make the mistake of rotating around the ball with the elbow moving outward away from the body instead of over the ball with the elbow staying tight against the side.

Although posture and weight shift are often overlooked in all the movement pitches, they are probably underestimated more with the drop ball. For the drop ball, the pitcher leans slightly forward and her weight lands completely forward on the stride leg when that foot is set firmly. A slightly forward posture allows the ball to be released at a higher point and still maintain a downward angle. After release, because of the weight shifted forward at contact of the stride foot, the pitcher comes through the stride leg and lands out in front.

Release point refers to the target and path of the ball at release. No pitch can be thrown against the break. In other words, a drop ball cannot be thrown upward at 60 miles per hour at a distance of 40 to 43 feet away and be expected to come back down because of the direction of the spin. Therefore, a drop cannot be released upward; a rise cannot be released downward; and a curve cannot be released on a left to right angle (for a right-handed pitcher), or a screw at a right to left angle. All pitches must be released at least slightly toward the breaking direction. The drop ball should be released toward a point that is downward from the pitching hand. Usually, the height of the batter's knee is the standard for the drop-ball release.

Speed of the spin of the ball, not the speed of the ball itself, dictates severity of movement in all movement pitches.

Rise Ball

The rise ball is one of the most popular pitches in fastpitch softball. The dominance in the strikeout tally of pitchers possessing an effective rise ball makes most pitchers eager to learn it. However, the lack of genetically powered forearms coupled with the required quick pass underneath the softball at release often makes this a difficult pitch for females to master.

Correct spin of the rise is often the most difficult skill of all. The desired straight backspin often turns into a torpedo or screwing spin because of a twisting wrist snap, crossover follow-through, or inability to maintain hip and shoulder positioning. Usually, in gripping the rise, the index finger digs into or rolls against the ball (figure 16.11a and b). If the digging method is used, the pitcher at release should put pressure on the ball with the index finger and push out and upward. If the rolling method is used, the pitcher should feel a slight pinching of the index finger toward the middle finger at wrist snap. Both methods help guide the ball off the back of the hand, as opposed to the fingertips or side of the index finger. The pitcher should try to place the middle finger and possibly even the ring finger on a seam to gain a better grip and snap. The answer to the four- or two-seam

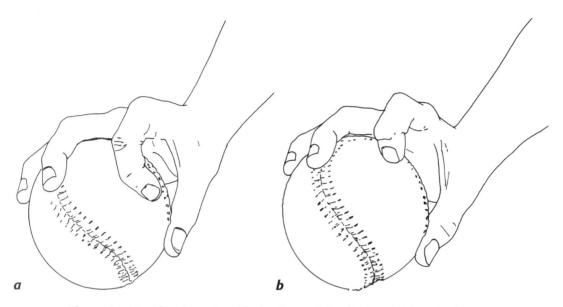

Figure 16.11 The rise grip with the finger *(a)* rolled and *(b)* tucked.

debate lies within the pitcher. After obtaining correct spin, each individual pitcher should experiment with two- and four-seam grips and decide which grip provides the best result on the softball.

Posture for the rise is slightly backward. Weight should remain behind the front leg. With the drop ball, the pitcher leaned forward and worked through the front leg. The rise is exactly opposite: The pitcher leans backward and works against the front leg. Once the position is set at contact of the stride leg, the pitcher should maintain the front shoulder directly forward and slightly higher than the back shoulder, which also remains behind. In turn, the hips remain open until release. This positioning is crucial to the backward rotation of the softball. After release, the pitcher's weight falls back on the drive leg, slightly behind the stride leg.

Release point of the rise ball must be slightly upward. Pitchers with correct posture positioning and strong legs (for a solid and long stride) are able to start the ball lower in the zone than pitchers who do not possess those skills.

Spin of the rise is complex and difficult. Therefore, when learning the spin, pitchers must always stress quickness of wrist snap to impart fast spin. This pitch is unique in its movement against gravity and requires plenty of spin speed to achieve its goal.

Curve Ball

The curve ball, if thrown correctly with a sharp break, can be an extremely successful pitch. However, unlike the drop and rise, the curve ball usually stays on the same relative plane in its path to the hitter. For that reason, pitchers usually try to keep the curve ball on the fringes of the plate, staying away from the meat of the bat. Swinging strikes are often located, at finish, beyond the reach of the bat itself. The curve ball is also effective in controlling the hitter by jamming the ball off the handle or causing a mishit off the end of the bat.

Correct spin for the curve ball should be in a sideways or horizontal direction. Often referred to as a flat spin, the ball breaks right to left for a right-hander and left to right for a left-hander. The grip of the ball places the middle finger and sometimes the ring finger on a seam. The index finger can be tucked or rolled if desired. Many pitchers grip the curve identical to their rise for uniformity in appearance. Some pitchers prefer to have the index and middle finger on a seam. Either way is effective, and like the rise, pitchers should experiment with two- and four-seam rotation after obtaining correct spin to check for optimal movement.

Posture for the curve should be slightly leaned toward the glove side or the direction of intended movement. Weight should be shifted mostly onto the stride foot with the head located slightly toward the movement direction. Throughout the pitch, the hand leads the body. Often, pitchers perceive a spinning of hips or shoulders to initiate the release instead of the release initiating the follow-through of the body. At finish, the pitcher falls slightly toward the direction of movement (right-handers slightly left and left-handers slightly right).

Release point of the curve ball must be slightly right to left (right-hander). A key technique that provides wider plate coverage is a slight crossover step with the stride leg. This stride allows the pitcher to start the pitch farther over for different location results. Speed of spin once again determines the severity of the movement and cut.

Screw Ball

Right-handed pitchers use the screw ball a lot to jam right-handed hitters or to throw away from slappers whose half swings sometimes make them difficult to throw past. Left-handed pitchers like to use the screw ball to jam slappers or throw off the outside corner against right-handed hitters. Although the screw can be thrown high and low into the zone, like the curve ball, it does not jump or cut to different planes. For many pitchers, the screw is a great pitch to mix with but not usually considered a dominant go-to pitch.

Correct spin of the screw ball, if it were true to the movement direction, would require the ball to spin inward toward the pitching arm. This spin is nearly impossible in an underhanded motion. However, to achieve inward movement, two variations of spins are used. One is a vertical screw or torpedo-like spin that when released left to right by a right-handed pitcher shoots nicely toward the side of the throwing hand. This movement is usually not cutting but remains consistent. To obtain this spin, place the index and middle fingers lengthwise along the seams or the ring and middle fingers lengthwise along the seams with the index finger rolled or tucked. The hand passes underneath the ball in a crossing direction right to left (right-hander) instead of a forward direction as with the rise ball. This spin of the screw ball is often what occurs when making a mistake with the rise ball spin.

The other type of spin for the screw ball is actually a downward spinning release. The grip should be located on the horseshoe exactly like the fastball. The pitcher should grip slightly tighter with the index and middle finger and emphasize release off the fingertips of those two fingers specifically. It is actually the makeup of the ball and the long seams rotating with the air that cause this pitch to veer inward. Severity of movement can vary with different ball types.

Posture for this pitch is slightly toward the throwing arm side with the pitcher's weight shifted to the stride foot and the head located slightly in the direction of movement. As with the curve ball, to increase plate coverage the pitcher should step slightly toward the glove side and away from the direction of movement. This adjustment allows for a greater angle of release.

Release point should be slightly left to right for a right-handed pitcher or right to left for a left-handed pitcher. Speed of spin has its impact on this pitch even though the direction of the spin is not exactly toward the direction of the movement.

Coaching the Mental Process

As mentioned before, the position of pitcher requires a mentally tough and focused athlete. In an average game, the pitcher throws 80 to 100 pitches, each requiring pinpoint accuracy and execution. Think about it: A shortstop can field a ground ball after a brief bobble, throw the ball in the dirt four feet below the intended target, and with a good scoop from the first baseman, still successfully complete the play and get the out. A pitcher can miss the intended target by an inch or two and fail by either giving up a hit or throwing a ball. So throughout the game, on every pitch, the pitcher must exercise immense concentration to succeed.

Take a look at the mental circle of the pitch (figure 16.12). This is an orderly example of the thought process of the pitcher throughout the game. It is based on where the pitcher may be located during the particular thought.

First, the pitcher takes the signal from the rubber to start the process. Location of the pitch according to the count is automatic because of a prior

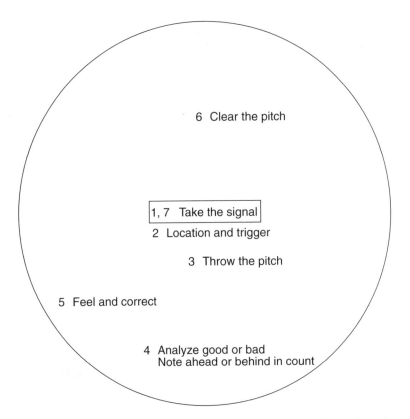

6 Clear the pitch

1, 7 Take the signal

2 Location and trigger

3 Throw the pitch

5 Feel and correct

4 Analyze good or bad
   Note ahead or behind in count

Figure 16.12   The mental circle of the pitch, showing the pitcher's thought process.

note of the count. A trigger is helpful in the execution of the particular pitch called. For example, if the signal was drop ball with a 1-2 count, the location would be the edge of the zone or lower because the pitcher is ahead in the count. The trigger may be to get on top of the pitch or shift weight forward to ensure that the pitch does not hang.

After throwing the pitch, the pitcher analyzes the pitch, either good or bad. This is automatic and leads into the next point. As soon as the result is known, the pitcher notes the count and whether she is ahead of the batter or behind.

The pitcher's analysis of the previous pitch leads her to feel and correct. If the pitch was not executed successfully, she decides what the correction should be for the next time. This mental acknowledgment becomes her trigger.

Now the pitcher clears the pitch. Good or bad, she cannot take the last pitch into the upcoming pitch. The most important pitch is the next one. She takes the signal, and the process begins again.

Teaching Strategy:
The Game Within the Game

The primary objective of the pitcher is to get the strikeout. No pitcher should be in the circle without that mind-set. Having said that, it is important to acknowledge that no pitcher strikes out every batter. Therefore, the secondary objective of the pitcher is to control the hitter.

To achieve either of these goals, pitchers must be proficient at working the zone and attacking the hitter's weakness. It is not the pitcher's responsibility to call the game; it's the catcher's or the coach's. However, it *is* the pitcher's responsibility to execute the pitch that is called. The following factors contribute to a pitcher's success at the elite level.

First a pitcher must define the strike zone. Unfortunately, what the rule book defines as the zone is not what every umpire defines as the zone. The pitcher needs to find out early on what zone she is playing with and work within its boundaries.

Every pitcher should know her go-to pitch. One pitch should be a consistent go-to no matter what the count is. Be sure the catcher and coach know each pitcher's go-to pitch as well.

The pitcher should approach each batter one pitch at a time. She should work to get ahead in the count and stay ahead. Put together a good "at bat." Remember, it takes three good pitches for a strikeout. One or two great ones can quickly become unimportant if followed by one mistake.

Pitchers need to set goals—for example, no hits, no walks, no one past second base, no runs, no consecutive hits, and so on. The pitcher needs a secondary goal to fall back on if her goal becomes nullified during the game. This backup plan can help her recover from a downslide when mistakes occur.

Pitchers and catchers should communicate between innings. Also, if a coach is calling the game, the pitcher needs to let him or her know if she is feeling particularly confident or insecure with a certain pitch.

Train pitchers to throw more pitches in the strike zone early in the game. This habit proves to the umpire as well as opposing batters that she is sharp and controlled, allowing her to move toward the edges and beyond in the later innings, gaining called strikes as well as swings.

Pitchers should always be prepared to compete. They need to make the most of practices and warm-ups. In game situations, relief pitchers should anticipate when they might be brought in, and they should be ready both mentally and physically.

Pitch calling plays a large part in the strategy of pitching. When deciding what pitch to call, keep the following factors in mind:

- How many pitches have been thrown by this pitcher in this game? This day? This weekend?

- At what point in the total pitch count does this pitcher start to lose control or movement of certain pitches?
- Which pitches are hit most often?
- What types of hits are typical: singles, doubles, triples, home runs, dribblers, ground balls, fly balls, line drives?
- What are the strikeout pitches?
- Which pitches can be thrown for a called strike in a behind or get-ahead situation?
- What is this pitcher's performance with a 3-2 count? Usually a hit? Usually a walk? Usually a strikeout? The answer to this question helps you decide what pitches to throw with a 2-2 count.
- How often is the pitcher ahead in the count, and how does that relate to hits, walks, and strikeouts?

In the event that a hitter makes solid contact, assess whether the hitter put a good swing on a well-executed pitch versus the contact being made on a mistake or on a poorly executed pitch.

Final Thoughts

One of the most difficult transitions for any pitcher is the jump from division to division, from 12U to 14U to 16U to 18U and then to college softball. If the elite pitcher continues after college, there will be even more challenging transitions to professional softball or to pitching at an international level. Each transition requires more speed, and the pitches require increased and refined movement. College pitchers must adjust to throwing their pitches from 43 feet and face denser and tougher lineups that make a pitcher pay dearly for mistakes. Some of the normal shortcomings that a pitcher routinely got away with in youth ball, such as being consistently behind in the count, can make for a long freshman year.

Transitions themselves are tough enough. Be sure that those transitions are not magnified by taking shortcuts in the development of a pitcher, building a shaky instead of solid foundation. Because if along the way we did not build it correctly, either out of haste or ignorance, the athlete suffers at the moment she has been working for all along.

CHAPTER SEVENTEEN

Charging Up the Battery

Lori Sippel

A team's success is directly related to the battery's success—a fact recognized when things are amiss and a concept taken for granted when all the cylinders are firing. So what allows some batteries to have consistently productive games versus those that live on the infamous roller coaster? Why can a pitcher have success at one level and struggle at the next? Many say it is the intangibles, those things that are specific to the person but not necessarily shared by all, something you cannot touch or teach but you can recognize when someone possesses them. I agree with this to a certain extent, but I also believe we leave too much to chance and we lessen our load as coaches by inferring that we cannot affect or bring out the intangibles in our athletes.

The game of fastpitch softball is often recognized as a pitcher-dominated sport. If this is true, then you must consider the duty of the catcher as well. A pitcher's ability to dominate is internal; however, her ability to apply her dominance is indeed mirrored by her catcher's ability to quarterback each situation and utilize the pitcher's repertoire. The pitcher's ability to consistently win in game situations is what gives her the mark of a dominating pitcher. A pitcher's ability to put her best pitch forward in every situation is critical and is as much a mental feat as it is a physical one.

Preparation

Physical mistakes are apt to occur in the circle, yet some errors are side effects of a poor mental game or a lack of a plan. A pitcher cannot dominate without having conviction. She cannot have conviction without first having purpose, and it is impossible to have purpose without having a plan. A plan can only be created with a goal in mind. Lack of conviction on the mound or behind the plate is often a by-product of poor understanding of role or goal.

A knowledgeable pitcher is a pitcher who understands the rules of her game. She knows how to work the count, she knows how to expose the hitter's weaknesses, and she knows how and when to use her defense. Basic game knowledge is built upon as the pitcher gains more understanding of her physical and mental strengths and fears. Why do I say fears? I believe a high percentage of a pitcher's weaknesses are fear-based rather than a lack of ability. A pitcher's fears cause her to do things that are not successful and over time she may actually believe that she is unable to physically execute.

One day I was working with a pitcher at a string apparatus, one in which elastic bands are used to create a zone to throw through. The pitcher sets up her zone, then sets up two football dummies to act as hitters, one on the left and one on the right. If all things are properly set, the pitcher sees a plate with a left-handed hitter, a right-handed hitter, and the string zone. During this particular session, the pitcher was working on a low curve.

After she easily succeeded in throwing the curve through her zone, I asked her if she was throwing to a left-handed hitter or a right-handed hitter. She smiled and said, "to a righty," indicating to me that this was a safe zone because not only was the ball thrown outside but it would move away from the hitter. So I removed the right dummy to leave the left dummy standing alone. In this context, that same pitch would be inside on the left-handed hitter and would break into the hitter. She hit the dummy on the first pitch and did not hit her zone for another six pitches. Understand, she had pitched three consecutive curves to that zone. All I did was remove the right dummy, forcing her to consider the left dummy as her hitter. Even though the left dummy had been there the whole time, she had ignored it until I forced her to consider it. Physically, she had proved that throwing the curve away from a right-handed hitter was no problem. Throwing the same pitch to the same zone was a problem if it meant throwing inside to a left-handed hitter. Her weakness, throwing inside on the left-handed hitter, was caused by fear, not by a lack of ability.

A coach needs to help players redefine what they can do so that they can take charge. In most cases, the pitcher is quite capable of more than she ever thought possible.

Understanding

To charge the battery is to prepare the pitcher and catcher to have a positive outlook in all situations. You want them to see every situation as the glass half-full not half-empty. You want them to believe they can win every given situation. The combination of being mentally charged and physically prepared is what people see when they watch a dominating pitcher on the mound. The pitcher cannot help but to seem offensive because she is always thinking about the next pitch, rather than reflecting on the last one. So how do we get our battery charged and keep them thinking forward thoughts regardless of the situation? Let's consider some facts of the game first.

Every game lends itself to a different mental and emotional challenge. A laissez-faire attitude is as much a challenge to a team's success as is an overcharged one. The infamous roller coaster is what allows the underdog to win and favorite to lose. If this were not true, a coach's pregame motivational speech would not be necessary. Additionally, past performances, opposing hitters, fans in the stands, and impact of the game are all items that may be in the back of the pitcher's mind, distracting her from reaching peak performance.

Every 15 to 20 seconds, a pitcher's circumstance changes. Every pitch changes the count and in turn changes the advantage within the at bat. The pitcher must be able to keep a next-pitch mentality and can only do so if she can be consistent mentally whatever the count.

A team's success is detemined by how many bad-day victories the battery can lead the team to. There are days when the cylinders just aren't firing; however, a dominating pitcher can still give her team an opportunity to win if she takes control of what is working and uses those pitches with conviction.

The pitcher is the only position where the player can actually plan and act on her response. Every other position on the field is one of anticipation and reaction. The luxury of being able to plan your response should not be taken lightly, and indeed the pitcher must be accountable for how she responds to each situation. We expect the pitcher to set the tone for her teammates, and the best way for her to accomplish this goal is for her to be accountable for how she plans and attacks the situations as they unfold throughout the game.

Focus

Together, the pitcher and catcher must put on their respective game faces. I like to define *game face* as that piece of armor that a player puts on to protect her from inefficient and ineffective thoughts. It is a face with a plan. This face is put on during pregame or prepractice and stays on throughout the practice or game. It is the tapering of thoughts from general thoughts and ideas to that of thoughts and ideas with respect to the game only.

Game focus is created through a warm-up that gets the player physically and mentally in tune to her upcoming task. The routine the pitcher and catcher use to put on their game faces must be one that works for both. Often, the pitcher's routine dictates the catcher's warm-up. The warm-up must be discussed to ensure that the catcher has time to fully prepare as well.

The physical preparation should initiate the mental preparation. We tend to warm up our bodies gradually, and we should relate our mental focus to the physical warm-up. As skill work becomes more game specific, so should mental focus. For example, an appropriate time for players to get task-oriented is during the jogging and stretching portion of the warm-up. Players need to throw the day's thoughts into a get-to-it-later file and clear their heads.

The throwing routine allows players to get snapped into the task. With each throw and catch, players can fill their heads with thoughts specific to the game. Working on each pitch allows the pitcher and catcher to work on the specifics of their positions. Mixing the pitches just before the start of the game allows the pitcher and catcher to work together at a game pace.

After their specific game skills have been physically toned, their focus shifts to managing the strategy of the game. Getting ahead in the count, reviewing the hitters, working specific counts, and identifying the pitches that are working well versus those that are not are all a part of sharpening for the game. Getting task-oriented is critical when a player is held accountable for her performance. It means letting go of thoughts that distract from the goal and focusing on those that are synonymous to the task. Putting on a game face is charging the battery. At this point, it is time to move on to maintaining that charge while in the heat of battle.

Execution

Game management is the creation of a routine that perpetuates forward thinking. The facts of the game could easily lead to self-destruction. Every at bat, the pitcher finds herself in a situation of advantage or disadvantage. If the battery does not have a plan of attack and one of counterattack, the game's outcome is of chance, not of action. The game routine ensures that the battery is acting with purpose. Being convicted in all your actions not only wins the battles but also gets the attention of the troops. A battery that consistently takes charge and is accountable to each outcome is guaranteed to have the backing of their teammates.

Forward thinking is the art of being reflective long enough to gain information to be put into the next pitch without overcritiquing or overcelebrating. There are 21 wars (21 outs) for the battery to fight each game. The battery's ability to take on one war at a time and deal with each war as a separate issue leads to more wars won at the end of the contest.

Critiquing and celebrating are part of the game, yet too much time spent doing either one only leads to players being too high or too low in the esteem department. Peak performance can be sustained only when emotions are in check. The game management routine helps the battery stay focused and stay in the moment. A pitcher without a consistent routine may actually telegraph her level of empowerment, whereas a pitcher with presence does not give away her position. She can be viewed at different points of the game—you would not know if she were winning or losing because her actions between pitches are consistent, deliberate, and viewed as attacking.

An effective game management routine allows the pitcher to gather information, plan her attack with her catcher, pitch to the hitter, and start the cycle over again. Specific steps must be taken to ensure that the battery is charged and ready to commit with purpose to every pitch. Every pitcher has her own pace between pitches; some pitchers like to work faster than others. The key, however, is that pace does not fluctuate. A pitcher in trouble tends to quicken her pace, which often leads to skipped steps in her routine. Trouble leads to trouble because the one safeguard—the routine—has been cast aside. The spiral effect occurs, and soon the pitcher is on the bench.

The game routine must include some specific steps if it is to encourage forward thinking (see table 17.1). First, the pitcher should never get on the

TABLE 17.1

Game Routine for Pitcher

Phase	Action
1. Ready zone	Ready for plan of attack
2. Plan	Receive signal
3. Breathe	Relaxation breath; visualize path of the ball
4. Deliver the pitch	Do it
5. Gather information	Critique/adjust, celebrate/sustain, counterplan
6. Breathe	Get rid of any residual thoughts of past pitch
7. Ready zone	Ready for plan of attack

mound if she is still considering her last pitch or is stewing over the last play. The pitching rubber must be viewed as sacred and should not be approached unless the pitcher is totally focused on the next pitch. Once the pitcher has approached or is standing on the rubber, she is in what I call the *ready zone*. She has gathered information, discarded the stuff she does not need, and is focused on receiving the plan.

The plan occurs when the pitcher and catcher communicate about the next pitch. Often, the pitcher receives the signal from the catcher and then continues onto the next step. However, it is important that the pitcher totally agree with the catcher's call. If a pitcher is to be accountable for her performance and is to throw with conviction, she must be able to veto a call if she is more certain of another means of attack. The wrong pitch thrown with conviction wins more often than the right pitch thrown with hesitation.

Breathing is critical to a routine that emits presence. The breath that occurs just after the plan has been received is what is going to fuel the pitch. Physical tension is a pitcher's biggest opponent, and this breath allows the pitcher to go into her motion fully relaxed. The breath is also a sign to the catcher that the pitcher has committed to the plan and is about to deliver the pitch.

The moment the pitcher has delivered the pitch, she begins to gather information. The pitcher can feel if the pitch is going to do its job as soon as it comes off her fingertips. She becomes aware of the hitter and how the hitter responds to the pitch. The pitcher then begins to critique her performance based on the hitter's response. She may celebrate a good pitch, or she may become critical of a poor delivery. The key at this point is that the pitcher brings herself back to a level where she can again harness the information she has gathered and focus on the next pitch.

It is very important that the pitcher find a level of equilibrium so that she does not overemotionalize the situation. Her ability to do so lies in her commitment to critique, then adjust, as well as celebrate, then sustain. In doing so, the pitcher is in control of her emotions and is able to maintain her presence. The roller coaster never gets started as the pitcher controls herself and her responses.

The final part of gathering information is in critiquing the game situation. The count has changed. Perhaps runners are aboard, and the number of outs may dictate her next move. Once she has checked into the game situation, she then completely commits to the next pitch by taking a big breath that discards any lingering thoughts of the last pitch. She indicates her readiness to receive the next signal by approaching the mound or by looking up to the catcher; she has returned to the ready zone.

Table 17.2 contains an example of an at bat with respect to a pitcher's routine. The middle column lists what a pitcher may say to herself under certain circumstances.

TABLE 17.2

Pitcher's Routine: Sample at Bat

Pitch (result)	What the pitcher might say to herself	After pitch
1st pitch (ball outside)	1-0 count. Find a way to even the count.	Breathe, signal, breathe
2nd pitch (swinging strike)	1-1 count. Swing was under ball but on time.	Breathe, signal, breathe
3rd pitch (hit, drive up middle)	1-1 hit. I'm better than that. Work the ball off the plate, work the black. Runner on first, I have third on the bunt.	Breathe, signal, breathe

Final Thoughts

Forward thinking is pitching with purpose. Pitching with purpose establishes the pitcher's presence on the mound, presence often viewed as dominance. Having the skill to get the strikeout when needed and the groundout when necessary is all a part of the game. Staying focused leads to winning more battles within the game, allowing a greater opportunity for victory.

A battery that can take control of the controllables and dismiss the uncontrollables becomes the heartbeat of the team. A battery that wears a unified game face day-in and day-out has the attitude that becomes contagious. Setting the tone is quite a responsibility. Educate those who start with the ball, and team success will follow.

Playing Situational Defense

Linda Wells

Photo courtesy of Alyssa Johnson, Arizona State University

Every elite team utilizes strategies for special situations. Teams practice fielding bunts, covering steals, executing double plays, and defending other plays that together constitute team defense. The ability of the defense, as a team, to respond accurately and efficiently to the offense often determines the outcome of a game.

Situational defensive strategies fall toward the top of the softball defensive pyramid, as shown in figure 18.1. As the pyramid indicates, ability in the basic skills—such as catching, throwing, and fielding—are primary for successful team play. Advanced skills such as covering bases and backing up are required before the introduction of team defense. Additional team

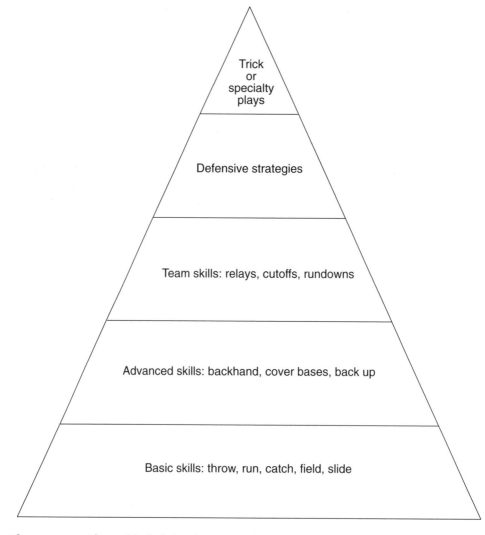

Figure 18.1 The softball defensive pyramid.

skills such as relays, cutoffs, and rundowns provide the final complement for execution of situational team defense. Success at team defense depends on proper technique and training of the lower pyramid skills. Coaches must plan practice regimes to reflect the skill level of their teams with the goal of achieving higher pyramid skills as ability allows. Remember, even elite teams spend daily practice time on the basic skills. The pyramid suggests time allotments with basic and advanced skills requiring the majority of training time.

Teaching Defensive Skills

To build a successful defense, you need to teach players the proper way to grip the ball and cover the bases. Teach players to press the ball into their gloves to get a firm grip. One of the most common and fatal defensive flaws is for a player to flip the ball from the glove to the throwing hand. This habit increases the chance that the ball will squirt away and allow the runner to reach base. Players should always press the ball into their gloves to get a proper grip and ensure an accurate throw.

Train players to properly cover bases. Opportunities for outs are often missed when the player does not properly cover the base. The player covering the base should align herself with her throwing teammate to create a lane whenever possible (figure 18.2). Also, she should position herself between the runner and the base to anticipate the pickoff of a runner who has rounded the base too far.

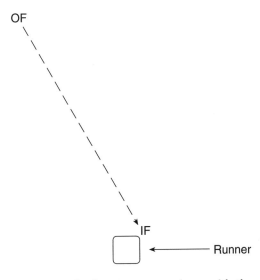

Figure 18.2   The infielder covering the base creates a lane with the outfielder.

Rundowns

Situational defense often exposes the offensive player to the jeopardy of the rundown. Great defense prompts the runner to get caught in the pickle. To execute the rundown, the player with the ball holds the ball with her throwing hand above her shoulder in a dart throw position. She creates a lane with her teammate by positioning herself in front of or behind the runner, depending on where her teammate is positioned. She runs at the offensive player, taking short steps on the balls of her feet. Whenever possible, she tries to get the runner to retreat to the trailing base and tags the runner well off the base. If she can't get the runner, she uses a dart throw to give up the ball to her teammate, who has taken a position off the opposite base. It helps if her teammate calls for the ball.

Try not to use fake throws, as they distract teammates more than opponents. Once the ball is given up, the player should get out of the path of the runner, allowing her teammate to pursue. Rundowns should create outs with a minimum of throws. Adjacent players should fill in to provide support and backup for the pursuit. Remind players to be aware of additional runners and cover any potential advancement.

Cutoffs

A variety of plays in situational defense use a cutoff. The cutoff player is positioned between the player with the ball and the player who is covering the base. If the throw is errant or untimely, the cutoff can cut or intercept the ball instead of allowing it to travel to the player covering the base. Any player can be used as a cutoff, depending on the play set. One or more players are assigned the responsibility of deciding whether or not the ball is cut—for example, the catcher calls the cutoff on plays at the plate.

To help the cutoff find her initial position, instruct the player to move between the two players involved in the play until her teammates are no longer in her peripheral vision. This adjustment puts her in a reasonable cutoff position. Sometimes she can adjust to the right or left based on information from a player involved in the play who does not have the ball—again, the catcher on the play at the plate, for example.

Relays

On play sets involving extra base hits, the relay is used to move the ball from a deep outfield spot to a base on the infield. The outfielder should surround the ball, keeping her body open in anticipation of the throw to the infielder. When the play develops, the infielder takes a position toward the outfielder, yelling *Relay! Relay!* The infielder holds her arms in the air creating the look of a football upright.

This becomes the target for the outfielder. As soon as the outfielder has released the ball, the infielder should turn her glove side toward the infield in an attempt to catch and throw the ball as promptly and accurately as possible. Although she requires the outfielder to make the longer of the two throws, she still has a long throw to her base. The infielder is assisted by her teammates as the play develops and is instructed to what base the ball should be thrown. A quick relay, or booster throw, can often turn an extra base hit into an out. As a rule of thumb, encourage the outfield to make 60 percent of the throwing distance on the relay. Sometimes the infielder has a tendency to go too far out to receive the throw.

After these basic concepts have been taught, situational defense can be introduced. Remember, all defensive sets require application of the skills in the lower part of the pyramid including basic skills, advanced skills, and team skills. Be willing to interject review or drill breakouts in the teaching of situational defense. Be patient as players attempt to add play coverages to their individual and partner skill repertoire. Novice teams do not need to incorporate all situational plays. Select and present material appropriate to age and expertise.

Teaching Situational Defenses

When teaching team defensive strategies, work on one play sequence or one series at a time. Fungo hit the ball to create locations of choice. Provide repetition as each play is introduced. Demand coverage of the most common play sets first, then allow coverage for balls outside the set. For example, on a short fly ball with a runner at first, there often is the option for a force at second. First have players work on defending the base hit with a runner at first. Then allow them to read and respond to special situations.

There are many different ways to defend a play. Perhaps you want the shortstop to relay balls on the left side and the second baseman to relay those on the right side. No problem. The purpose here isn't to make you use these exact play sets, only to reinforce that your players need to know what to do with the ball and practice it. Hopefully, they know all the time. Play sets give them the potential to know in most situations. Decide the coverages and teach them. When a team is great on defense, modifications are easy. When they are novices, structure helps.

Basic Defensive Alignment

The basic defensive alignment for player positioning and coverage is shown in figure 18.3. The corners play about 15 feet in front of the bag. Middle infielders play behind the baselines as deep as their throwing ability allows. Outfielders evenly divide the outfield, with the center fielder playing a couple of steps shorter than left or right fielders.

Figure 18.4 shows the common configuration for defending a slap hitter. Notice the shortstop and second baseman move forward, playing in front of the baseline. Exact depth depends on the speed of the runner. The faster the runner, the closer the defense plays toward home.

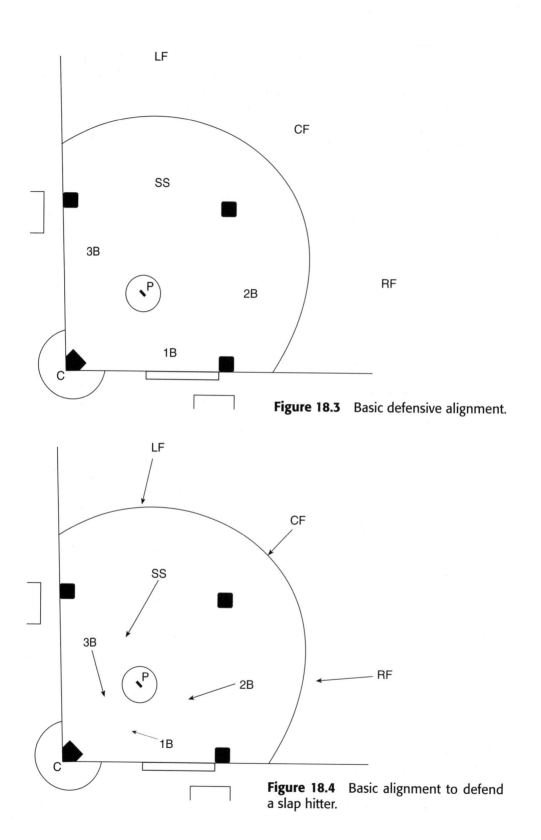

Figure 18.3   Basic defensive alignment.

Figure 18.4   Basic alignment to defend a slap hitter.

The third baseman moves off of the line and also shortens for a potential bunt. Likewise, the first baseman plays short but is always aware of her necessity to beat the runner to the bag. The outfielders are also drawn in, with the left fielder near the line (assuming the slapper is a lefty). Center and right fielders shift toward left and play short.

An alternative is to put the second baseman short (between the pitcher and first base), leaving the first baseman at the bag to cover. Additionally, with a slapper who can also hit, you may need to play the center and right fielders deeper, depending on the hitter's ability.

The idea of the defensive alignment is to stand where the offensive players are most likely to hit the ball. Adjustments to the basic defensive alignments are based on a variety of factors.

Pitcher and Pitch Count

Consider the speed of your pitcher in relation to the opponent's pitchers. The faster your pitcher, the more the defense shifts to the nonpull side (to the right for a right-handed hitter).

As the pitcher creates a pitch count, the outfield and infield can adjust by count. From her initial position, an outfielder might move one step back and to the pull side for every ball in the count, one step in and to the nonpull side for every strike. With a 1-1 count, the player regains her initial position.

Infield and outfield might be assigned to take an extra step back on a full count, or outfielders may move back for each ball against a power hitter. The infield and outfield also take a step back and to the pull side for a change-up. Outfielders may take two steps back. Outfielders typically move toward the pull side on a screwball with a righty–righty combination. Although two steps are the norm for the outfield and one step the norm for the infield, additional factors may affect the adjustments.

Ability of the Outfield

General alignment adjustments can be made for the strength of each outfielder. Usually the center fielder captains the shift of the outfield defense. Considerations for a left-handed player may prompt the center fielder to play closer to a right fielder who is left handed with a pulling left-handed hitter at the plate. Sometimes alignment can help cover for a weak or injured arm. If one outfielder is a great diver/slider for the ball, you might try to adjust the initial alignment to allow her to play shorter whenever possible.

Ability of the Infield

Initial adjustments can be made by the middle and corners as well. The shortstop usually captains and moves the infield. The shortstop and second baseman adjust to the possibility of a double play (shift toward second base), the shortstop deep in the hole for a right-handed power hitter, or the corners moving together up or back, depending on the bunt threat.

Middles and corners also adjust by pitch count. Their depth increases with a high ball count or in the late innings of a starting pitcher. A rule of thumb is for the corners to guard the lines, especially late in the game.

Game Conditions

Initial defensive alignment is continually adjusted based on the playing field and weather. Outfielders must play deeper when there is no fence or the fence is very low. They would play deeper when the wind is swirling or blowing out. Infielders would play up on a soft diamond but back on a harder, faster infield. Distance to the out-of-play area may affect the ability of the corners to play off the lines, and they would also adjust on a muddy or slow field by further guarding against the bunt. Of course, if the batter is having difficulty getting out of the box, this factor may cancel itself.

Opponents

Knowing how your team stacks up to the opponent's team on paper can give you significant hints about defense alignment. If you are unlikely to outscore your opponents, you may try alignments in which you risk the long ball but have a chance to keep runners off bases.

Against base runners, the defense usually shades toward the anticipated play. Middles shade toward second base with a runner at first in anticipation of the double play. Outfielders move in with a runner at third or in any winning-run situations. The same is true in a close game with runners on base.

With a lead, the opposite is true. Infielders (one step) and outfielders (two steps) are able to play deeper and protect against the long ball in the outfield as well as execute a cutoff with an infielder.

The tendencies of the opponent's batters, the team's strengths and weaknesses, and individual and team speed also determine initial defense alignment. Outfielders play deeper and to the pull side for the power hitter. The defense shortens for bunters and slappers. Most importantly, the defense positions itself to cover the tendencies of the individual hitter. It is fun to watch the defense make a great diving play, as long as the defensive player doesn't have to make the heroic play because she was out of position.

Game Situations

All players should be alert to adjusting their defense alignments based on circumstances in the game. Consider the inning, score, and outs as you adjust for each batter. Factor in changes for the hot hitter or cold temperature that can change the strategy of the game.

Teams should take their best shot at the defensive alignments that give them the highest probability of being in the right position at the right time. Communication among pitcher, catcher, infield, and outfield must occur continually. When the ball is not hit right at them, their situational strategy supports the team to turn hits into outs.

The following play sets have a high probability of occurrence in a game.

No One on Base, Base Hit

When no one is on base and the ball is hit to left field, the second baseman covers second and the shortstop lines up to cut off the throw from the left fielder (figure 18.5). The left fielder throws through the cutoff to second. The center fielder backs up the left fielder while the right fielder backs up the second baseman. The first and third basemen cover their bases; the catcher backs up first base. The defense needs to stay alert; a strong throw to first may be able to pick off a rounding baserunner.

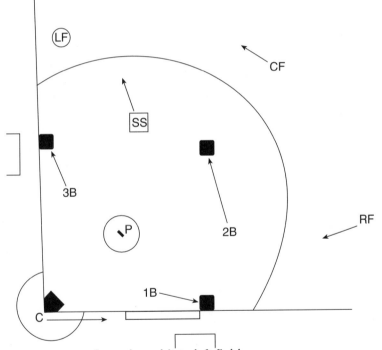

Figure 18.5   No one on base, base hit to left field.

When no one is on base and the ball is hit to right field for a base hit, the shortstop covers second base and the second baseman lines up as the cutoff. The right fielder fields the ball and throws through the cutoff to second base. The center fielder backs up the right fielder, and the left fielder backs up third. The first and third basemen cover their bases; the catcher backs up first.

When no one is on base and the ball is hit to center field for a base hit, either the second baseman or shortstop can cover second while the other lines up as the cutoff for the center fielder. Who does what depends on the abilities of your infielders and where the ball is hit in center field. The center fielder fields the ball and throws it through the cutoff to second. The left and right fielders back up the center fielder. The first and third basemen cover their bases; the catcher backs up first base.

Runner on First, Base Hit

With a runner at first and less than two outs, the shortstop lines up between the outfielder and third and acts as the cutoff. (Figure 18.6 shows a base hit to left field.) The throw should go to the cutoff if the runner from first is not advancing to third. If the runner is trying to advance to third, the cutoff should let the ball go through to the third baseman for a tag at third. The shortstop should be alert for a runner who rounds second too far. On balls hit right to the outfielder, the runner probably will not attempt to advance to third, but she may round the base, making her vulnerable to a pickoff. The first, second, and third basemen cover their bases. The pitcher backs up third base while the catcher covers home plate.

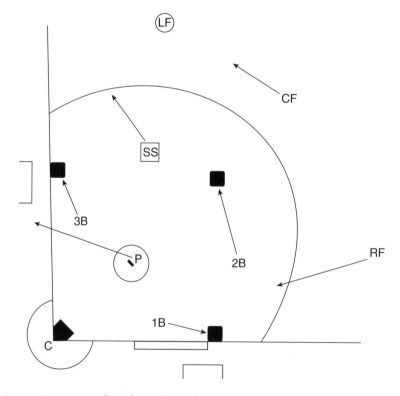

Figure 18.6 Runner on first, base hit to left field.

Runner on Second, Base Hit

To defend a base hit with a runner on second and less than two outs, the third baseman acts as the cutoff between left field and home plate on balls hit sharply to the left side (figure 18.7). For hits to center and right field, the first baseman is used as the cutoff. Balls from the outfield should be thrown home through the respective cutoff. If the runner is holding at third, the cutoff catches the ball with the possibility of a play on the trailing runner. If the runner at third is attempting to come home, the cutoff lets the ball go through to the catcher for a tag at the plate. The catcher covers home plate while the pitcher backs up throws home. The first baseman covers first, the second baseman covers second, and the shortstop covers third.

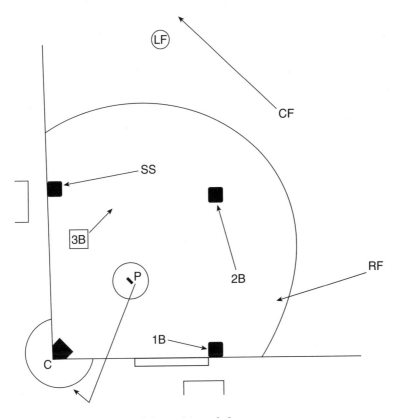

Figure 18.7   Runner on second, base hit to left.

No One On, Extra Base Hit

Defending extra base hits requires relay throws. If the bases are empty and the hitter gets an extra base hit, the shortstop is the relay, except on hits down the right field line (figure 18.8). Often the second baseman has a weaker arm than the shortstop, and the team wants to use the shortstop's stronger arm for relay throws on most plays. The second baseman, however, is in better position to act as the relay on balls hit down the right field line. On all extra base hits with no one on, the pitcher backs up third base, the catcher stays at home plate, the first baseman covers first, and the third baseman covers third. The outfielder who fields the ball needs to hit the relay with a good, solid throw. The relay, whether the shortstop or the second baseman, needs to be a big and loud target for the outfielder.

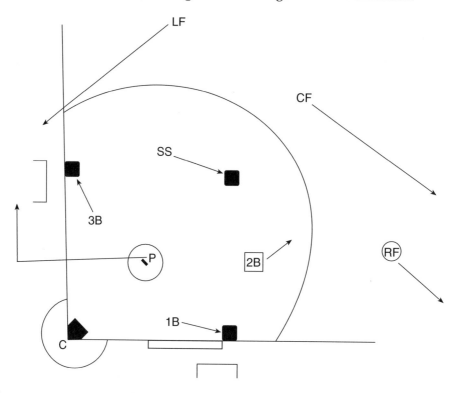

Figure 18.8 No one on base, extra base hit down the right field line.

Runner on First, Extra Base Hit

With a runner on first, defending an extra base hit requires the use of the relay as well as the cutoff. The shortstop acts as the relay, except when the ball is hit down the right field line. On hits down the right field line, the second baseman is the relay (figure 18.9), and the first baseman acts as the cutoff for all hits. On all extra base hits with a runner on first, the catcher covers home plate and the pitcher backs her up. The third baseman covers third. The relay needs to be a big, loud target for the outfielder.

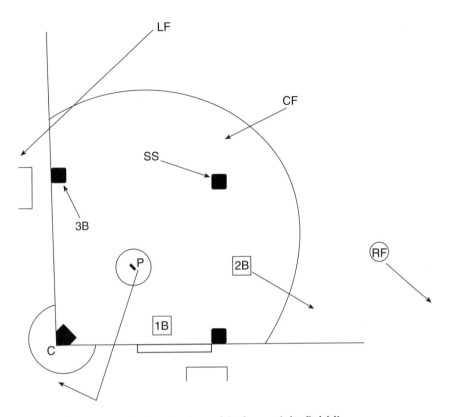

Figure 18.9   Runner on first, extra base hit down right field line.

Defending Steals

On a straight steal, first to second, the shortstop typically covers second. With a right-handed pull hitter at the plate, you may want to change the assignment and have the second baseman cover second.

To defend most second to third steals, the shortstop covers third base. She should attempt to round out so that she places herself in line with the throw. The shortstop should anticipate by "cheating" closer to third in her ready position. With two outs or when there is no threat of a bunt, the third baseman can be assigned this coverage.

Defending the first and third double steal is a challenge. Some teams combine this play with predetermined fakes or pickoff moves to anticipate the movement of the runners. The play set shown in figure 18.10 is the most common but requires an alert second baseman and a shortstop gifted with a strong throwing arm.

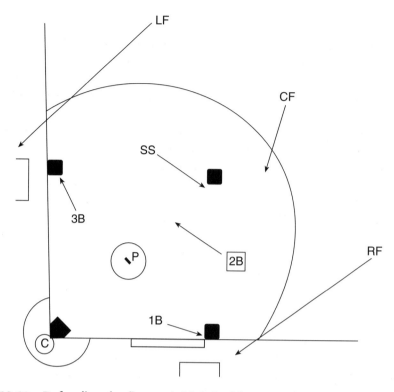

Figure 18.10 Defending the first and third double steal.

If the runner from first breaks on the pitch, the catcher throws the ball to the shortstop covering second, through the second base cutoff. The catcher should be aware of the runner at third, usually seeing her on the throw with her peripheral vision. Obviously, the throw should go to third if this runner can be picked off. The second baseman moves to the cutoff between the pitcher's mound and second base. If the runner is attempting a straight steal and the runner at third holds, let the ball go through for the tag play at second. If the runner at third breaks for home, yell *Cut!* The second baseman should then cut the ball and be alert for the instruction *Three!* or *Four!* from the catcher or third baseman, indicating she should throw to third base or home.

If the runner from first attempts a delayed steal, the shortstop should use her rundown skills to make the runner retreat toward first. The catcher and third baseman, meanwhile, watch the runner at third and yell *Watch three!* when she is off the base far enough to be put out. If the runner from third breaks home, the catcher yells *Four!* for the anticipated play at the plate.

Covering Bunts

Offenses attempt the bunt in an effort to surprise the defense or advance runners. Defensive assignments are made for area coverage with no one on. With a runner on base, a combination of area and base coverage assignments is made. With a runner at first, the catcher covers third if the third baseman fields the bunt. With a runner at second, the shortstop covers third. On a squeeze play, the catcher may not leave the plate to field the ball. She must depend on the charging infielders to get her the ball.

With no runners on base, the corners move in an additional 10 to 15 feet in anticipation of a bunt while the second baseman moves closer to first base. Players read the hands of the hitter to continue to reposition, creep, retreat, or hold their positions during the pitch. Primary bunt responsibility is with the first and third basemen while the second baseman moves over to cover first base for the out. The catcher fields a bunt in front of home plate or calls to the first and third basemen who should field the ball and where the play is. The pitcher fields a hard bunt hit right at her.

With a runner on first and fewer than two outs, the defense needs to look to get the lead runner. The catcher fields a bunt in front of home plate or calls who should field the ball and where the play is. She also covers third base if the third baseman fields the bunt. The shortstop covers second base while the second baseman covers first. The first and third basemen have primary responsibility for fielding the bunt. Elite level infielders often are able to get the lead runner at second base.

With a runner at second and fewer than two outs, the shortstop covers third, and the second baseman covers first. The center fielder moves in to cover second base. The pitcher fields a bunt hit hard right at her. The catcher fields a bunt in front of home plate or calls who should field the ball and where the play is. The first and third basemen charge to field the bunt. Fielders need to take care when throwing the ball to second base: since the center fielder is to cover second, there is limited backup.

Fewer than two outs and a runner at third should always prompt the defense to be alert for the squeeze play (figure 18.11). The catcher should be reminded to stay near the plate, as she will have to put a tag on the runner. Fielders need to listen for the catcher's command and position their bodies for the throw to the plate. The pitcher fields a bunt up the middle. The first and third basemen charge to field the bunt. The second baseman covers first. The shortstop covers third until she realizes there is a play at the plate. Then she sprints to second base to keep the bunter from advancing.

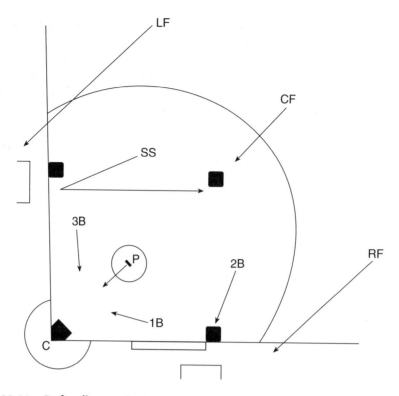

Figure 18.11 Defending against a squeeze bunt.

Advanced Plays

Your team's defensive talent and growth allow you to incorporate more plays of greater difficulty. The following situations and coverages test your defense's abilities.

Right and left side switches can produce quicker base coverage and are more efficient with multiple runners but can be used for other situations as well. For example, imagine that the bases are empty and the ball is hit in the hole between the third baseman and the shortstop. Both infielders try for the ball, but neither can get it. The momentum of the shortstop is toward third, so she goes there and covers. The momentum of the third baseman is toward second, so she goes there and covers. They have just executed a left side switch.

Fakes can also be effective, but the defense has to practice the timing and signals. For example, imagine a base hit to right. The right fielder realizes the only play she has is a close safe play at first. She pretends to bobble the ball, alerting the first baseman to leave the base—this is a fake giveup on the play. This deception clears the path for the catcher to sneak in behind the rounding runner and receive a throw from the right fielder. The right fielder pretends to throw to the first baseman but whips the ball to the catcher instead in an attempt to pick off the rounding runner.

Like that one? Try faking out a runner who is attempting a straight steal of second. The catcher, realizing there is no play, throws a pop up, high and around second. The shortstop and pitcher both loudly call the ball as though the batter hit the pop up. Believing the batter has hit a pop up, the runner retreats to first.

The ability to devise and implement specific plays is limitless. Work to evaluate the abilities of each individual and team. Defense wins.

CHAPTER NINETEEN

Competing in Tournaments and Playoffs

Margie Wright

The most interesting aspect about consistently participating in the postseason is that the planning for it must start in the preseason. Success in the postseason is nothing more than executing the basics at the right time after a long season of those very same skills.

Preseason Preparation

In softball, postseason preparation begins in the nontraditional season—the fall. Before practice begins, there should be a team meeting for goal setting. What does this group of players really want to achieve? What does the coach believe they can achieve? For this to be a successful meeting, the coaches and team must combine their desires and design appropriate goals that address all expectations.

One key area that must be addressed is the difference between goals and expectations. Goals are the realistic beliefs of the individual; thus, goals are internal. Expectations are what everyone else expects of the individual; therefore, expectations are external. Softball parents are notorious for living their lives and dreams through their daughters, so it is key that players not get wrapped up in the often unrealistic expectations of others.

Goals need to be realistic. Once the team goals have been determined, the coach should meet with each player to set individual goals based on the team goals. Individual goals must coincide with team goals, and the coach may help point the player in the right direction. It is crucial, though, for the coach to allow the player to set her own goals . . . or at least believe she made the final decision, that is.

All goals, both team and individual, must be broken into daily, weekly, and monthly goals and should be reevaluated regularly. Several things can happen over a year (injuries, for example), so regular evaluations are crucial in order for goals to be achievable. Once goals are in place, the coach should address ways to deal with any failures and the necessity of rethinking and reestablishing goals based on where the team is at a particular point in the season.

Some expectations are needed for a team's success. Expectations that address each individual's role within the team are needed, so all team members know their roles and each other's roles. The coach, school, and players also have non-softball-related expectations that must be fulfilled to develop trust and respect within the team. These types of expectations often come in the form of external rules, such as team rules, academic, instructional, NCAA, and Federation rules—all of which give more power to the accomplishment of team goals. Once the expectations are in place and the players realize they will adhere to a code of accountability, the team can move forward to becoming prepared physically.

With goals and expectations in place, the coach must develop a practice and game plan that gives the team the best chance to succeed. In the preseason, weight training, conditioning, individual mechanical development, strategies, and scrimmages develop valuable characteristics and skills for players to take into the season. All practices must be structured to the abilities of the players, so they can reach a high level of success and move toward the postseason in a positive direction. The coach's creativity is part of the challenge, but if you adapt your training to the needs of your personnel, the postseason becomes the most exciting part of the season.

Game Plan

Once you have established your goals and have developed a practice and conditioning plan that fits your athletes, put your plans into action by developing a game plan of success for the season and, more importantly, the postseason. Anticipate the abilities of the teams you play during the preseason, in conference play, and in the postseason. Discuss every potential scenario with your team and make sure they know that your practice and conditioning plans prepare them for each of these scenarios.

It is essential that physical preparation give confidence to the athletes. They should know that they are prepared for every situation they may face because they have previously performed it in practice.

Make sure each player performs enough repetitions of these skills at 100 percent of her ability so that she develops an edge. If she performs drills at only 80 percent, it will be too easy for her to give in at the challenging time of the postseason.

Be sure to allow for adjustments as the season progresses. When players make these changes, it is important that they see them as physical adjustments rather than emotional ones. It's not about what is happening to them; it's about finding a way to fix the skill so that bad things won't happen.

At various times throughout the year, ask the team to review their strengths and weaknesses and continue to formulate a plan for each player to improve so that the team can peak during the postseason.

Preparation During the Season

This preparation is similar to that in the preseason. The team experiences both success and failure through competition, so goal setting and preparation at this point can be more specific.

If postseason success is the team's ultimate goal, it is key for the team to reestablish or reaffirm goals on a daily or weekly basis. Constant evaluation needs to occur so that players can continue to succeed and work toward tournament time. It is important that the ultimate goal established in the beginning remains the same. They may now have to change their preparation or game plan in order to fulfill it, but keeping the ultimate goal is key.

Once the postseason is a reality, the focus shifts to handling pressure, preparing to play better opponents, and dealing with the possibility of facing elimination. Since the strategy in a game usually can change the outcome, it is essential to design a specific strategy against each and every possible opponent. This strategy should be explained to the team and practiced to develop confidence and a competitive edge. At times, it is also wise to change the strategy at times during competition. Think ahead to as many different possibilities and make sure you are prepared for each one. Softball is a game of adjustments, and the team should be prepared to make them in the postseason. The team that is prepared for those adjustments is the team that comes out on top.

Game Day During Tournament Play

The game plan on game day usually can make a big difference in the outcome of the game. Developing a successful game plan includes making sure there is balanced behavior by everyone involved. That includes trainers, assistant coaches, athletes, and, of course, the head coach. Any unusual or extreme behavior may take away from peak performance.

First and foremost, adopt the one-game-at-a-time philosophy. Looking past an opponent is self-defeating. Focus for each game must be finely tuned toward that one opponent, the weather, and everything relating to the events on just that one day.

Consistency is very important to maintaining that balance and focus. Allow players to behave as they normally do the morning before a game, and assure them that they don't have to do more just because it's a big game. Each individual's rest and diet are important, as is maintaining a routine in those areas. Allow each player to consistently prepare in her own way and remind players to accept how others prepare for competition. Also, allocate the maximum time needed by the slowest player to get ready, and do it from game one so that everyone is able to judge their time accordingly.

Warm-up should be structured, to the point, and done the same way throughout the season. Pregame talks by the coach should be consistent no matter whom you are playing. Talks should be highly intense all season (if that is how you would do it in the postseason), and they should be consistent. Your talk should be the same intensity before a weaker team as it is before a stronger team. Players change their emotional level from opponent to opponent, but the coach should keep a more even temper throughout the season so that the players don't develop a I-gotta-do-more-in-this-game attitude. Let the players perform. Realize that once the tournament starts, each team you play is a great team, even when you are seeded number one and your opponent is number six.

Once the game is completed, keep the postgame activity the same and keep it short. Obviously, when the team wins, there is more excitement; but remind them that although what they did was great, it was just another step toward the ultimate goal. The same would be true if the team lost in a double elimination setting. Use the loss in a positive way by finding areas to improve. Remind the team of the elements of the loss that make them better and make the ultimate goal more attainable.

Postseason Performance Plan

When it is time for the team to be tested in the postseason, there are several areas that should be incorporated into the team chalk talks, practices, goal-setting sessions, and so forth. This time of the season is when the pressure is greatest, and how your team handles that pressure usually determines the outcome. When the structure of the program is consistent throughout the season to what is expected in the postseason, it is easier to handle the pressures facing a team when each game could be their last.

In tournament play, you play your best players *every* game. The players you expect to use as role players (pinch hitters, for example) should have been used in that role all year so that their jobs become routine in the postseason. This is no time to shuffle lineups or batting order. The team should know before the tournament begins what the lineup is going to be, who is pitching, who is in relief, who is pinch running or pinch hitting, and what adjustments to the lineup may occur if necessary.

The preparation needed for playing against top-notch teams is the same preparation that should have been used all season long. If your team is used to approaching each game of the season with the same intensity needed in the postseason, they have half of the battle won.

The one factor that is different in tournament play is the possibility of elimination. This should be discussed ahead of time because it is a reality—but it should not be something to focus on. The focus needs to be this: When the team does the things they are prepared to do, elimination is not an option. The discussion about elimination should focus more on ways to prevent it and about the confidence needed to face it only when it happens, not before it happens. The reality is that only one team does not have to deal with facing elimination, and the focus of your team should be on being that team.

When you step into the tournament setting, the strategy you are prepared to use against each opponent is extremely important. Having access to your opponents' tendencies, strengths, and weaknesses is necessary to develop a strategy to defeat them. You can secure that information by talking to someone who has played them. If you already have played them, analyze the strategies that worked and those that didn't work and make the adjustments. An example of this would be if you played a team before the postseason and lost to them. Use positive strategies to exploit the areas in which they beat you before. Convince your team that you now have the answers and if the team is able to execute the adjustments, they will be successful.

For example, one season we faced the top pitcher in the country, who threw only rise balls. I secured the videotape of the regular season game and edited it to show how most of the rise balls were out of the strike zone. I also showed my team a few of the pitches that were hittable and explained the adjustment we were going to use to better recognize the difference. That analysis allowed us to be successful against her. We practiced the adjustment and ultimately defeated that team to advance in the tournament.

Another key is to recognize your opponent's strength and plan what your team intends to do to neutralize that strength. For example, we knew the way to defeat one of our opponents was to keep their first three batters off the base paths. Our focus went to which pitches to throw to accomplish that goal. Then, if they still managed to hit the ball, the defense knew it was crucial to get them out. We believed that if we took away their strength, it would force them to change their strategy and give us a better chance to win.

There are many adjustments your team can make to be successful. The key to that success is inspiring your team to believe that if they execute, they will be successful.

Another key area in fastpitch softball is pitching. I have found over the years that usually one pitcher on the team can get on a roll and pitch at her top level. If this occurs, that pitcher should throw until she runs into a problem. Recognize who is stepping up and go with her. Plan to forego your pitching rotation in the postseason, and put your best pitcher on the mound every game unless you have two pitchers who are equally talented and the best in the nation.

Other elements that may occur in the challenge of postseason should be focused on throughout the year, like having to play back-to-back games in the loser's bracket, for example. If your team is in its best condition and realizes multiple games are possible, it is easier for them to compete in those scenarios. What can also make the difference is the way you handle the situation if the team does lose and thus goes into the multiple-game mode. In one College World Series, our team got killed in our opening game. Everyone on our team made an error, and the game was over in five innings. That loss was so devastating to the players that I believed how it was handled would determine whether we lost the next game or continued in the tournament. When I walked into the room to talk about the game, I was greeted by the most crushed players I had ever seen. The worse thing in the world I could have done would have been to focus on anything negative, so I decided to move forward in a positive way. We had put on new batting gloves before that game. I walked into the room and told everyone to pass their batting gloves to me. When I collected them all, I tossed them in the garbage can and told the team those batting gloves were the problem. Everyone breathed a sigh of relief, and we moved forward to our next opponent. We also talked about the fact that even though we lost, we could still win the tournament and how great it would be to have had such an embarrassing performance in our first game and then win the whole thing. We were then on our way and consequently finished second in the nation. We didn't accept defeat; we handled it. And it made just the difference my team needed to succeed after the loss.

Final Analysis

Building a program that is successful in tournaments and postseason is not an easy task. The preparation and goals are only part of developing that success. The philosophy of the coach and program help do the rest. There are some specific suggestions that may be able to help if they fit your philosophy. These suggestions can work at all levels and abilities.

- The coach should focus on the athletes first.
- A positive approach is effective; make sure anything negative is dealt with properly and turned into a positive.
- Surround your program with the best of everything within budget restraints (i.e., facilities, fund-raising, booster clubs, fan support, staying in top-notch hotels or motels).
- Make sure the players give back to the community as role models (e.g., children's hospitals, Special Olympics).
- Attitudes need to be the best; players should carry themselves with a great deal of class.
- Work harder than everyone else.
- Make partners of academics and softball.
- Be flexible and adjust.
- Goals, dedication, loyalty, responsibility, accountability, trust, respect, and confidence all allow for a refuse-to-lose attitude.
- Quality not quantity. Do things right every time.

There are so many more suggestions that could be mentioned, but keep this in mind: When you want your team to overachieve, they must only believe.

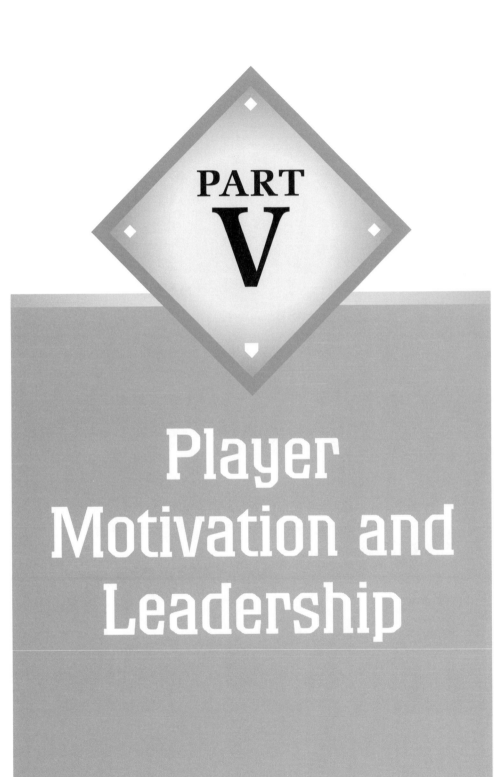

PART

V

Player Motivation and Leadership

Winning the Mental Game

Jeff Janssen

Coaches know that a variety of factors go into building a championship team. Obviously, proper mechanics, sound strategies, and physical factors such as strength, speed, and agility play a critical role. However, the teams that consistently achieve the most success are the ones that also have the mental edge.

How much do mental factors play in your team's success? A survey found that Olympic athletes attributed roughly 70 to 80 percent of their success to mental factors such as confidence, attitude, focus, competitiveness, and dedication. Interestingly, they attributed only 30 percent of their success to physical talent. Thus, it seems that while mechanics and muscles are important, it is often your team's mental game that ultimately determines success.

While most coaches and athletes believe that the mental game determines at least 50 percent of their team's success, few coaches invest more than 10 percent of their time developing and strengthening it. Imagine what would happen if you spent only 10 percent of your practice time on hitting. Obviously you couldn't expect much out of your hitters because of the little time devoted to it. Similarly, how can you expect your players to be focused, confident, and mentally tough when you only invest a minimal amount of time on it?

You and your players achieve two primary benefits through working on the mental game.

First, your athletes begin maximizing the potential they have inside them. When athletes mentally commit themselves to set inspiring goals, practice with quality, stay focused on the game, play with confidence, and stay mentally tough in pressure situations, they consistently play well.

Second, by winning the mental game, your players cut down on the number of frustrating mental mistakes that often cost games. If your team is like most, in some games last season your opponents didn't necessarily beat you but you lost to yourself. In these games the teams physically match up, but mentally, your players just weren't ready to play and compete: they were intimidated by the pitcher; they tightened up and couldn't get a bunt down in a critical situation; they didn't cover or throw to the right base; or they didn't adjust to the umpire's strike zone. The most frustrating losses for coaches are those attributed to mental mistakes. Although talentwise you could have won, a lack of mental toughness led to the loss.

Odds are that many of your losses can be traced to one or more breakdowns in the mental game. Fortunately all of these problems are correctable and can be avoided if you invest a small amount of time to develop your team's mental game. Just as you spend time teaching your players how to place their hands and feet for success so, too, can you teach them how to place their heads and hearts for success. If you win the mental game, you force teams to beat you rather than losing to yourself.

The Five Fundamentals of a Winning Mental Game

The mental game revolves around five important mental characteristics: commitment, composure, concentration, confidence, and consistency.* These five skills are the critical elements athletes need to be able to perform at their potential. They form the basis of the mental training program I use with athletes. Let's examine each of these mental skills and discuss some strategies for developing each of them.

Commitment

Getting athletes to perform to their potential really starts with commitment. Players must be committed in order to work hard, practice with quality, and improve their skills. In essence, commitment means that players play with passion, are intense competitors, and put their hearts into the game. Unfortunately, commitment can sometimes be difficult to find in today's athletes. How can you as a coach get your players to be more motivated and committed?

In our fall ball meetings with our freshmen at Arizona, one of the first things we have them do is think ahead to the end of their careers. They project ahead four or five years to the end of the year banquet following their senior seasons. As they imagine this future event, we ask them to think about and note what they would like the coaches to say about them when their college careers are over. We also ask them to consider how they would like to be remembered by their teammates, support staff, parents, and fans. In essence, we are asking them to explore what type of impact and legacy they would like to leave on the program. We encourage them to envision their legacy before they even see their first pitch on the college level.

When your players examine the kind of careers they want to have, you begin to discover their reasons and motivation for playing. This exercise reveals what drives each player to succeed as well as keys to motivating them. Many players want to be remembered as being hard workers, team players, effective leaders, and winners, as players who are committed and have a great attitude. Some talk of the desire to win conference and national championships during their careers. Others may talk about All-Conference, All-American, and even Player of the Year honors. Not surprisingly, virtually every player wants to leave a positive and lasting legacy on the program. Your challenge as a coach is to harness the power of these

---

* If you would like to evaluate your athletes on each of these categories, I encourage you to visit my Web site at www.jeffjanssen.com to take a simple online evaluation.

motives and encourage your players to commit to working on their long-term legacy now.

The difference between wishes and mission is commitment. Commitment is the single most important factor that differentiates champions from the average. While every athlete wishes she could be successful, only a few make the commitment to pursue their dreams. Commitment entails action. It means deciding your destiny not by fate or luck but by determination, sweat, and hard work. Inform your players that a commitment is a promise to themselves that they will consistently do what is necessary to achieve their mission.

If your players want to be remembered as being dedicated and successful at the end of their careers, show them how they can start working on that legacy today by setting daily goals. Each day they are presented with numerous opportunities to become the players they would like to be. They can commit to being leaders in conditioning workouts or they can choose to slack off. They can commit to coming to practice early and taking extra batting practice, or they can choose to show up just seconds before practice starts. They can commit to approaching drills with a positive and enthusiastic attitude or they can choose to be lazy and cut corners. Help your players understand that the commitments they make on a daily basis either build or erode the legacy they want to leave.

One of the saddest things I see is when seniors look back on their careers with regrets. They regret not working harder during the off-seasons to improve their game. They regret not taking advantage of practices and coaches who were willing to help them. They regret not being more confident and aggressive when they stepped in the box. They regret how they cheated themselves and their team because they did not start giving it their all until it was too late.

Invest the time to sit down with each player and ask her about her long-term goals and how she would like to be remembered. After you discover what she wants to achieve, help her set short-term goals to improve her skills. Then encourage her to commit to working hard on a daily basis.

Composure

To perform successfully, players must maintain control of themselves. Great players have the poise to handle pressure situations rather than tensing up, becoming frustrated, or playing scared. Thus, in addition to teaching your players hitting, fielding, and throwing skills, you must also teach them how to remain composed, especially under pressure.

At Arizona, we use an analogy of a traffic light, originated by sport psychology consultant Ken Ravizza (Ravizza and Hanson 1995), to discuss and strengthen our team's mental game. A green light mental game means that the player is focused, confident, positive, aggressive, in the flow, and in control of herself. Mental green lights lead to players who have their heads in the game, have quality at bats, and consistently make routine plays.

A yellow light mental game means that a player is frustrated, distracted, stressed, tentative, and losing control. Mental yellow lights show up on the field when a player is pressing at the plate and swings at pitches out of the strike zone; when she forgets to check the signs, runners, or number of outs; or when she tenses up and can't seem to throw a strike. Yellow lights decrease the player's chances of playing to her potential because her mental game gets in her own way.

A red light mental game means the player has lost control, is extremely angry, and is very frustrated and negative—or she may be totally apathetic and have given up. If the player is still on the field when she is in a red light, she is worried about looking foolish at the plate, praying the ball is not going to be hit to her in the field, and scared to death as a pitcher of getting hit hard. When a player is in a red light, she gives herself very little chance of playing well because her head is not positioned for success.

Composure means getting the player into a green light before practices and games. It means helping her stay in a green light despite distractions, pressures, mistakes, and criticism. Mental toughness means staying in a green or quickly getting back to a green light even when it is very easy to go into a yellow or red light. We encourage players to recognize when they are slipping into a yellow light and work to mentally change it to green before allowing themselves to drop into red. Mental strategies for doing this are presented in the following sections.

Concentration

Concentration is another critical skill for athletes. Because focus is so important for hitting, let's examine the role it plays. Imagine this scenario: Bottom of the seventh, you're down one run, you've got runners on second and third with two outs. Would you rather have a batter at the plate who has a few mechanical flaws in her swing but who you know is mentally tough, confident, focused, aggressive, and looking forward to the opportunity to come through for the team? Or would you rather have your most mechanically sound hitter standing in the box physically, but her mind is a million miles away because it is filled with doubts, distractions, and fears?

While mechanics are definitely an important aspect of softball, a poor mental game can cause them to break down, especially in pressure situations. How many times have overanxious hitters cost you games because they swing at bad pitches? How often have you seen a player freeze up and not be able to pull the trigger because her mind was too cluttered or distracted?

While you spend countless hours in the cages and on the field trying to perfect a player's swing, more often than not a weak mental game is the cause of poor at bats. The good hitter whom you see in relatively stress-free practice situations is not always the same person who shows up at game time. Rather than spending an extra 10 minutes in the cage perfecting her mechanics, perhaps your time is better invested in strengthening her mental game.

What your players choose to focus on both before and during their at bats is a key factor in determining their success (Janssen and O'Brien 1997). Successful hitters learn how to focus their minds in ways that maximize their chances of being successful. To help your players have more consistent quality at bats, encourage them to focus in the following ways.

Focus on the Controllables

Often players let factors they have little or no control over get into their heads and take them out of their game. Umpires are a good example. How many times have you seen a player blame an umpire's strike zone for her failures? While umpires' zones can fluctuate, your players have little to no control over their calls. Instead help your players focus on adjusting to the umpire's strike zone rather than constantly blaming and battling him or her. Convince your players it is a battle that's out of their control and one that they therefore will never win. Don't allow them (or yourself) to use terrible umpiring as an excuse for why you can't perform. Make a mental adjustment.

Focus on the Present

The most important at bat of the game is always the present one because it's the only one your players can do something about. Too often hitters drag thoughts of previous bad at bats into their present focus. Dwelling on the past only clutters their minds and divides their focus. The key is to take it one at bat, and even one pitch, at a time.

One way to teach this concept is to talk about bad at bats as bricks. Just as a player would have a tough time hitting well while holding on to a brick, so too would she have a difficult time mentally hanging on to a previous at bat. Have your players let go of bad at bats by encouraging them to convert them to mental game lessons, such as thinking, *The pitcher is going outside to me, so I need to go with it and drive it the opposite way.* Lessons help players focus on what they want to do right for the next time rather than dwelling on what went wrong the last time.

Focus on the Positive

One of the most common but easily correctable mental errors is when hitters try to negate the negative. For example, they negate the negative when they step into the box thinking, *Don't strike out* or *Don't swing at bad pitches.* What hitters fail to realize when they rehearse this self-talk is that their minds have a funny way of disregarding the *don't.* These words actually register in their minds as *Strike out* and *Swing at bad pitches.*

Since the body seeks to fulfill the wishes of the mind, have your players focus on the positive things they want to execute. Tell them (and have them tell themselves) to *See the ball, Hit the ball, Hit your pitch,* and *Put a good swing on a good pitch.* Helping your hitters focus on the positive things they want to accomplish is much more effective than focusing on the negative things they want to avoid.

Focus on the Process

Being obsessed with outcomes such as batting averages is often a hitter's worst downfall. Batting averages can distract hitters so much that Arizona Coach Mike Candrea never lets his players see them (Janssen and Candrea 1994). Instead he has them focus on quality at bats where the goal is to see the ball well and hit it hard somewhere. The focus is much more on the process of successful hitting—seeing the ball well, being balanced, having relaxed hands and a calm and clear mind. If your hitters can take care of the process of successful hitting, you are much more likely to get the results you want.

To help your players focus on and acknowledge the importance of the process, congratulate them when they hit the ball hard, regardless of whether it is a hit or an out in the scorebook. Our players realize the power of the process and celebrate hard hit outs as much as hits.

Confidence

At some time during a season, a player may find herself at the plate with the game on the line. Runners are in scoring position, and you and your team are relying on her to get the clutch hit to tie the score or get the game-winning RBI. Why do some players tighten up and fall apart under this kind of pressure, while others remain calm, cool, and collected? The answer is confidence.

Believing you can be successful is more than half the battle. Ty Cobb once said, "The great hitters operate on the theory that the pitcher is more afraid of them than they are the pitcher." Your hitter must believe she has what it takes to perform in the clutch. She must convince herself that her ability to hit the ball is greater than the demands of the situation.

There are four basic sources of confidence that your players can draw from to help them perform in virtually any situation both on and off the field: strengths, past successes, preparation, and praise (Janssen 1996). By developing and reminding themselves of these four areas, your players have the mental tools necessary to cultivate and create confidence. Furthermore, one of your biggest roles as a coach is that of confidence builder (Janssen and Dale 2002). Use these four sources for building confidence to help your players create the mental toughness necessary to come through in the clutch.

An effective source for building confidence is to have your players reflect on and remind themselves of their strengths. Because players are often too critical of themselves, they have a tendency to forget about the good things they can do. To help your players remember their strengths, have each player list them on a sheet of paper. Or taking this exercise a step further, have your players go around and list each other's strengths. Not only is this a great way to build a player's confidence, but it is also a good team building activity (Janssen 1999).

One of the more powerful sources of confidence comes from past successes. If a player has had success in a previous similar situation, she is much more likely to feel confident when she is in the situation again. If she's done it once before, then she can do it again. Have your players list all of the great games they have had as well as their clutch hits. Reflecting on past highlights is a great way to create the confidence necessary for future successes.

Quality preparation could be considered the mother of confidence. When players work hard in the cages, off the tee, in soft toss, and on the field during practice, they earn the right to feel confident during the game. Confidence is earned and built through hours of hard work and gallons of sweat. Additionally, quality preparation can take the form of studying a pitcher's tendencies, talking to teammates who have already faced her, and developing a consistent mental hitting routine. Hard work and quality preparation help your players feel like they deserve to be successful.

A final source of confidence comes from praise. Have your players list the compliments and encouraging words that have been said about their games. These words might have come from teammates, parents, opponents, and most importantly you. The feedback you give your players has a tremendous effect on them, some more than others. Ask yourself and your coaching staff, "Are we building or eroding our players' confidence?"

While Arizona coach Mike Candrea is an expert at the mechanics of hitting, he's perhaps better at helping players build their confidence through his positive and encouraging feedback. Remember, the level of confidence you show in a player often has a big effect on the confidence she has in herself.

Consistency

One of the telltale signs of being a great player is consistency. Some players may occasionally have a game or two where they play well, but the truly great players perform well on a consistent basis. It doesn't matter whether it is a scrimmage situation or the seventh inning of the national championship game of the Women's College World Series; great players are ready to do battle.

How can you help your players become more consistent? The key to consistent hitting begins with proper preparation and thinking before each at bat. Proper mental preparation allows your hitters to be more focused and confident when they actually step into the box. It is this focused and confident mindset that allows your hitters to have more quality at bats. When your players can have more quality at bats, they become more consistent hitters.

To help our players become more consistent hitters, we encourage them to develop a consistent mental routine before each at bat (Ravizza & Hanson 1995; table 20.1). This routine typically involves a certain sequence of thoughts and actions that are done before every at bat. The primary goal of the mental routine is to help your hitter properly prepare herself and create the mindset necessary to have a quality at bat. The routine helps the player focus on the process of hitting, which if done well, maximizes her chances of getting the outcome you both want—hits.

TABLE 20.1

A Hitter's Mental Routine

Phase	Goal	Location	Methods
1	Assume control	In the dugout	Deep breath, focus
2	Plan	On deck	Watch pitcher, time warm-up swings with pitcher
3	Trust	In the batter's box	Deep breath, turn off thinking, fix eyes on pitcher's thigh

The first phase of a mental routine for hitting involves making sure that the hitter is in control of herself. A player who is not in control of herself may be dwelling on past problems or letting things outside her control take her out of her game. A player who is not in control of herself has a distracted mind and a tense body. This stressed-out mindset does not make for good hitting. Thus, the player needs to be able to control herself before she is able to control her hitting. She should assume control in the dugout before she is in the hole.

If she finds herself somewhat distracted, frustrated, or tentative, she should use her time in the dugout to regain control of herself before bringing this ineffective mindset into the box with her. She can regain control by taking a deep breath and using the refocusing ideas covered in the concentration and confidence sections.

The second phase of an effective mental routine is planning. The planning stage occurs as the player is on deck and until the time she steps in the box. During this time she can be watching the pitcher and timing her swings with her delivery. She also should be scanning the field so that she begins to get a feeling for what she might be called on to do for her upcoming at bat. By the end of the planning stage, your hitter should understand what she wants to accomplish with her at bat and have the confidence to do it.

The final stage of an effective mental routine for hitting is trusting. Trusting means that the player has a clear mind and is focused only on the release point of the pitcher so that she can pick up the ball as early as possible and see it well. In essence, she is turning off the thinking and analyzing part of her mind and allowing herself to trust her hands to react. Most problems occur when a hitter is still thinking and analyzing when she steps into the box. Too much thinking causes a hitter to be overanxious or freeze up. A trusting mindset is the key to letting her hands (and the rest of her mechanics) react naturally.

To help your hitters get into the trust mode, encourage them to take a breath before they step into the box. This breath should symbolize to them that they are emptying their mind of the thinking and analyzing and are now stepping in with a calm and clear mind. Have them fix their eyes and fine-tune their focus externally on the pitcher's thigh area, so they pick up the ball as quickly as possible.

Even though I used hitting as an example, pitchers, infielders, and outfielders can also use mental routines. The key is to help your players run through a quick mental checklist to make sure that they are in control of themselves, focused on the situation, and ready to trust themselves and react naturally.

Final Thoughts

Obviously mechanics and physical skills are important in the game of softball. However, mental skills like commitment, composure, concentration, confidence, and consistency are absolutely critical for allowing your players to perform to their potential. In addition to your time working in the cages, catching your pitchers, and hitting fungoes, be sure to invest some time developing your team's mental game. In doing so your team gains the critical mental edge by minimizing mental mistakes and consistently maximizing its potential.

References

Janssen, J. 1996. *The mental makings of champions: How to win the mental game.* Tucson, AZ: Winning the Mental Game.

Janssen, J. 1999. *Championship team building: What every coach needs to know to build a motivated, committed, and cohesive team.* Tucson, AZ: Winning the Mental Game.

Janssen, J., and M. Candrea. 1994. *Mental training for softball: A guide and workbook for athletes and coaches.* Tucson, AZ: Winning the Mental Game.

Janssen, J., and G. Dale. 2002. *The seven secrets of successful coaches.* Tucson, AZ: Winning the Mental Game.

Janssen, J., and L. O'Brien. 1997. *Psychology of sensational hitting: How you can become a more focused, confident, and consistent hitter.* Tucson, AZ: Winning the Mental Game.

Ravizza, K., and T. Hanson. 1995. *Heads up baseball.* Indianapolis: Masters Press.

CHAPTER TWENTY-ONE

Building Team Chemistry

Rhonda Revelle

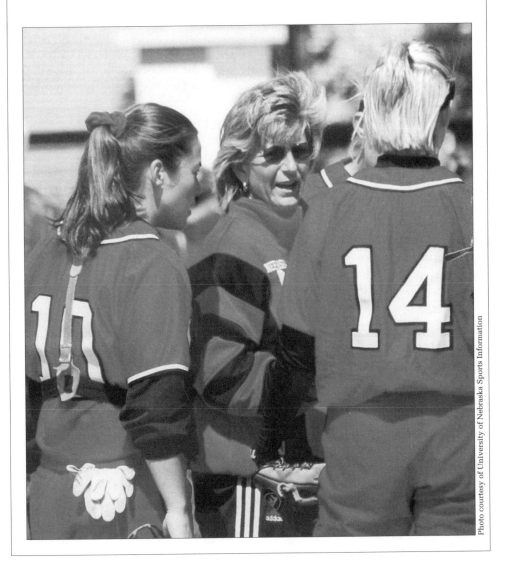

Players repeatedly express their desire to play on a team that has unity, cohesion, and respect for one another. However, one of the greatest challenges of a coaching staff is building and maintaining a team-first philosophy among the players.

Like any other living thing, team building is a constant work in progress. It takes the same focus and energy that any healthy relationship would need to grow and maintain trust, communication, respect, commitment, and love. People need to be motivated to build a team, just as they need motivation to reach their physical potential. Team building, like physical skills, can be improved with proper practice, persistence, and discipline. Pat Summit, University of Tennessee women's basketball coach, says, "Teamwork is taught. You don't just lump a group of people together in a room and call them a team and expect them to behave like one."

We have all coached both the team that has one collective vision and the team that has as many focal points as players on the roster. It is without question that the team working toward a common goal is the more rewarding and enjoyable to coach. Generally, this is the team that also achieves the most success.

As an athlete, I enjoyed the feelings associated with committing to a team mission, battling in the trenches together and rising above adversity and conflict. Working, struggling, and experiencing the pain of defeat and the joy of victory are what develops the loving family-like bonds. Victories were the most humbling because I reflected on the sweat, persistence, and dedication that went into the realization of those goals. My spirit would soar, and my love of and for the team filled my being. It is an addicting feeling, one you want to share and one you want everyone to have the opportunity to experience. But, it cannot be achieved alone, for it is a feeling born and cultivated with a team.

Trust

I don't know that anyone is an expert on team building because individuals are as different as snowflakes, and each team is as distinct as the day's sunset. However, I do believe that there are some absolutes to good team building, the first of which is trust. Tom Osborne, retired football coach at the University of Nebraska, said, "Trust is the cornerstone of a team. Without it, a team cannot function to it's potential. Once trust is broken, it is never fully regained."

Trust is developed by sharing experiences and time, gaining knowledge about an individual, and self-disclosure. We spend a considerable amount of energy on creating trust among our team. It starts with recruiting talented people of sound character who value honesty and a strong work ethic.

We have a team meeting to discuss the significance of the recruiting process in determining who meets our standards and fits into our program. We talk about what it takes to be gracious hosts and what qualities we are looking for in potential teammates. The players trust that the coaches are doing their jobs by screening prospects academically, athletically, and socially. In turn, the coaches trust the players to provide a genuine and thorough report after the recruits have left campus. I always ask the players to ask themselves these questions: Would I want this person as a teammate? Would I want this person to represent the softball program and the university? Do I trust that this person has similar values, goals, and intentions that we do? We have had players approach us with red flags about recruits. We have trusted their information and on occasion have ceased recruitment because of the team's feedback.

Trust is developed both on and off the field. In practice, we try to create an environment that encourages risk taking. Coaches understand the stages of learning and are patient in allowing that maturation process to unfold. Errors (unless careless in nature) are not seen as a deterrent, but rather as an opportunity to push the learning curve. Players also learn to trust their teammates. For example, when a player makes a bad throw but a teammate makes a great catch, she thanks her teammate for helping her out. Teamwork helps people know that they are not out there alone and that they can trust a team member to put themselves on the line to ensure the success of the team.

Trust needs to be reinforced constantly, which is why our daily routines are so important. The players know what to expect; there is a consistency of behavior, preparation, organization, and expectation. One day, I posted practice just like I had every day for many years, but I changed the font style of type. Several players said something to me about it. Now, changing the font is not any violation of trust, obviously. The point I am making is that disciplined athletes have a healthy obssession with ritual and routine—that's what establishes trust. I couldn't care less what the font style is, but I am glad they called it on me. It showed me that they craved routine, and it is always my pleasure to give it to them, no matter how small the request is.

Players want to know that you care about them as people, too. There is a saying: Players don't care how much you know until they know how much you care. We see this consistently, and when players know that their coaches care, they trust us more. In the fall, we run a coach-supervised study hall. Although the university athletic department has a monitored study hall, the coaches take the time, so student athletes know that the coaching staff care about their academic success. We also have 30-minute meetings twice a month to discuss many aspects of life. This is where many tears are shed, but with every fallen tear, trust is nurtured.

Communication

In my experience, team unity is most often threatened by lack of communication, by miscommunication, or by malicious communication (i.e., gossip, slander, or rudeness). Thus, effective communication is a critical element to team building. You cannot build a trusting team without honest and consistent communication, both verbal and nonverbal. "If you can't communicate with people, you have dramatically narrowed your chances for success. Effective communication is the best problem solver there is," says former Boston Celtics coach Rick Pitino. Communication takes many forms, including discussing goals, strategies, fears, concerns, joys, and other personal and professional items. We believe in the importance of communication so much that our team is on information overload at times.

Our communication starts in the summer when players receive two or three letters from the coaching staff. The letters cover general information, debrief the season that just finished, preview the upcoming year, and set goals and strategies both individually and from a team standpoint. The communication process is a two-way street, as we always give the players a writing assignment that involves answering meaningful philosophical questions. Summertime is also when we take applications for team captain. We believe that being a team captain is a job, so we have people write an essay applying for the job. The applicants are screened and interviewed, and then selected by the coaching staff. This is a surefire way to communicate to your captains and team the importance of the position.

The communication process continues the first week of school when we have a meeting detailing the necessary ingredients to running a class act. Players take notes because they are tested on the material before they ever step onto the practice field. We want to be sure they understand that being a member of our team is a privilege and not a right, so they should conduct themselves accordingly. At our kickoff picnic, they divide into four groups, and each has a series of questions they discuss among themselves before they report back their responses to the entire group.

Once practice starts, several routines play a part in being in the system and having pride in the tradition of the program. First, a different player each day starts practice with a theme, thought, or quote. Second, before they begin their group jog, their gloves all have a ball in them and are clustered uniformly together. After they stretch, a team captain has a players-only huddle to discuss the goals of practice that day. When the coaches get too close to their circle, they are asked to move away. Players are routinely sought out for information regarding what they feel they need more or less of in the practice setting to help the team reach its potential. At the conclusion of practice each day, after closing remarks by coaches and announcements, the players are given the opportunity to make remarks or observations. Again, it is a two-way flow of communication between players and coaches.

Every couple of years, we take a personality inventory and have a master teacher interpret the results to enhance our knowledge of one another and assist us in communicating better among and within the group. This use of psychology has been an extremely valuable tool because we gain awareness in how we and others perceive and translate verbal and nonverbal stimuli. We get ideas of how we best respond to someone approaching us on a subject and also how we receive ideas as to how to deal with a person who has personality characteristics dissimilar from us. Bottom line, it gives us baseline language and a framework with how to engage dialogue with one another.

Finally communication is about listening effectively. A coach or teammate who is an effective listener is known by all as someone who really cares about people. It is critical that coaches not only solicit and listen carefully to the words of their athletes, but it is also imperative that we hear the tones and read their body language as well. Phil Jackson, Los Angeles Lakers coach, reveals, "Over the years I've learned to listen closely to players, not just to what they say, but also to their body language and silence between the words." Some players communicate more thoughts and feeling through nonverbal cues, and it is our responsibility to recognize and respond to those.

In my 30-minute meetings with individual players, I shut the door, forward my phone to voice mail, sit facing the player, lean forward, and look her in the eye. (I also keep a supply of tissues nearby.) I want her to know that during that period of time, she is the most important thing going on in my life. It is her time, and I am locked in and ready to listen. Pat Summit, University of Tennessee women's basketball coach, confesses, "The more I have listened to our players, the better I have known them and understood them. Listening has allowed me to become a better coach."

Respect

Like communication, exercising respect—including respect for self, the game, opponents, coaches, and teammates—does much to enhance team building. Respect is most precisely described in the biblical verse called the Golden Rule: "Do unto others as you would have them do unto you." Those words are all about respect and love. We believe in the magic of *please* and *thank you*. A sentence started or finished with a *please* or a *thank you* is a breeding ground for mutual respect among those involved in the conversation.

Respect for self is shown through our habits in nutrition, sleep, academics, time management, physical training, emotional/spiritual training, and social behavior. Coaches and specialists in these areas talk to our team about how to improve these aspects of their lives. We encourage development of the entire person. A softball career lasts only for a short period of time, compared to the lessons that can influence them for a lifetime.

To respect the game is an act of humility and civility. Respect for the game is displayed in many ways on our team. After practices, our players rake, manicure, and water the pitcher's mound, batter's box, and bull pens. On game day, we clean our cleats, organize our dugout, and handle our helmets carefully by setting them down rather than tossing them (in fact, a thrown or dropped helmet results in your removal from the game). After the game, whether on the road or at home, our rule is to leave all environments (dugout, locker room) in equal or better shape than how we found them. We do not allow our team to eat sunflower seeds because they get on the infield dirt and cannot be removed, and it is a deterrent to the grounds crew and their ability to maintain an immaculate infield.

We show respect for our opponents by shaking their hands before and after the game. Our cheers are about our team instead of being about the opponent. At home games, our fans are required to be sportsmanlike, and if they are not, a member of our booster club asks them to conform or leave the stadium. It is simply a value statement of our program to do everything we can with a classy attitude. Sometimes, the umpire is considered the opponent, but we still insist on treating the blue with respect. We find that players are a direct reflection of coaches in this regard. It starts at the top because if coaches are respectful of the umpiring crew, players tend to follow.

Showing respect to teammates and coaches on the field is a necessary ingredient to successful team building. Coaches and players take their sunglasses off so they look the person in the eye when they are having a conversation. When a player lays down a sacrifice, the entire team congratulates or thanks her. If a pitching change is being made, the pitcher coming out of the game hands the pitcher coming into the game the ball, and they have a short discussion about the opponents and then have some kind of physical contact (slap hands) before the original pitcher leaves the circle.

Every team is built by its everyday starters and its role players. The starters are the bricks and the role players are the mortar. You cannot construct a building or a team without both bricks and mortar. People do not drive by a house and say, "What beautiful mortar." No, the bricks get all of the attention. But can you imagine where the bricks would be without the mortar?

This is the lesson we try to teach our team. The respect with which the mortar is treated by their teammates and coaches is key in maintaining team chemistry throughout the season. We coaches keep these people at the forefront of our minds, and we publicly recognize or thank them for their contribution anytime it is appropriate to do so. Also from time to time, we pull them aside to let them know their meaning to the team. We believe people need to be needed and noticed, and we attempt to make sure we do both for these valuable team members.

Sincere compliments are a tremendous method of enhancing mutual respect. It sounds simple, but it is uncanny how many compliments that are thought in the head or felt in the heart are left unsaid. I encourage players to seize the moment. While visiting with some players about team issues, I found them to be very complimentary about some of their teammates. I said, "That is so kind. Do your teammates know that you feel that way? Have you ever told them?" I was surprised to find out that they had not even thought to tell them. Capturing the moment myself, I jumped in and asked, "How would it make you feel if someone said that to you?" Of course, they would be deeply touched. What an opportunity to sincerely and genuinely exchange respectful expressions from one teammate to another. Mother Teresa said, "Kind words are short and easy to speak, but their echoes are truly endless."

We also feel compelled to support our support staff. Our secretary, manager, laundry person, academic adviser, strength coach, nutritionist, massage therapist, field crew, booster club, sports information director, video technician, marketing specialist, and senior women's administrator are all integral cogs in our entire wheel. Our coaching staff's goal is to do random acts of kindness so that they know how appreciated they are. It could be an e-mail, stopping in their office just to say thanks, a Christmas gift, an invite to lunch on your dime, and so on. So often these people do not get the recognition that they deserve, but a sincere thank-you goes a long way.

Responsibility

In a team environment, having a committed coaching staff is as important as having committed players. Motivation breeds commitment, and committed, consistent, competent, and caring coaches escalate motivation in players. What also enhances motivation and commitment in players is when they are given responsibility for the team. Responsibility is empowering, and it gives the team a sense of ownership.

We always tell our team, "This is your team." However, if you say that, you need to back it with your actions. The coaches set a system of operation in place, and the players assist in defining the contents within the system.

A team is as strong as its leadership. Great leaders need to be self-controlled, hard working, accountable, good listeners, and effective communicators through adversity, conflict, and celebration. When players embody these characteristics, they earn the trust and respect from their teammates. Leaders have a lot of responsibility because all eyes are on them, and they are expected to walk their talk. This is why we have our captains apply for the position and write an essay explaining why they want to be team captains. Applicants have to answer these questions: What qualities do you possess that you feel would make you a strong team captain? What visions or aspirations do you have, and how would you make those visions or aspirations a reality? Their teammates understand the rigors team captains went through in the selection process, and the expectations of the position are known by all.

With input from the team, our captains make many team decisions. They work directly with me every year in writing our team code of conduct. They have input in the rules we should establish and the consequences for noncompliance. This has been an effective means of discipline because the team knows that the rules were greatly influenced by their peers. They more readily commit to the conduct regulations and hold each other accountable because it is the team's rules for the team versus the coaches' rules for the team. What has been interesting about this process is that the captains set just as strict if not stricter rules than the coaches.

We also have a team meeting at the same time each year to define team goals and the team theme and profess our commitment level to one another. Each player speaks to the group and states what she believes we need to do to achieve our team goals and how she plans to contribute en route to the team achieving its goals. This is a powerful gathering because each player is required to state her intentions, which in turn puts a responsibility on her to work to fulfill her goals for herself. Following the meeting, we send our most common team goals to a sign company to have them professionally made into a goal board. The goal board is then hung in the locker room so that it is the first thing they see when they walk in. It is a daily reminder of the team's commitment to team.

We realize that not all players have the same level of commitment and that several factors play a part such as playing time, maturation, level of ability, and so forth. Regardless of where they start on the commitment continuum, we attempt to manifest an ongoing pledge to being committed to the team. Our program's battle cry is "There is no single person more important than the team. We conduct a six-week course in the fall called Team Building Thru Me Building, where it is our aspiration to strengthen the level of commitment of each individual. If we are truly only as strong as our weakest link, then our desire is to internally stimulate a person to become more invested in the team. We define, discuss, role play, and strategize about topics as they relate to the team and how they relate to the self—topics like respect, trust, commitment, discipline, honesty, and the difference between self-love and unconditional love. There is so much sharing of ideas and self-disclosure going on in these sessions that we have found this to be a valuable team-bonding tool, one that binds them and deepens their sense of commitment to the team and to each other.

Love

With all the effort to form a trusting, communicating, respectful, and committed team, my greatest personal hope is that these young adults experience the wholeness of unconditional love during their careers. In my opinion, the greatest gift a coach can give an athlete is an environment in which she witnesses, participates in, and feels the giving and receiving of unconditional love.

Each year we have a team exercise that involves sharing the love. During the first semester, each team member privately writes in her journal about the positive traits of each of her teammates. At our Christmas party, we bring our journals and share the special qualities each person possesses. We discuss one person at a time, and that person takes notes (as do the coaches) in her journal so that she can capture the feelings of her teammates. The coaches have the list laminated, so the player not only has these observations in her own handwriting in her journals but also in print to be displayed in her locker, carried in her ball bag, or posted wherever else she deems meaningful. This annual event is much anticipated, the results are long lasting (a lifetime in many cases), love and tears flow abundantly, and it really sets the stage for the true meaning of the holiday season.

Some of our most loving moments have originated with conflict. This is a critical life lesson to learn. It often takes differences to get to the heart of the matter or to seek a solution to a problem. However, it also takes courage and vulnerability to risk speaking up in honesty. Conflict can be resolved if handled with civility, and the relationship can actually improve because of the adversity. A strong foundation of trust and respect is essential for the positive to come out of the negative.

Our team had a three-hour blowout meeting after a tough loss during the middle of a season. Before the meeting, many were angry, sad, disappointed, and dejected. But the meeting ended with a renewal of faith in each other because it was structured to air out the issues with the intent to communicate honestly and work toward resolve, compromise, and solutions. It actually turned the corner on our season, and we went on to win 38 of the next 42 ball games despite the fact that we experienced three key injuries that caused us to work nine different lineup combinations in the infield alone.

Another example of unconditional love was displayed when tragedy struck one of our players who learned of the suicide death of her mother. Her mother was a single parent, and the team understood that the player's financial and emotional state was dismal. They gathered around her and would not allow her to be alone. They cried with her, held her, and just sat with her in the silent times. They made her a videotape letting her know how much she was loved. When she was out of the state, they sent her a care package of their own personal belongings (stuffed animals, favorite sweatshirt, Bible) so that she could have a piece of them with her at all times. They had a prayer and phone chain that kept in constant contact with her, and they raised over $1,200 on their college budgets to help her in her financial crisis. They did all of this and more out of pure love. I honestly do not know if I have ever been more proud of a team in my entire life.

Final Thoughts

Team building is really about relationship building. When we nurture trust, respect, communication, responsibility, and love for and with one another, we have a cohesive and unified team. When we have a team with cohesion and unity, we also have a team with synergy and passion. And that, for most of us, is truly what successful coaching is all about. As so eloquently stated by our pitching coach, Lori Sippel, "As the years roll by and the scoreboard fades, it is the people, the friendships and love shared, and the remembrance of the journey that will glow ever brighter."

CHAPTER TWENTY–TWO

Developing Responsible Athletes

Elaine Sortino

Photo courtesy of Tim Winn, Rapid Eye L.L.C.

Teaching your players to be responsible and accountable is an ongoing effort. It requires a great deal of time, attention, and communication on many levels. Not only in the sport of softball, but in every arena of our lives, responsibility and accountability are necessary components as we strive to achieve success.

We refer to responsibility and accountability (the R&A words) on a daily basis in our program. To us, they represent how well we achieve as individuals and as a team both on and off the softball field. As we built our softball program, we found the following elements necessary in building a responsible and accountable team.

Identifying Individuals With a Solid Core Value

In the recruiting process, we work eagerly to identify a pool of young people who are talented and athletic. This is where the process should really start as we work with equal intensity to identify a solid core value in the people we bring to our program.

Our definition of a solid core value encompasses many traits, including honesty, trust, determination, intelligence, unselfishness, diligence, compassion, and, of course, a true love of softball. It is a lot easier to recognize athleticism and talent than it is to find the core value of the individuals we recruit. We need to work hard at trying to learn the core of the person we are considering. It requires a lot of communication, which is not always easy, as time and the amount of contact available to us is limited.

Admittedly, our contact, telephone conversations, and e-mail can be extremely superficial, so it takes a great deal of listening, watching, and inquiring to try to get to know what makes up the individual. As athleticism is necessary to teach a player to be skillful, it would be impossible to teach responsibility and accountability without some base of solid core value.

It seems obvious that a straight-A student would be a sure bet for having a good core value. Yet we all know that there are many players who work diligently, but their best might be only a C in the classroom or a .275 batting average for the year. Their core may be just as solid as our leading players and best students. Neither talent nor intelligence has any effect on diminishing their capacity for being able to exemplify the R&A words. Players who are accountable and responsible share similar core values, and over the years, our most successful teams comprised a majority of such individuals.

While it is possible to teach R&A to an individual without core values, it is extremely challenging. It is difficult for an individual to leave her core to become something she is not.

Making the Investment

As coaches, we tend to expect (or readily assume) coaching staff and players share the same investment. When players are deficient in their capacity to invest, coaches typically find themselves frustrated with their teams.

Teaching our players how to make an investment is paramount to the level at which they are responsible and accountable to the program, to their careers, and most importantly to their lives. Their ability to sustain their investment is challenged and nurtured both by their successes and failures. Most importantly, throughout this process our players need to understand that this is pefectly okay.

Whenever we buy something or commit to what we value, our level of responsibility and accountability is raised significantly. We need to talk with our players frequently about the level of their investment in their goals and mission throughout the season.

We remind our players about the rental car versus the dream car, borrowed from Jeff Janssen's book *Championship Team Building*. As he points out, there is little initial investment in the rental. We just stand in line, sign some papers, and leave with a brand new car. Often, these cars are abused and mistreated. When the rental car is finally brought back, it doesn't really matter how it looks or what kind of shape it's in. We just turn over the keys and walk away.

The dream car is a different story. It takes a long time to work and save to make that initial down payment. We have to remain accountable and responsible to that car in many ways—keeping up payments, washing and waxing it, and maintaining the engine. When something goes wrong with the car, we quickly take care of it because it really matters and is important to us.

We remind our players frequently of the different ways they have made investments throughout the season. It is important to remember all that has gone into the making of one single season. We believe that the level to which our players are capable of investing directly reflects their capability to remain responsible and accountable throughout the season.

Creating this awareness and acknowledging their investment is a critical part of the process in teaching and enhancing a player's level of living up to the R&A words.

Making the Commitment

Players who are heavily invested become quickly and deeply committed and as a result are accountable and responsible to our program's goals. The hard part is when our players are faced with the regular challenges that inevitably present themselves.

The challenge of running early in the morning or weightlifting on a Friday afternoon, especially in the off-season, is a lot easier for a player who is committed to her team than the player who is not. It is critical to frequently remind players that these difficulties are a normal part of the process. A player's ability to persevere forecasts her level of investment and commitment to the team.

Checking in with each others (reality checks) and reflecting on why they are here and what they have at risk are key to helping our players evaluate their commitments throughout the season.

We periodically ask them to assess their individual commitments and those of their teammates. Our evaluation is anonymous and confidential. The players are given their own particular results from their teammates and coaches.

These reality checks are often revealing and help players understand how their individual commitment is perceived by fellow team members and the coaching staff. Looking at yourself through the eyes of others can be a helpful self-reflection. More importantly, the repetition of this exercise hopefully teaches them to perform reality checks on their own, which is useful later in life.

Learning about commitment makes them do things because it is the right thing to do, not because of negative consequences. When players capable of making strong commitments dominate a team, the R&A words become the team's standard.

Setting the Bar

Whatever level program we are trying to establish, our players can only be accountable and responsible if they are involved in setting the bar for that particular season. We believe it is important to directly involve players in making their commitments during the season. It is a given fact team members are most responsible to standards that they feel are important. As coaches, we need to be open and encourage our players to set their standards. This identity formation takes time and communication among them as a group with and without us.

At the beginning of each season, we talk about what we have previously accomplished, how we would like to be better, what we need to keep, and what we need to change. Having players directly involved helps keep them accountable and responsible both on and off the field to achieve their goals. It is also important as the season goes along to give the team the opportunity to reevaluate the bar so that needed adjustments can be made.

Over the years, we have found that our best teams have handed out their own commandments, rather than our coaching staff making the presentation from the top of the mountain. In the end, the team that is responsible and accountable does what is right for that reason and not because of a list of consequences.

Communicating Honestly

Let's face it, being honest is one of the hardest things to do. Over the years we have stressed to our staff and players to really buy into just how important communication is for the team to be responsible and accountable to each other.

On teams, as in life, peer acceptance and approval are very important. Additionally, we have found that sensitivity to how another person is feeling is critical, especially in times of difficulty. We try to teach our players to be honest with each other because it is one of the most important requirements for being responsible and accountable to each other.

We encourage players to be compassionate with each other and try to put themselves in each other's shoes before saying what may need to be said. Over the years, it has taken a great deal of time to be able to achieve clear communication, not only among the team but also from coaches to players. In the end, there is no possible way that responsibility or accountability within the system can be achieved at any level without continual and understandable communication.

Developing Leadership

In trying to teach our players the R&A words, the role of leadership remains paramount, and the coach needs to be the role model in this area. It would be difficult for players to exemplify behavior that they do not see emulated by their leadership, and that example starts with the head coach. Assistant coaches need to be an integral part of that system, too.

Our team always selects captains, but before that process takes place, we spend considerable time discussing the qualities necessary for good leadership. Once the team has chosen captains, we always make time for them to come in and discuss just how their responsibility and accountability may be played out through the course of our season.

We have found that developing the R&A words with our captains takes time, constant direction, and cultivation. Their ability to be accountable and responsible to the coaching staff and the players is critical to the positive effect of their leadership. They need to understand their charge is from the players and coaches, and they should not be discouraged if there is conflict. They need to learn how to communicate honestly and effectively to successfully lead the team and carry out their responsibilities.

We also believe in empowering others on our team who have strong leadership qualities. There are always other individuals in the group who have strengths that are key in keeping the R&A of the team on track. These players frequently contribute to the good of the group and are committed to keeping things moving in a positive direction.

The collection of good leadership leads to the manifestation of an R&A team that can truly take care of its own problems without requiring the intervention of the coaching staff.

Creating a Family

The greatest demonstration of R&A is manifested in the setting of the family. Within that system, it is obvious that the actions of any family member reflect upon its nucleus—good, bad, or indifferent. We talk about the team as our family all the time.

Our players are aware of the fact that when they buy into being a part of our softball program, they have truly become a member of our family. Whether they are attending class, going to a football game, or just out with other people on a weekend, their behavior reflects back on our family, our team. Not only on the playing field, but wherever they go, they are no longer individuals but are labeled as softball players. Whenever they do well in class, show great presence as a group at an airport ticket counter, or are just polite to individuals they meet, they have been very R&A to our family.

Final Thoughts

As coaches, our dream is to have a team composed of players who are responsible and accountable. The greatest and most recent example of how important these qualities are for a team's success is the USA National softball team and their performance in the 2000 Olympic Games. Their individual capacity to be responsible and accountable led to their selection to the National team. Furthermore, these character traits enabled them to train physically and mentally on their own until the team began its playing tours. At the Olympics, they faced possible elimination from the medal round, but their individual and collective levels of responsibility and accountability helped them regroup and achieve their ultimate dream—winning the gold medal.

Responsibility and accountability require all the components discussed in this chapter, namely a solid core individual who is willing to make a significant investment and commitment to reaching the bar that has been established. Through constant communication and with the help of strong leadership within the family, our teams will be more likely to achieve goals.

We would never dream of going through a season without spending time on the mechanical aspects of the game (i.e., pitching, hitting, bunting, fielding). We take great pains in investing the time to prepare our players in every conceivable way to play the game physically. Likewise, making it a priority to work with our players to recognize the vital and absolute value of bringing their own responsibility and accountability to our team produces a greater sense of satisfaction and achievement throughout the seasons that lie ahead.

CHAPTER TWENTY–THREE

Building Loyalty and Tradition in Players

Carol Hutchins

Photo courtesy of the University of Michigan

When you think of a great athletic program, concepts like *loyalty* and *tradition* come to mind. Unfortunately, merely describing a program with these words is not enough to instill their qualities into your program. Building loyalty and tradition within a program requires a great amount of effort. As winning a championship doesn't just happen, neither does establishing the powerful traits associated with the values of loyalty and tradition. The process of genuinely getting the members of a program to take care of the program, to completely and unquestioningly buy into its values and beliefs, is a feat that requires continual teaching and nurturing through its coaches and team leaders.

The values of loyalty and tradition must be inherent in a coach's philosophy. The personal beliefs that ultimately guide the actions of the coach must include these values to consciously integrate them into the program on a daily basis. The coach needs to believe in and demonstrate the traditions of the program to expect that any members of the program will interpret them as valuable and internalize them as part of their core value system. One thing is certain: Should you be successful at integrating these traits into your own program, you will have a solid fundamental belief system, a set of core values that can give your athletes a true sense of ownership. Loyalty and tradition help maintain focus at critical times and build a common bond that can be built on over time. Programs that capture the essence of loyalty and tradition are those whose names become synonymous with the sport: Michigan football, UCLA softball, Duke basketball, Iowa wrestling, Tennessee women's basketball. Winning is a common theme in programs that are successful in establishing a strong history of loyalty and tradition, but winning is not the only important ingredient.

Loyalty

Developing program loyalty among athletes begins with the coach. The coach must be considered faithful to the school, players, staff, and fans. I bleed Michigan blue, and there is little room for doubt. Not only am I devoted to my institution, but my players know I am their greatest advocate as well. A sense of trust and respect is paramount in developing this relationship. Loyalty is not automatically given, and for a coach to develop this quality with her players, the players have to believe that the coach truly cares about them as people. They must trust that you care about more than their batting averages or their ERAs. Athletes play their heart out for coaches who show that they are just people, too!

As mentioned, what is imperative in developing loyalty is establishing a relationship built on trust. Athletes must trust you as a coach, and ultimately this faith in you comes down to being honest with each one of them. Trust must be built over a period of time, and no athlete, or coach for that matter, is loyal to anyone they do not believe is honest. Coaches have a difficult time preaching loyalty unless they indeed are seen as faithful to all parts of the program. Loyalty is something to be constantly and consistently demonstrated; it shows an appreciation of all those involved in the program. Being loyal means being dependable, able to inspire trust and faith, and having a desire to do whatever it takes to serve the team.

Loyalty is a two-way street between players and coaches. It is pervasive throughout an entire program, and it includes the announcer, the trainers, the managers, the grounds crew, and the diehard fans as well! Demonstrations of loyalty can extend beyond the actual playing field. My players know that if they miss a tag or miss a class, I will demonstrate my loyalty by first giving them the benefit of the doubt. I argue the call for them if I believe the tag was really put on, and I ask them first if they did indeed miss class. I ask them rather than accuse them. I also ask what the circumstances may have been, should there be any appropriate explanation for the situation. Loyalty requires honesty, and my players learn early in their careers that no matter what, I respect and am faithful to them when they are honest. If they miss a class, they may suffer punishment, such as being dismissed from practice. If they lie about it, they suffer a worse punishment by losing my respect and being forced to earn it back. In any of these situations, a constant education about the entire process is always in place. We discuss with the athletes what value is most important, and although missing class is not appropriate, we allow for mistakes. We do not allow for dishonesty. Loyalty requires faithful adherence to the people in a program, as well as their values and ideals. Therefore, loyalty demands respect and honesty.

Loyalty within and to a program is an unconditional state of being, both when times are good and when times are bad. If you have members who have differences, the ability to put the program above all else becomes a major indicator of a program's loyalty.

Many talk of loyalty when speaking in terms of an athletic program, but it is truly demonstrated when an athlete can remain on speaking terms with one of her teammates when they in fact are fighting as roommates. Great teams, in terms of inner dynamics and regardless of talent, take care of the values of the program.

A team reacts positively to conflicts within the inner team more often when the coach takes the time to use teachable moments when identifying and defining loyal behavior. Loyalty requires team members to have and demonstrate a sense of the larger picture. A common complaint coaches make regarding their teams is that they don't see the broader perspective. However, educating your players to that perspective takes time and effort from the coaching staff. Teams can often get caught up in the small picture of protecting a particular team member from the coach's wrath when violating a team policy. Teams that react by handling the situation, be it internally or by contacting the appropriate authority figure, are teams that understand that loyalty is to the program, not individuals in the program. Loyalty is best served by ensuring the success of the entire program.

This self-policing effort does not come about by itself and must be taught over time by the coach. When a member displays disloyal behavior, such as breaking team policy or not attending class, the coach can use this opportunity as an example to teach the team where the loyalty factor really lies while dealing with the situation. Once team members understand that an individual who doesn't attend class and becomes ineligible undermines the opportunity the team has for success, they become better at self-policing and understand the larger picture of being loyal to the program. Even though the small picture has uncomfortable moments, like teammates who become mad at one another, the team understands how important it is for the group to display loyalty at all times to parts of the program like team rules. Inspiring loyalty requires teaching it and directly affects a team's ability to be successful. Average teams that are loyal to the program and to the coach play hard and find ways to win, and thus they become excellent teams!

Tradition

Just as loyalty to a program must be taught and nurtured, so must the traditions that define the program. Each and every program has its own nuances that can be built on and molded into tradition. Although tradition may seem to be inherent in some programs, it actually must be born, bred, and fostered. Central to a team's tradition is its history, comprising athletes who competed in or were members of the program in the past. It includes championships (and near championships), rituals, and superstitions that have evolved over the course of the program's history. Handing down customs, information, and beliefs creates a sense of history for your program and a connection for all members, past and present, to that history.

> Tradition is something you can't bottle. You can't buy it at the corner store. But it is there to sustain you when you need it most.
>
> Fritz Crisler, former Michigan coach and legend

As a coach, you can recognize and create your own tradition. I realize that the unique events or new routines that occur each year have become part of the traditions and rituals of the Michigan softball program—whether it is our annual first practice, which historically includes only the freshmen and their first jog to the top of Michigan Stadium, or these seemingly insignificant events that become the things that are talked about by former teams and anticipated by future teams. I have discovered that by making that annual jog to Michigan Stadium with the freshmen, I have created something more vital to the program than taking one more batting practice. I have created a sense of familiarity year after year—a custom, a ritual—and it brings with it an immediate connection to our program because these freshmen are participating in something that every other Michigan softball player has experienced. All outgoing seniors remark fondly (or not so fondly) on their first tour of the stadium.

Annually our seniors are required to cook dinner for the entire team before our first road trip of the year. This tradition was in place before my arrival in Ann Arbor, and to my knowledge every senior class in our history has celebrated this ritual. I regularly joke that the mark of each senior class hinges on its culinary skills. While these events in their own right do not seem significant, their continued practice transmits custom and familiarity from one team to the next.

The beliefs, tenets, creed, and code of conduct of our team are also handed down from one generation to the next. My assistant coach, Bonnie Tholl, who graduated from Michigan in 1991, recently competed in a practice scrimmage. As is common in softball, after a big out, there was the usual infield huddle at the mound. After huddling in the circle with our present-day infielders, Bonnie was amazed that many years later some of the same sayings and hand gestures were still being executed. Little did our team know that one of the original participants in the huddle ritual was listening in.

Over many years it has been a team rule to wear the team game uniform or practice uniform with nothing less than total pride. Shirts must always be tucked in, shoes polished, and one must always wear the Michigan name properly. I have found that many of my former athletes who have gone on to coach at various institutions have taken this tradition with them. They tell me tales of starting similar traditions in their new environments; the tradition of wearing the block M properly is so ingrained in them. Recognize practices or rituals of your team that you can promote as tradition, such as how the uniform is worn and rituals performed on the field or in the dugout. These are practices that can give your team ritual and help your players feel connected when they need it most. Practices that are recognized as tradition and customs that are continued year after year help instill pride in your program.

Creating a sense of tradition should definitely include telling stories to the team. Whether the stories are factual in nature or even slightly embellished bits of information, I have found that communicating with the team in this way creates some of the folklore of our program. The Horsemen of Notre Dame is one such piece of folklore, and it captures a certain spirit associated with the Notre Dame football tradition. You see examples of this in football often, where former greats are immortalized into the history of the program and every player who ever competes in the program learns the tales of their careers.

Michigan folklore includes the tales of many harrowing van rides with Coach Hutch (along with the many tales of near misses). Former players never miss an opportunity to reminisce about conditioning, lining up for sprints, or other experiences that become legendary with a little color commentary. One tradition that is present at every Michigan softball game, home or away, includes the doll Bert from the TV show Sesame Street. Bert is actually a former player, who was nicknamed after the TV character, and she remains (in spirit) with our team to this day. A team member is designated to carry Bert to each game and put him in a visible place in the dugout.

Some of the current standards and practices of our current team were actually enforced and taken to a higher standard by our alumnus Bert when she was in the program. Things that seem trite, like tucking in shirts, wearing the uniform properly, or being on time, became even more central to our program because Bert not only enforced them, she helped the entire group connect the pride factor to these rules.

The Michigan seniors traditionally hand down the various duties of the program at the annual awards banquet, such as carrying the Bert doll throughout the next year. Other duties that are traditionally passed on include the duty of counter, the person who counts all bags during every airport trip; the cheerleader who is responsible for organizing our traditional *Go Blue* chant; and even someone who is delegated the duty to count our game day sprints. All these duties are a tradition of our program. They have become a ritual, and they keep each new team connected with teams of the past. And most important to all of this, the players take every one of the traditional duties that a team member becomes responsible for very seriously. They respect their tradition.

This year in an effort to really connect past players to present players, we put a placard in each player's locker that had all of the players listed who wore that particular number. Each current player must be able to identify something unique about everyone who ever wore the number she now wears. For instance, three different athletes, all of whom were NCAA All-Americans, have worn number 44. Some players discover that they have numbers of those on our first-ever Big Ten championship team or our first ever College World Series team. The purpose of this exercise is to emphasize that there is a significant history associated with Michigan softball, full of many outstanding individuals. The placard's inscription—"Honor those who wore the uniform before you, respect tradition"—implies that your uniform is not yours alone but also belongs to those who paved the way before you. Honoring players who helped build the program is now one of our traditions, and doing this has helped create and highlight a sense of Michigan softball history and pride.

Another exercise we developed to help our players remember the past was having them take a simple quiz early in the year. The quiz asked them to find answers to questions related to the history of Michigan softball (they were allowed to use the team media guide to find the answers). Who was the first-ever Michigan softball All-American? What was the first year Michigan softball was a varsity sport? What was the previous name of Alumni Field? All these are pieces of softball history that both present-day players and incoming freshmen might know nothing about. We hoped and succeeded in having our team consider the historical perspective of the Michigan softball program, and it evoked a lot of thoughtful discussion on top of it. Learning the history of a program can help the players in the program truly appreciate the traditions that you are now teaching them.

Many women's sports programs are relatively new and within the sport of softball, some are newer yet! Creating tradition in these instances, although not as easy as in a program that has years of history, can be done! Buying into themes that are already a part of the larger institution's tradition is a good way to get started. Michigan football's winged helmet is a good example of a tradition to borrow, as well as their credo "Those who stay will be Champions." That particular phrase is found on many Michigan teams' locker rooms in all the different sports.

Nurture some of these traditions and look to recognize some of the various rituals that can be utilized as you begin building your own program's traditions. Recognize key rituals and even superstitions that your team may have and embrace them. Realize that tradition is simply a sense of connection to both the past and to each other. Teams, programs that feel connected, that have players with a sense of the whole program, produce players who more likely buy into the whole program, who invest more of themselves in team effort, who are more productive and more successful in the long run. Winning is an important aspect in creating team traditions; however, the truly successful program produces people who are involved in, who represent well, and buy totally into the values and the ideals associated with the program.

I have tried to illustrate some of the examples of program loyalty and tradition that we have utilized at the University of Michigan. Without doubt, the intangibles associated with both characteristics have allowed our program to compete and succeed. Many times I have heard colleagues make reference to my team as "knowing how to win." I attribute this to the many traditions we have created over the years and to the fact that players who stay in the program and alumnae who have graduated from the program are intensely loyal to University of Michigan softball. Individuals, teams, and programs that can create and cultivate a culture of loyalty and tradition truly can reach and achieve their maximum potential. Establishing a program that has rock solid faith in itself, and in the members themselves, can happen over time when attention is given to the daily cultivation of the concepts involved in creating loyalty and tradition. As a coach, one must buy into and build upon those values associated with both. The coach is integral in creating the sense that team traditions are valuable. The coach must be seen as the most loyal of all, to the program, to the players, and to all members associated with the program. Programs with great tradition, with loyal players and fan base, are often those programs you see year after year winning softball games.

CHAPTER TWENTY–FOUR

Inspiring Today's Players

Mona Stevens

Photo courtesy of Steve C. Wilson

Before we can begin to think about motivating or inspiring athletes, it is important to understand what they want. Why do they go through the difficult hours, tedious routines, frustrations, anxieties, injuries, and other challenges presented in sport? A study done on younger athletes questioned their reasons for becoming involved in sport. There were obvious answers such as "Because all my friends are," "My parents want me to," "It looks fun," and so on. However, the number-one reason was "I wanted to see how good I could be."

It has been my experience that whether you are coaching youth, collegiate, professional, or Olympic softball, the answer is the same, especially when players find success early and progress to higher levels. How far can they go? What are their capabilities? Will they be the one to hit the winning run, pitch the championship game, or make the game-winning defensive play? That drive is one of the greatest buttons a coach can push. Nurturing players within that atmosphere can be one of the most rewarding experiences for coaches as well as players.

Inspiring today's athletes is about helping them realize their potential. You have to break through self-doubt, failure, fear, setbacks, and limiting beliefs, and move toward a higher level of thinking and eventually performing. You have to learn to tap into their passion and spirit. It takes time, some research, and a constant effort.

The sport of softball is challenging in the way golf and baseball are challenging. Aggressiveness needs to be controlled, and there isn't a time that you can use a surge of emotional energy to produce an extraordinary effort. Imagine defensive linemen on a football team pounding on each other's shoulder pads, jumping up and down, yelling at each other, and working each other into a frenzy before taking the field. That surge of adrenaline could inspire the defensive line to literally push the offense backward. In softball, adrenaline to that degree isn't typically desirable. A pitcher who worked herself into a higher state of emotion through the same shoulder-pad-like bashing before taking the mound wouldn't last long; she needs to keep her emotions in check. In a sport based on finesse and pinpoint accuracy, too much energy can result in poor performance. Watching a pitcher between innings as well as between pitches is an accurate indication of the focus and control needed.

Inspiring and motivating athletes in this sport is challenging because of the delicate nature of the skills involved. However, I find it most rewarding because the skills and emotional lessons learned are similar to those we need for living a fuller and more rewarding life. Teaching those life lessons is the desire of most coaches.

Inspiration uses methods and techniques that help an athlete grow to a higher level of emotional power. Ideas and techniques need not be original; we can borrow and adapt them. Although the ideas may not be original, the implementation always is. Organizing the pieces of information and putting the puzzle together is as unique as the athletes involved. Techniques and emphasis may change every year, but that challenge is the reward of the journey.

Character and Credibility of the Coach

The first and most important factor is the coach. Coaches are contagious. When the coach's character is questionable, all attempts to inspire the team fall short. When I think back on all of the coaches and teachers in my life, the ones with the most impact and influence held high standards and expectations of themselves. I wasn't expected to be something that they themselves weren't a good example of. I understood they were human, capable of mistakes and shortcomings but that they also strived for excellence. Before any of us can inspire our athletes to higher levels, we must establish a certain level of character and caring. The result is trust and respect from the athletes. We cannot inspire an athlete if we are lethargic, uncaring, or lack passion and energy. It is impossible to influence commitment if we are not committed. You can teach a diving catch without ever having done one, but you can't inspire passion when you have none.

Developing trust and relationships with athletes takes time and consistency. Athletes find it comforting to know what to expect. There are certain things I try to do all the time. Habits such as posting practice every day, having regular office hours, and having an open door policy may seem small, but they are important to my team. Remember: Even on busy days, the players are the purpose, not the distraction. I have an assistant oversee the equipment for practice, so I can use the time before and after practice to mingle and talk to the team. For some players, it is the only one-on-one time I have with them that day. I try to keep that as dependable as the starting time of practice (another biggie on the consistency chart). We have routines in setting up equipment, transitioning at practice, and even checking our bags at the airport. The consistency and routine keep a lot of confusion at bay.

Trust can be a by-product of consistency, especially when players know what to expect from your moods. It is quite a challenge to maintain a positive and enthusiastic demeanor every day, yet it is a key ingredient in gaining the trust of the team. At Utah we ask our athletes to check their mental and emotional baggage at the gate when coming to practice, which is a challenge for college students. They have so many demands, and stress is common. However, practice is freedom from the demands. Having athletes who are consistent in their moods reaps obvious rewards, but it does not happen when the coach doesn't set the example.

Consistency in how we treat each athlete is also essential. They need to know what to expect from you on positive days and challenging days. They need to know that the personality you have on game days is the one that loves them before and after. It is essential to know them as people. What is important to them? Why are they struggling this week? Who is important in their lives? When an athlete knows you care and that your concerns and feelings for them are real, the level of trust increases. In his book *Bringing Out the Best in People*, Aubrey C. Daniels states, "Once trust is established, people will give you the benefit of the doubt if you make a mistake. If you are not trusted, they will not believe you even when you tell the truth."

Athletes need to feel that they are understood. When that happens, an athlete respects and trusts her coach, and a coach's ability to inspire that athlete increases. Understanding involves listening, and often for myself that means creating opportunities to listen.

Be authentic. Have a human side. During the NCAA Regional Tournament in 2000, I drove one of the vans with my players in it. My junior pitcher was in my van for the first time in her career. At the end of the tournament, she told me everyone needed to ride in my van at some point in the season. My first thought was that she was suggesting that everyone needed to share in the sheer joy of riding with the coach (sarcasm intended). But she went on to say that she was able to see a different side of me that helped her know me even better. I was more relaxed and talked about things other than softball. She also felt on safe and fertile ground to do the same.

The most effective coaches are the coaches who have high standards for themselves, work hard at their jobs, stay current with the game, constantly try to improve, are organized with a vision of where the team needs to go, show authentic concern for the players, love what they are doing, and work at clear communication with everyone in the program.

Creating a Vision

Tony Robbins has made a living helping people discover how to live their lives with passion. He does it by helping them create a vision and breaking through limiting beliefs. He gets people fired up by helping them see what is waiting for them when they decide to look at life and circumstances differently, by helping them understand that they are in charge of their own direction. Steven Covey teaches about paradigms: How we view and choose to think about things controls our reactions. Victor Frankl has given us the gift of understanding what a person can endure and how she can hold onto whatever she is striving for if she attaches some meaning to it.

Vision is the center of all of their contributions—creating a reason, a meaning, and a goal. Our job as coaches is to create the vision of what accomplishment can look like. That leadership takes thought and honesty. It takes articulating all the steps and all the joy that can come from the journey. Inspirational talks from coaches usually center on a vision of success. The best speeches come from those who can articulate that vision with some emotion, some personal connection to it, some personal energy. Martin Luther King's speech "I Have a Dream" is probably one of the most inspiring speeches in history. He describes a vision with emotion and personal attachment. No one questioned whether or not it meant something to him. You can listen with your eyes closed and feel his desire and his passion.

In his book *Lead to Succeed*, Rick Pitino writes, "Present the vision. Then get people excited about it." As coaches, we may not have the full vision in our heads on the first day of practice. Sometimes we have a more clear picture develop as we go through the first weeks. However, we usually have an understanding of what the talent level is and what it can become.

My experience coaching youth, college, and Olympic athletes has shown me that the greatest dividing factor between those who achieve and those who don't is their perception of themselves. You become what you believe. There have been some great stories about athletes who have turned a corner at some point in their athletic lives. It is almost always due to the belief of a coach, family member, or friend. How many times has an interview of a great performer revealed the information that he or she had someone who believed in him or her. One of the most inspiring things we can do for our athletes is to believe in them. We see what they cannot yet see. We know what they can become.

Get them excited about it. Describe it to them. A clear, exciting vision can tap into their hearts and spirits. Every year before we begin practice, before we step onto the field, or before we pick up a ball, we go on a camping trip (one of the many assets of living in the Rocky Mountains). The staff have two goals during the two days: First we want the players to get to know each other and begin establishing their bonds. Second it is our time to paint the picture as we see it. It isn't just about the results we seek as a group, even though that is always there. It is more about what can be and how we plan to get there. It is one of my favorite times. I get to map out the year. I describe what can happen only if we want it to happen, and I also describe those things that keep us from that reality. It takes a lot of preparation, but right out of the chute I want them to understand that our expectations are high.

In 1999 after coaching the National Team in the Pan American qualifying tournament in Columbia, South America, I used my USA Softball parade warm-up to make a point with my Utah team. On our camping trip, I pulled out the jacket and put it on a few of the team members. I asked each one of them to describe how she would act if that were her jacket and this was the USA Softball team that she was a part of. Each one talked about how tall she would walk, how she would be on her toes and demand the best effort of herself every day because she knew that everyone around her had the same high expectations. The pride would be obvious and the discipline would be unwavering. Each player saw herself at her best. Next I had them put on a Utah game jacket. My question was, "What is the difference in you?" The answer: "Nothing but perception and expectation." Exactly!

Part of the excitement in the vision of a journey comes from a knowledge that the discipline will be sound. We coach knowledgeable athletes who understand that you can't get anywhere without discipline. They want it because they know it takes them where they want to go.

Laced in the vision are the high expectations we place on our athletes. We expect them to do the little things—tuck in their shirts, pick up after themselves, take care of their equipment, be neat, always say thank you, walk tall, breathe deeply, and make eye contact (a biggie on my list). Then we expect the big things—control what you have control over, your effort and your attitude. That learning process is constant. It is a daily goal and one that we feel ultimately has the greatest impact on the outcome of individual games as well as the overall season.

After the vision is clearly established and the heart has been stirred, the next step is to develop goals that lead to the full picture. Each athlete and part of the team needs to have a ladder of steps to show that they are getting closer to achieving the vision. Goals need to be broken down into steps that create small victories. Celebrate those victories; it's where our own passion needs to express itself. Getting genuinely excited about an athlete's progress drives both you and your athlete to work harder, to focus more deeply. It shows your personal investment in her.

Patience is important, but pushing an athlete through those times also shows that you expect her to be able to perform a skill. That is one way to let an athlete know that you believe in her talent level. Accomplishing small goals leading to the larger ones keeps us excited because we see progress. It can be measured. My mother has always said to me, "It is better to aim for the moon and miss it than to aim for nothing and hit it." Goals help us constantly set our sights and check our aim. Vision is powerful. An individual's vision can be the lifeline to her potential.

Eventually they begin to get glimspes that are more real than a dream. That can be season defining; that can be life altering. They may need to lean on yours to begin, but as they grow, they form their own inner belief and vision. Constant reminders and subtle comments keep their hearts alive and committed.

Atmosphere of the Team

For players to reach their potential as athletes as well as a team, there needs to be a healthy atmosphere. Being able to inspire athletes takes a fertile ground that depends on the relationships between each player and between the players and the coach. No dream or goal is fully reached in the presence of bad feelings or animosity. This isn't to say that bad feelings won't come up, but they need to be worked through. Women can create incredible bonds with each other, and they can also get caught up in emotional issues. It is a constant project to keep the atmosphere supportive and healthy during a season. Our effectiveness to inspire and motivate depends on it.

To help create that healthy atmosphere, it is important for players to accept that they need to take care of each other and create bonds together, on the field and at practice. It does not necessarily mean that their social structure needs to be centered on the team, but it is important for women to know that they can be a great team and not necessarily be best of friends off the field.

To develop that sense of team, we have a motto of serving each other: *Lift someone today.* Leadership is about an attitude of service, and it is about elevating those around you. *Lift someone today* is a gentle reminder that can be put on the wall, in the dugout, or just spoken. Some athletes I have coached were ready for and were needing those leadership responsibilities, those opportunities to serve.

Inspiring a team is also about identifying leadership characteristics in certain members of the team and helping them to develop those skills. Once established, trust is there, even when they make mistakes—especially when they make mistakes. It is not only important between the coach and player, it is important among the players themselves. The best way to gain trust is to be consistent, unselfish, and service oriented.

For the first part of the season, we have the upperclassmen watch over the freshmen until they get comfortable and established. They are there for the freshmen when they set foot on campus. They show them around campus, help them find classes and books, and survive the parking and ID lines. But that support and concern goes further. We don't allow demeaning comments about freshmen. We try to bring them into the group as soon as possible, so they understand that where the team goes depends on them also. They aren't our slaves; they are part of this team. We want to help them get their oars in the water and start paddling alongside the returning All-Americans. This is their team, and they have as much influence as all of us do. The sooner they understand, the sooner they start to contribute. Service starts with the coaching staff and trickles down to the upperclassmen and eventually filters throughout the team.

Just as all game skills require practice to improve, so does the atmosphere of the team. It doesn't just happen; it is developed and created.

I am a firm believer in the journey being more important than the destination. That idea can be difficult to understand because it makes it sound as if our goals of being conference champions, going to the NCAA tournament, and then the World Series are not important. That is certainly not true, but to reach that goal, the steps to getting there are much more important: They are ultimately what is remembered and are exactly what makes them feel successful. To win or lose the last game of the season should not determine how you view the complete season.

To help my team understand this idea, I use sayings such as "You don't dance to get to the other side of the floor," and "You don't travel on a great journey to sleep at the hotel at the end of the day." Without the journey or the dance, the hotel and the other side of the floor are meaningless. They are important when they are preceded by a wonderful process of getting there. With that being said, we focus on each other and our journey knowing that if we do it right along the way, the result should take care of itself.

Driving the Bus

From my own playing and coaching experience, I am convinced that for an athlete or a team to reach their potential they need to be involved with every step. They need to become thinking players. As coaches it is easy to make their decisions for them. It is less work to call the pitches ourselves, to adjust defenses, and to help them adjust on the fly in a game. However, if they are solely dependent on you for everything, you become the limiting factor. One of the greatest things you can do to tap into the commitment level of your athletes is to train them to think and adjust. It gives them ownership. Part of the fun of sport is to outwit the competitor. They never experience that fun when you are the one making the call.

I tell my teams that I want to get them to a point where *they* drive the bus. That doesn't relinquish my responsibility or my influence; it actually takes it further. For example, when new slappers enter our system, I work with them at first then let the upperclassmen who have trained with me for a couple of seasons step in. I am close at hand and keep a watchful eye on what is being said, but more times than not they are right on. It creates a special atmosphere that wouldn't fully exist if it were completely dependent on me. The slappers get the information from me to begin, then they run with it. It creates a special bond when they coach each other. They then celebrate each other's victories and have a vested interest in each other's progress.

In his book *Leadership Wisdom of Jesus*, Charles C. Manz shares this insight: "Thus the most effective leaders are often those who lead others to lead themselves. By guiding and developing people to be competent self-leaders, a leader is able to spread strength throughout the entire system."

To inspire your athletes, give them some responsibility, give them the reins when you trust them. They now feel that they are influencing the success of the team. They are not pawns but cared-about athletes who are recognized for their intelligence and leadership as well as their athleticism. At the collegiate level, it is a powerful tool a coach can use to put some decisive power in the hands of the leaders on the team. When I give them the bus, I make sure the engine is cared for, the map is correct, and we are traveling down the right roads; but I want them to drive the bus as much as possible.

In his book *Positive Coaching,* Jim Thompson states, "The best teachers and coaches are developers of people as lifelong learners. They help their pupils embrace the act of becoming better at whatever they choose to do or be. And a big part of this is being able to surrender control of the process to the player rather than trying to direct everything from the coach's perch."

A colleague of mine uses the statement "Practice is mine, the games are yours." It is my job to teach them, so they can become independent of me. I am a resource, a guide. In practice I teach, then step back and let them discover. If after a sufficient period of time, they are still asking questions, I answer them with the same question. Many athletes are reluctant thinkers. They have been taught to take in information and then spew it out. To inspire them, give them the information, develop their skills, give them your confidence, then stand at their side and push when needed, hug them when needed; but let them feel that the journey is theirs and they have some control.

The athlete today is different from a decade ago. They need to know why. It wasn't that long ago that we could say, "Because I told you so." That won't fly with today's athletes. They want to know why the way they've been doing it won't be enough to continue to be successful. I think they have a right to know. I never feel questioned as a coach when an athlete asks me a *why* question. I should be able to answer it. And if I do so in a clear and logical way, that player is much more committed to working through the difficulty of learning something new or relearning something they felt they did well already. When you answer their questions and have discussions with them that are timely and appropriate, players gain a respect of your knowledge and trust in what you want for them. They may even stop asking why, but don't count on it. I actually like it because it lets me know they are thinking.

Having Fun

Having fun can serve a team throughout the season. It is worth noting what a college athlete may consider fun compared to a high school athlete or younger. My team has helped me to understand that for them, the most fun they have is when they are in a highly competitive situation yet can use their witty one-liners and healthy sarcasm. It isn't fun to just be funny. It needs to be coupled with hard work and competition. But a sense of humor keeps a team on track and makes the season even more enjoyable.

We laugh a lot on my team. A sense of humor serves you. Coaches need to be able to laugh at themselves as well as the team. The book *Thinking Body, Dancing Mind* states, "Research now shows that not only laughter but all positive emotions cause the brain to secrete endorphins that relieve pain and tension. Happiness is one such emotion; like laughter, pleasant, happy thoughts relax the mind and lower stress. Happiness is a habit . . ."

In difficult, stressful, demanding, and tense times, humor can cut through the atmosphere. Laughter is the best medicine. Laughter changes the atmosphere that can be created when facing difficulty—laughing at how many times we have to make U-turns during our travels, at the obnoxious habits we all have, at the silly mistakes that we make in practice and in games. Laughter makes the season pass quickly and with joy and wonderful memories. Laughter can make a team healthy. It helps keep things in perspective.

Working Hard

Another important aspect of a team that plays inspired softball is the knowledge that they have prepared well. Hard work is rewarding. Players are motivated when they know in their hearts that they gave the time and effort necessary. A team that knows they pushed themselves through difficult workouts knows they are capable of more in games. Being physically fit and strong creates confidence and a stronger self-esteem. Players walk taller, breathe deeper, relax more easily, and think more of themselves.

Being prepared and physically ready helps a team take the results of a game in stride. It is easier to deal with whatever might happen. Softball is unique in that we play so many games. It is very unlikely that any team will ever have an undefeated season. The nature of the game itself requires us to deal with failure. Even a great hitter needs to deal with not getting on base more times than she actually does. What players do with failure ultimately determines how successful they are. Being in great shape creates a mental edge and attitude. Pushing through the grueling moments and pain establishes a mental toughness. If players can make it through that, they can handle the game pressure. They have a higher sense of belief in themselves and their ability, which keeps them coming back when they are knocked down.

Developing Professional Standards

The last point in dealing with the atmosphere of the team deals with being professional and creating an image. Webster's defines *professional* as "To be engaged in or worthy of the standards of a profession." Professionalism is about high standards and self-image. For my team, professional means we dress well, we aren't sloppy, we are neat and clean up after ourselves, we are prepared for practice, we are on time and never miss appointments, we are respectful of each other and anyone serving our team or coming in contact with our team. It is how we view ourselves and the standards we operate under.

I influence that image not only by directing actions and thoughts throughout the season but by making sure the facilities are as clean and organized as possible. What a difference it makes when players have pride in where they work and where they spend so much of their time. It is important to me that the locker room, dugouts, bull pens, batting cages, and equipment storage areas are all neat and clean. It creates an atmosphere of professionalism, one of high standards and expectations. We don't spit seeds and make a mess. We clean each dugout before we leave it. We want any team entering the dugout after we left to know that Utah was here; therefore, it is clean and professional looking.

Lucky for me, the grounds crew feel the same way I do: The grass lines are crisp; the infield is manicured impeccably; even the warning tracks are dragged for practice. A visiting team walking onto our field sees a clean and perfectly groomed field. The team loves the field, and it makes them feel proud. In a very real sense, the grounds crew set the initial stage for our home games and practice. This is the team's home, and they are very proud of it. My relationship with the grounds crew is ultimately important. We are a team, and they need to know how much they are a part of our effectiveness. The team knows them all, and they have their own relationship with them. They are a part of our family.

Inspirational Tools and Methods

We need an arsenal to aid us in touching the hearts of our players. Movies, songs, books, videos, stories, and other types of media give our messages a proverbial punch. A wealth of information and resources exist for us to use as they fit into our design and our goal. Athletes can be very moved after seeing movies such as *Rudy, Gladiator, Remember the Titans, White Squall, Love of the Game, The Natural, Field of Dreams,* and *Hoosiers.* These movies tell stories of difficulties that are overcome and the rewards that are there for those who endure. They tap into emotions and when that happens, it can be powerful. When my team was struggling to find their identity this past year, we went to see *Remember the Titans.* It was inspiring, and it also gave them a few slogans to take with them and make their own.

Music has the effect of stirring, calming, and creating an atmosphere. We use music in some practices. In hard conditioning workouts, music helps push them through. It also taps into the spirit of their workouts. Using music with a driving beat drives players to a higher level of activity. At the end of a workout, calm and peaceful music soothes them as they cool down and stretch. Used well, music is one of the best tools for setting the stage.

Video clips of great plays are a great motivator. Highlights of our team or other great players have the ability to motivate players into thinking that if someone else is able to do it, surely they can learn too. It is exciting, it looks great, and it taps into the original motive of *How good can I get?* It makes them want to get out on the field right now and make a highlight play.

Some of my best thoughts and lessons come from the books I read. I have such a long way to go as a coach. I can't possibly gain the knowledge of all the coaches before me through my experience alone. Books not only give me ideas and help clarify my own philosophies, but they give me stories, poems, quotes, and metaphors I can use daily. I have a resource to use when dealing with tough times. Barnes and Noble loves to see me coming. I live in the martial arts, self-help, sport, biographies, and business sections.

I keep a notebook of the things I run across that might be used later. I date the notebook so that I know when I have used those ideas and when I can come back to them with a completely new team. I use the ideas whenever it fits our needs, whenever there is a learning moment, when I feel we need an emotional shift in one direction or another to map out our path.

Quotes of the day are one way to start. This is a small thing that may stimulate conversation and tap into the heart. The quote usually has some connection to both sport and life. Quotes probably don't affect everyone, but the players they do affect are usually the more emotionally influential ones, the ones who can help turn a team that isn't going in the direction you want. They are also the ones who lay the emotional groundwork for the team; they are the emotional intelligence of the team.

Inspiring players is more about taking pieces of information and completing your puzzle. The puzzle is as original as each team. Using the wisdom written or produced by others can be a great help to us in times when we don't have anything in our own well.

In 2000 we began our season in Arizona against a very good field of teams. We felt confident in our ability and were looking forward to a good year. We opened against a talented Fullerton team, losing 8-0 in five innings (the wonderful yet awful mercy rule). Then we faced Oregon State. I knew Oregon State didn't have the advantage of practicing outdoors, so I thought the ground might be more equal; but we lost in five innings again. It was a tough loss that wasn't easy to take. We regrouped and faced Wisconsin the next morning. I thought we were ready, and the team seemed in good spirits. We stepped onto the field with confidence, but again, it seemed we couldn't do anything right. One inning took over an hour. We could not get them out. We could not hit. The players were looking around at each other and wondering "Could we really be this bad?" They looked to me for answers, but at that moment I had none. The only thing I could do was help them focus on each inning, each pitch. The outcome was well out of our reach. Wisconsin beat us with a score of something like 15-1.

After the game, I had a team of defeated athletes. They were embarrassed and troubled. Their frustrations spilled over to each other. I asked them to get in the vans and not to discuss the game. I told them I wanted them to meet me in my room in 45 minutes. That gave me enough time to collect my thoughts, ask for some divine help, and detach myself from the moment. I reviewed some literature that I had brought with me. Sometimes the right things just find their way to you when you need them. I read a passage from *The Leadership Wisdom of Jesus*: ". . . when people suffer dramatic failures that are clearly of their own doing and recognize and acknowledge their responsibility, it may be the best time to provide encouragement and support rather than condemnation."

When the team arrived, my points were simple. During the tough times, it is easy to point fingers. But that destroys us in the moment and in the future. Have faith in your ability and in each other. These moments become a springboard for what we are ultimately to become. How we choose to use it or how we choose to let it determine our direction is what life and sport are all about. I then read them a portion of a book called *The Invitation* by Oriah Mountain Dreamer.

When I finished reading, there wasn't a dry eye in the room including my own. I then painted a picture of what our year-end banquet would look like. I described the team remembering today's pain. We would reread this verse and would feel again the questions that arose on this difficult day. That would make the success that we would have that much sweeter. Our road would be filled with the knowledge of a painful struggle, and if we stood together like the gladiator, our achievements would not be hollow but filled with the understanding of what we had to go through to get there. It became such a powerful moment that it changed our attitude.

I was hoping to simply compete in the game that evening against a very good Mississippi State team. We won. It wasn't pretty, but we won. Then we beat Kansas. The next weekend we got another shot at Oregon State and beat them. We were on our way. The year was filled with tough times and it was never easy, but the team became the regular-season conference champions, won the conference tournament, and finished in the top 16 of the NCAA tournament. They were one game away from the World Series. At the year-end banquet, after all the individual awards and recognition had been handed out, I stopped and looked at them carefully. I asked all those in attendance to bear with us for a moment because what I was about to say was something for just those of us who had lived in the trenches.

"Who would have thought?" I started. "Who would have guessed that after losing our first three games by the mercy rule that we would be here? Remember that I told you that at the end of the year your victories and successes would be all the sweeter because of the difficulty. It is sweet, and it is sweet because you had to fight for it. It is sweet because you rose above the temptation to cave in and paint a picture of yourself that wasn't real. You overcame. You won. You are champions."

And then I reread the excerpt that I read in the hotel room in Phoenix. It was a powerful moment for all of us. It put an exclamation point on our year. It made it something we will never forget.

There are so many ideas that we can use to help our teams bond and grow. There are so many inspirational books, videos, interviews, stories, slogans, metaphors, and symbols. It is our job to collect them, using them to create an atmosphere that moves our athletes to a higher level of thinking. To a higher level of living and performing.

Final Thoughts

For me personally, an important concept is one of detachment. If I stay removed from the emotion of a loss or a win, I can keep a view of the big picture. When I do that, my attempts to inspire my players and help them grow are more than likely to be clear and appropriate. They are also more effective because I am grounded and I am more of a foundation they can trust. They can see hope, vision, confidence, and even dissatisfaction when necessary. They trust in it and can look to it when they need it.

To inspire my team, I need to live by the concept that "love and faith are the ultimate ingredients for mountain-moving leadership," as I read in *The Leadership Wisdom of Jesus*. Sometimes that love is a tough love. But my goal is to touch and awaken their hearts and let that become part of how they play and maybe even how they live.

PART VI

Off-the-Field Opportunities, Challenges, and Pressures

CHAPTER TWENTY-FIVE

Learning and Developing As a Professional

Rayla J. Allison

My first job interview after graduating from college was for a position as 10th grade biology teacher and junior varsity basketball coach in Plano, Texas. I'll never forget the panic I felt when the high school principal interviewing me asked what my teaching philosophy was. A memory flashed in my mind of some education assignment in which the professor asked us to write our teaching philosophies. For the life of me, I could not remember what I had written. I fumbled through the question, but gratefully I was offered the job.

Although I couldn't tell the principal what my specific teaching philosophy was, I could tell him my general thoughts about teaching, learning, discipline, and life skills. It was in that explanation that I shared my philosophy. A key to success in coaching, as in other careers, is establishing your philosophy and consistently following it.

Developing a Philosophy

Early in my career, I was fortunate to have two highly successful Hall of Fame coaches as my mentors: One of my college coaches was Jody Conradt, one of the most successful coaches in college basketball and the current University of Texas women's basketball coach and athletic director. My undergraduate adviser and mentor was Dr. Carla Lowry, currently dean at Southwestern State University and a former basketball coach. Both women are ultimate professionals and continue to set the standards for the rest of us.

One of the many lessons I learned from these great coaches was to be the coach I am innately. Do not try to emulate someone else's coaching style if it does not fit your style, personality, and beliefs. Such copying only comes across as insincere and ill fitting, and you eventually appear inconsistent to the athletes. The Cliff Notes lesson is to be consistent with your coaching philosophy.

As a young professional in coaching softball, I looked to coaches who were recognized as the best in the sport. What did Sharron Backus, Dr. June Walker, and Carol Spanks have in common? Was there a formula for success that could be patented? Whether it is the year-in, year-out district championship coach in your local high school league or the perennial NCAA Women's College World Series contender, all top coaches know and follow a few central themes.

Each successful coach identifies and follows his or her philosophy. Philosophies develop over time and reflect the way coaches conduct themselves on and off the field and how they interact with others. Their philosophies reflect their personalities, style, beliefs, and the sum of their experiences. The teams they coach throughout their careers mirror their philosophies. Former USA National Team coach Carol Spanks, who also coached at UNLV and Cal Poly Pomona, was known for coaching teams that had a never-say-die attitude and the ability to make something happen. Dr. Walker's teams were always a sure bet to have honed the basic skills in all areas and to be students of the game. Coach Backus annually fielded teams that were solid up and down the lineup. Each coach develops his or her own philosophy then remains consistent to the broad principals under which he or she acts.

It's Not Set in Stone

Your coaching philosophy is not so narrow as to only involve aspects of the game of softball. Your philosophy includes principles such as your approach to hitting styles, baserunning techniques, the role of the short game, and defensive strategies. It may also include your belief regarding work ethic, teamwork, sport as a mechanism to teach life lessons, or sport participation relative to classroom performance. The teams you remember are the ones who fit your coaching philosophy. We all remember the teams that comprised terrific athletes whom we truly enjoyed being around and with whom we may have shared competitive success. These teams are the teams that matched our coaching philosophies. These teams were in sync with who we were as a coach and with our beliefs. No wonder they were a delight to coach.

An athlete who falls outside the coach's philosophy is viewed as a problem or ill fit. To use an example from another sport, imagine a football coach who believes the quarterback needs to be tall to see over the defense, should set up in the pocket, and should never scramble. The current quarterback is a short scrambler who is always on the move. Given time, the scrambler will be traded. The shoe doesn't fit. The coach planned, recruited, and signed the other players for the type of system he wanted. Does he change his coaching philosophy? Does he try to change the athlete? How rigid and inflexible is one's coaching philosophy?

Your coaching philosophy is not set in stone. Truly great coaches recognize the capabilities and limitations of each athlete and of themselves. Great coaches also recognize immeasurable qualities such as positive personality, strong work ethic, loyalty to a common team goal, and leadership abilities. The best coaches are like business leaders during the '90s. They adjust to the times, recognizing the total combination of all the pieces of the puzzle.

The coach who began coaching in the early '70s must realize that he or she cannot coach today's athletes the same way athletes were coached three decades earlier. Today's athlete doesn't ask how high to jump; rather she wants to know why to jump, how to jump, and what she can do to perform a better jump. Accommodating individual differences among athletes and coaching the individual as well as the team are not inconsistent with your philosophy; rather, this philosophy allows for adjustment within the broad principles that govern your coaching.

You Coach Because You . . .

The core of developing your broad guiding principles is knowing what motivates you, excites you, and drives you to do what you do. Whatever motivates you, knowing it helps you to recognize those times when tension exists between your motivation and other factors. Finding a balance between your personal motivation and what is best for the team and all parties involved is possible when you recognize such influences as motivation. For instance, seeking personal fame and glory may be your fire to win the championship but not at the cost of berating players, humiliating assistant coaches, and cheating.

Another illustration of different motives and how they affect a team is the conflict that may exist between winning and the pursuit of an education. Whether you are a high school coach or college coach, you must recognize the fact that you coach student athletes. One of the criteria of their playing eligibility is maintaining a certain academic standard as defined by either the school or the governing body.

The student athlete's education may also be a motivator for you personally. Coaches who place a high value on education give greater emphasis to ensuring an athlete's academic success. Such a coach may try to avoid class and practice conflicts, or the coach may closely monitor the student athlete's attendance and progress during the semester. All the motivators that influence your coaching help you make day-by-day, season-by-season coaching decisions. You will ultimately have a clearer and broader perspective of what you are doing, why you are doing it, and how it will affect the team.

Earning a Good Reputation

As a youngster, I practiced shaking hands with my mother as though I were meeting someone new. My mother, who was also my first coach, emphasized the importance of shaking hands with confidence and a firm grip and looking the individual square in the eye. As I learned, putting your best foot forward creates a lasting image in those you meet. Image includes not only a handshake, but also your presentation and demeanor, which all adds to building your reputation as a professional.

Put another way, would you be comfortable with the local 10 o'clock news broadcasting your discussion with the team from the afternoon practice, what you wore that day to your coaching office, or the private conversation you had with a recruit's parent? If the thought of thousands of people watching you in these situations makes you uneasy, then there is room for improvement in your behavior and actions. Your reputation gradually forms from how you conduct yourself day in and day out.

When I think of coaches who set a standard for professional demeanor on the field, in meetings, at clinics, or one-on-one with coaches or recruits, I often think of Kathy Veroni at Western Illinois University and Margie Wright at Fresno State University. Both are Hall of Fame coaches with coaching records to go along with the honor. However, a good reputation is not simply about wins. Coach Veroni and Coach Wright are consistent in their behavior toward others and in a variety of environments. They are known for their honesty, integrity, class, high standards, work ethics, fairness, sharing, caring, and, yes, their excellence in coaching. They have built solid reputations by being consistent in these traits over the span of their careers. They took notice of how they wanted to be perceived and how athletes, administrators, parents, fans, and other coaches perceived them. Their reputations withstand the 10 o'clock news test. Does yours?

Looking for Role Models

Role models come in all sizes, ages, and both genders. While coaching at the University of Hawaii, I was in northern California on a recruiting trip. I made it a point while recruiting at softball games to seek out a coach I was unfamiliar with to sit beside him or her. I eventually would turn the conversation to coaching theories and techniques. I found not only could I recruit, I could continue to learn at the same time. One of my favorite goal-setting techniques I borrowed from Rhonda Revelle, the current NFCA president and head coach at the University of Nebraska, with whom I had struck up a conversation on a recruiting trip. She shared what she was doing with her team in helping the athletes learn to set and obtain goals. Coach Revelle was my role model and continues to be so to this day.

We think of a role model as being an older person who is highly successful in his or her career, or we think as ourselves as role models to our athletes. Both of these are true; however, a role model may be one of your athletes, an assistant coach, or someone outside the sport. A role model is the person you want to emulate. We hope the example we set for our athletes is positive and that the role models we look to provide healthy and positive images.

During the time I was coach of the team, an All-American outfielder for the University of Hawaii was unknowingly a role model for myself and the team. Both of her parents had died when she was young. She lived with her siblings and was helping to raise the younger children. She was a smart student and a phenomenal player. Her ability to keep things in perspective, overcome adversity, and work hard while maintaining an upbeat attitude was inspirational to all of us.

Look for role modeling opportunities in others and yourself. Recognize the influence you assert on others, keeping it helpful and positive. Finally, encourage your staff and athletes to be role models for one another.

Seeing the We in the Big Picture

Quotes such as "We climb the ladder of success on the backs of others," or "I'm successful because I was lifted up by others," or "We play up to a better team" highlight the fact that we are only as successful as those around us. Therefore, it is prudent that we work to ensure we all are successful. Step back from the singular view of you and your team to a global perspective of the sport across the United States, better yet around the world. As the sport matured over the years, individual players excelled, teams became powerhouses, and dynasties were created before other players, teams, and dynasties took their place. Each incremental effort that led to surpassing the skill of a previous player or team resulted in the slow but sure improvement of the sport overall.

Why is it important? As coaches we contribute to the improvement of the sport within our own team and on a larger scale. I have always felt a responsibility and duty to give back to the sport that has given me so much. To keep the sport strong and vital, coaches and players need to share information, speak at clinics, write articles, and be active in the coaching associations. You can give back and contribute in your local community and on a larger scale.

The number-one selling book in softball is *Winning Softball Drills* by Dianne Baker from Texas Woman's University. Coach Baker is a Hall of Fame coach and one of the most prolific authors and speakers in the sport. Coaches and athletes for years have benefited from her good-hearted and sincere efforts to preach the sport. Thousands of coaches have attended her coaches clinic in Texas. To her it is not about Dianne Baker promoting Dianne Baker; it is about improving the sport. She recruits and brings in the best and brightest coaches from all levels to speak at the clinic. She is just as willing to spend hours with a youth coach as she is with a college coach. The sport has grown because of coaches like her who continually give back to the game.

Hall of Fame coach Gayle Blevins created the running slap when faced with speedy right-handed batters who were getting thrown out by a step. Then the head coach at Indiana, she knew if the batters could put the ball in play, they could possibly beat out the play or put pressure on the defense to force an error. The new technique was highly successful and is today synonymous with the sport. Coach Blevins did not sit on the new skill. She taught other coaches how to teach the running slap to their players. She wrote about the running slap, spoke at clinics, and made a video. Others coaches improved on the running slap, and the number of coaches teaching and sharing with other coaches grew.

Hoarding improvements, insights, new strategies, or refinements of skills only weakens the sport overall. By each of us working on a better running slap or training technique and sharing that knowledge, we keep the sport strong. When we teach others, we give back to the sport that is our passion and has given us so much.

Your parents probably taught you to give credit where credit is due. This simple life lesson goes a long way with athletes, assistant coaches, managers, trainers, and parents. Recognition of the work and efforts of others is remembered and taken to heart by the recipient. You and I know coaching is a team effort. It is impossible to coach a squad of players, practice, play, travel, and train without the contributions of many. A pat on the back privately or publicly showing your appreciation of their contribution is worth a million bucks to them and to you.

Remaining a Student

As coaches we are also students. To stay abreast of the innovations in the sport is as much of a coaching responsibility as being prepared for practice. Even the national championship coach does not remain stagnant. Sitting on one's laurels only gets a coach dethroned. Attend coaching conventions and clinics. Review the latest coaching books and videotapes. No single coach, no matter how successful, is immune to complacency and doldrums of status quo. You'll be left in the dust if you are not current.

Each year I enjoy attending the National Fastpitch Coaches Association convention. Though I no longer coach, I enjoy the opportunity to visit former coaching colleagues and keep current with what is happening in the sport. What a terrific opportunity to learn from the great names in the sport and the up and coming coaches. At each NFCA convention, it is a given that NCAA Women's College World Series champion coach Mike Candrea is in the audience listening to other coach's presentations. Coach Candrea, a Hall of Fame inductee, is a perennial attendee at the convention. His on-the-field consistency in excellence continues off the field as well. He continues to be a student of the game, and he continually is giving back by being a presenter.

Wisdom that can be applied to fastpitch can be found outside of the softball world. Expose yourself to knowledge and skills of other successful people and industries. The crossover knowledge gained from other sports is valuable whether it be baseball, track, or volleyball. Where do you think speed training and plyometrics came from? What worked for training athletes to be faster in track and field works in softball.

Be willing to search for knowledge outside of the sports world. Consider business, management, and sales videos or books as a starting place. If you're a college coach, you know how important it is to identify recruitable talent and to close the deal. People in the business of negotiating and selling for a living turn to some of the following books to improve their selling and closing skills: *Strategic Selling* and *Conceptual Selling* by Miller and Heiman; *You Can Negotiate Anything* by Cohen; *Getting to Yes* by Fisher,

Ury, and Patton; and *How to Master the Art of Selling* by Hopkins. In the business and management fields these books are terrific resources: *The Seven Habits of Highly Effective People* and *Principle-Centered Leadership* by Stephen Covey; *Leadership Is an Art* by Max DePree; and *The Leadership Challenge* by Kouzes and Posner. After all, as coaches, we are in the business of managing people. The people we manage are athletes of all ages. The better we are as managers, the better the athlete and team.

Lastly don't forget to look in your own backyard for a learning experience. Our coaching is judged best by those we coach. Look to your athletes and assistant coaches for feedback. Create an environment in which assistants and athletes feel free to communicate. Otherwise you end up coaching in a vacuum lacking crucial information. Finding out something was not working after the fact is too late. So go to the source—those nearest you.

Learning From Setbacks

While watching a game a few years ago, I overheard a coach say to a dejected player who had struck out on an inside rise ball, "Stay off the rise ball." For the player, this was worthless information. Of course the player knew she had just whiffed at a rise ball. What she needed was information to help her avoid swinging at the rise ball. She needed the how-to information, not the let-me-tell-you-what-you-already-know information. Just as importantly, the athlete needed to focus not on the negative, the mistake or the error, but rather on the analysis of why she swung at the rise ball and how to keep from repeating the same behavior. She then needed to leave the disappointment and anger behind when she stepped up to the plate the next at bat, and she needed to keep the empowering lesson.

You've heard the story of starving people who received donated shovels, picks, tillers, and seed so that they could begin farming. The idea was to supply these people with the tools they needed to farm so that they could grow their own crops, harvest the crops, and put food on the table. But the starving people continued to starve. They didn't know how to farm. When you supply bats, balls, and gloves to your players, teach them how to coach themselves as well. Teach them how to move from failure to success by analyzing the failure to gain a lesson. Teach them to keep the lesson, but leave the loss and negative distracting emotion behind.

Maintaining Balance

While I was coaching at the University of Texas at Arlington during the '80s, the NCAA adopted a rule limiting how many weeks a team could practice. Up to this time, a coach could hold practices every single day of the school year, and some coaches came pretty close to doing just that. I was one of them. My rationale was that if we were going to compete with the top 20, then I would have to mold the players into top players through hours of practice. I had a couple of really good players on the team, a few not so fair, and a number of mediocre players. So we practiced and practiced and practiced, day in and day out. I was concerned when the new rule passed. How could we compete with the best if we didn't keep up the grueling practice regimen? The year the rule went into effect, the team was ranked for the first time in the history of the program. How did that happen with less practice? I found out that I looked forward to less practice. If I didn't want to practice, you can imagine how much the athletes appreciated having some downtime. It's called balance.

We coaches are intense and driven to a state in which we don't allow recovery time in our lives or our athletes' lives. We know the need for physiological recovery in training. Why is it so hard to recognize the need for psychological and emotional recovery time? To be a productive and healthy coach, plan for balance between coaching and the rest of your life. You'll find a little time away from the field rekindles your energy and enthusiasm. You'll return to the field with renewed vigor and a fresh way of thinking. You and those around you will benefit.

Getting There From Here

Around the time Title IX passed, the path to coaching was through teaching. This seems odd now, but at the time the introduction to coaching was to teach physical education and coach a girls' or women's sport. Those of us who started coaching in the '70s most likely began our careers as teachers. Many of us coached up to three sports, a sport for each season—fall, winter, and spring.

Today the path to coaching may or may not include teaching. So how does someone enter the coaching field or advance in coaching? How much softball knowledge is required to be a softball coach? Should a coach have been a player of the sport? Should a coach of girls' and women's sports be of the same gender? These questions may seem idiotic to some, though in actuality they are excellent questions with no one right answer.

Coaching T-ball to five- and six-year-olds at times requires a similar level of knowledge and skill as does coaching Olympians. Both situations require knowledge of the game, the rules, the basic skills, patience, a desire to impart knowledge, the ability to provide a safe environment, and an ability to work with a group of people. The T-ball coach is no less valuable and important to the sport than the Olympic coach. If it were not for thousands of T-ball coaches who successfully provide an entry into the sport for young girls, we would not have the athletes at the Olympic level. Both coaches play a valuable role in the life of the athlete and to the sport.

I would encourage male and female, former players and newly introduced individuals, to get involved with coaching our young female athletes. The rewards are many, and the need for coaches is great. If you are interested in coaching, step to the front of the line and get involved. Educate yourself on the sport. We are fortunate to have excellent books and videos on softball. Tune in and watch college and women's pro softball games on ESPN or your local cable channel. Attend fastpitch games in your community. Attend coaching clinics, join the National Fastpitch Coaches Association, and subscribe to available magazines that cover the sport. There is an ample base of knowledge available to make you well versed in the sport. I would also encourage you to read about not only the Xs and Os of the sport but also educate yourself in the areas of sport injuries, mental training, conditioning and physical training, and teaching theories. Feel comfortable seeking out experts in the field and attend their practices.

Those interested in coaching at the collegiate level should be aware that in the current marketplace a college coach often was a player and started his or her coaching career path as an assistant. For some reason, fewer coaches take positions at NCAA Division I schools without first starting as an assistant at that level. It is more common for a head coach at the NCAA Division II and III and NAIA junior college levels to move within those levels than to move to an NCAA Division I position. There are exceptions to this trend, but they are exceptions. This is not to say one level of a national governing body calls for a better coach; it is simply recognizing what is happening in the marketplace.

If you are currently a student athlete or a youth or high school coach and want to pursue coaching at the college level, then get the word out. Speak with your college coach and ask if there is a position available or if he or she will be a reference on your behalf. Write, e-mail, and telephone college programs inquiring about possible assistant coaching or graduate student coaching positions. Read the NCAA News or go online to **www.NCAA.org** to check college coaching job listings. Prepare your resume and have a letter of introduction ready to send when a position opens. Tailor both the resume and letter to the position, addressed to the correct person. If you are able to, attend the NFCA convention to meet college coaches. Work college softball camps and clinics as a way to work with college coaches. You can list the camp or clinic on your resume and possibly the head coach of the program as a reference. In short, market yourself starting early. Getting your foot in the door is just that, an avenue to a coaching career.

Network

Always keep a lookout on the market, what positions are open and what the opportunities are. It is also imperative to keep in contact with those in the sport and in athletics generally. Drop a line, e-mail, or occasionally call these contacts. If you are out of sight, then you are out of mind.

A few years ago when I was involved in launching the women's pro softball league, we had an opening in the league office for a person who would work closely with me in all aspects of league operations. I called coaches whose opinions I respected inquiring as to anyone they might have in mind for the position. Jacquie Joseph, head coach at Michigan State University and current NFCA president had just the person in mind, an athlete she had coached at Bowling Green State University. This former player, Karen Appelbaum, had contacted Jacquie the week before to touch base. She was on Jacquie's mind when I called. Karen and I worked together for three years. She became a role model for me in many ways, including her networking capabilities. I marveled at her skill of keeping in touch with people from her past. When she left the league, it was to work with someone with whom she had maintained contact. Networking only works if you keep the connection open.

Play the Market Game

If you are a current college coach and are considering making a change, whether it be to improve your current situation or to coach elsewhere, then consider playing the market game. On the whole, college softball coaching salaries are low because of a lack of marketplace demand. It is possible to inflate college coaching salaries by creating demand. Every time you leave a position, the person hired to replace you is paid more than you were. A dynamic market creates demand. Leaving a position and accepting a position elsewhere helps create a demand for softball coaches. Unfortunately in women's sports, we tend to stay put and not test the market; thus, we keep a lower ceiling on the job market in our sport.

I encourage you to apply for coaching positions that would be considered a vertical move. The simple act of applying for another position places you in a demand position for your current position and helps you improve your current situation. It also increases the pool of applicants for the open position. Too often in women's sports, administrators say there is not enough interest in the position and select a candidate with less experience and qualifications.

If you apply for a position you have no serious interest in, then consider withdrawing and telling the administration the salary is too low and there is not enough support for the program. It says to them, "Get with it, you're not keeping up with the Joneses." I also encourage you to call and recommend coaches to the chair of a search committee. The recommended coach's administrator places a greater value on the coach when he or she gets a call from another athletic director wanting to invite the coach to apply. By doing these two things you help raise the ceiling and expand the market. Your position is improved as a result and so are others.

Going for It

If you are serious about applying for a position, then have your resume in tip-top shape. Try to begin the search process after a relatively successful year. Your introduction letter should be persuasive and highlight your accomplishments, abilities, and what sets you apart from the other candidates. Your references should know they are being used as a reference, and they should be able to provide an outstanding reference. Ideally your references should be people who know your work and are respected by the search committee. If your references know members of the search committee or decision makers at the school, then have them call members of the search committee on your behalf.

Be proactive in the process. Call the search committee chair about the position and discuss it over the telephone. This introduces you to the individual, and you can gain additional information allowing you to tailor your resume to the position. Once you have sent the resume and introductory letter, telephone the search committee chair two or three days later to confirm it arrived. This is another opportunity to promote you.

The Interview

If you are selected for an interview, then do additional research on the search committee members, the athletic department, athletic director, school, and reputation of the program. Consider possible questions that you may be asked and prepare responses. Approach the interview as an opportunity for you to gain information about the school and future colleagues. After all, should you be offered the position, you want it to be fit for you and the school.

If you receive an offer, say you need to think about it and to discuss it with counsel. Plan on asking for more in more than just one area. Consider asking for increases or addition of perks such as direct salary, benefits, freedom to conduct outside camps, vacation, retirement, and ownership of copyright of any books, videos, speeches, or articles you prepare. The two most important things you could do to improve your contract are to make sure it is for a fixed term of years and that you may be terminated for cause only with cause narrowly defined. I recommend you select those areas that are of the greatest importance to you and ask for what you want. It is much easier to get an increase at the beginning of the employment relationship than later. It also lets the athletic director know that you will negotiate to improve your position.

If you come to terms on the offer, then ask for a copy of the contract to share with your attorney. I encourage you to have an attorney review the contract. You don't necessarily need to have an attorney negotiate the contract or make changes to it. You should however know the positives and negatives of the contract and the legal implications so that you make an informed decision. Only an attorney can provide this legal analysis. It is money well spent for an hour or so of the attorney's time. After all, you will be living with the results of the contract for years.

Creating a Career Plan

Create a short-term and long-term career plan. What are your competitive ambitions? What type of institution provides the resources to enable you to achieve those goals? How much stability do you want in your career? Do you also want to teach? Create a career road map. Determine your action steps to reach your career goals. Annually reassess your progress and make adjustments at that time to the plan. Over time we all alter our objectives. Circumstances change and our desires and needs change as do our perspectives. It is because of these changes that it is wise to step back and take another look at your career plan each year. Then pursue your dreams and become the coach you already have within you.

CHAPTER TWENTY–SIX

Conducting Camps and Clinics

Judi Garman

Photo by Mel Franks, courtesy of Cal State Fullerton

When I got my first coaching job in 1971 in the Los Angeles area, I was so excited because I would be able to attend clinics and listen and learn from speakers whose names I knew from the sports pages. My first baseball clinic was at USC and featured Ernie Banks. There are two things memorable about my first baseball clinic. First, I got to listen to a major league ballplayer whom I had only seen on TV. One of the tips I still remember was how this great Chicago Cub player said that he would stand at home plate and hit bags of balls over second base to "groove the perfect swing." The second memory is that of the other woman at the clinic coming to sit with me at break and asking what school my husband coached at.

I learned a valuable philosophical lesson at a UCLA basketball clinic. I still remember the thrill of learning from some of the top men's college coaches. These coaches would diagram the offense they would use, with opposing coaches taking notes. When a coach asked if they weren't worried about sharing their offensive plans with their opponents the answer came back: "No, if we do it right they can't stop us!" We learned so much valuable information, as the next speaker would then tell us how they intended to stop that offense.

Sadly I have had several poor experiences with coaches of women's sports. A number of years ago I had the opportunity to share a room with a coach from the first professional softball league. I couldn't wait to pick her brain. As we talked softball, we were discussing the infamous first and third base running play. When I asked her how she defensed the first-and-third play, I was shocked when she answered, "I won't tell you." The next evening she was working on a presentation she was to give at an upcoming clinic and made the remark that it was "very difficult to give a speech and not to tell them what I really do." I must admit I lost it and gave a rather passionate speech about how can we ever learn and improve both our coaching abilities and the game if we don't honestly share. The room was very quiet for the next several days. To her credit, a few days later she decided to share her ideas. I have found current coaches very willing to share both in clinics and one on one. What a valuable resource these coaches are.

A Softball Clinic Is Born

My dream when I was growing up was to coach a college team, live in a big city, drive a sports car, and give speeches around the world. Dreams do come true. I have had the privilege of speaking at clinics all over the United States as well as Japan, Czechoslovakia, Holland, and Italy. My first speaking engagement and first softball clinic were at Golden West College. This was the first softball clinic I was aware of and it started rather informally. It was 1975 and many local high schools were adding softball. There was a chance meeting with a panicked drill team leader who was just told she had to coach softball. When she found out I was a college softball coach, she asked for help. Realizing there were many other teachers in the same boat, we decided to do a clinic on a Saturday. She would get the word out, and JoAnn Zwanziger and I would conduct a four-hour clinic. Cost would be $7.50 to cover duplicating materials and buy us dinner for our effort. Thirty-five dance teachers showed up and a softball clinic was born. Within three years the clinic had grown to 300, and in 2001 it will be held for the 27th consecutive year. (Price has gone up a little!)

The value of clinics is best illustrated by someone I will call Rosie. Rosie was another dance teacher who attended her first clinic about 10 years ago and sat in the front row. She asked many interesting and off-the-wall questions, making it obvious she had no clue about softball. She kept returning and three years later shared that she had won her first game. It was another two years before she won the league championship. At the clinic the following year during a question and answer period just before lunch, a new coach stated, "I am completely overwhelmed. I am a dance teacher and don't know where to start." Rosie, still sitting in the front row, jumped up and said, "Honey, you are having lunch with me!" And Rosie began her mentoring role.

Conducting Clinics

The true value of clinics is in the exchange of ideas. Most attendees agree that if they learn one new idea or tip, the clinic is well worth it. Clinics also provide an opportunity for each coach to reaffirm that what they are doing is correct. It is also an opportunity for the clinic director to improve his or her own knowledge. I have often invited speakers to speak on areas that I need help with. Clinics also provide a great community service and outreach. As your local coaches improve, so does the athlete whom you may eventually recruit. Clinics also provide a great opportunity for you to promote your program and staff. Offering academic credit through a college may also help coaches and teachers move up the ranks. Offering Amateur Softball Association VIP credit can certify ASA coaches and provide $1 million liability coverage. Conducting a clinic is also a chance to give something back to the game. Lastly, it can also be a great moneymaker.

Where to start? The following section comprises the nuts and bolts of organizing a clinic.

Speakers

First, identify your market. If you live in a metropolitan area, you may be able to draw enough people, while limiting it to coaches. In smaller communities, you may need to appeal to both athletes and coaches to get the numbers necessary. Decide if you want a hands-on clinic with some participation or an all-lecture clinic. Determine the level of coaches that you want to attract (youth, high school, college) and the speakers who are most appealing and beneficial for them.

While big names can be an attraction, their ability to present meaningful and useful material should be your main criteria for selection. I have walked out of sessions where big-name people do not know how to teach or even how to do the skills. And many major leaguers love to tell stories and drop names, while giving little information.

With the many clinics now offered and the demands on the speakers' time, you should secure your speakers six months to a year in advance. Have a signed contract so that there are no misunderstandings. Speakers are usually asked to provide four to five topics they would like to speak on, then the clinic director can choose the topic that best fits and rounds out the program. The contract should include the date, times, length of presentation, and the days the speaker is required to be there. Standard lecture sessions are 50 minutes long with the last five minutes used for questions and answers.

The contract should also state remuneration and expenses paid by the clinic, and whether a Saturday night stay is required. If the speaker is flying, the costs of the airline ticket can be much lower with a Saturday night stay. Make sure it is understood who makes the travel arrangements. And because many clinics are held in the winter months, make sure you allow time for delayed or cancelled flights. Should flight cancellations occur, the clinic director can often make the necessary changes to the program if kept informed of the problems and new arrival times. If weather can be a factor, the speakers should arrive the night before. However, with all the flight problems that seem to occur, this rule is probably a good one for all speakers.

If there are other competing clinics in your area, you may want to include a clause in your contract prohibiting the speaker from speaking at another clinic in your area within a certain time period. You would not want a popular speaker to appear at another clinic in your area just before yours. In addition, attendees love to get printed materials. Establish the deadline for when such materials need to be provided by the speaker for you to duplicate.

Providing the speakers an opportunity to sell their books or videotapes is a big plus for the speaker. It may help you land speakers that you did not think would consider your clinic. If the clinic is in a hotel, it is often easy to get comp rooms for the speakers. Meals can be handled several ways, but I recommend one of the following: speakers are either on their own or are given a voucher or credit to use at specified restaurants. This way, you can safeguard your budget more closely.

Make sure the speakers know the level of knowledge of the audience so that they can present the appropriate material that can be both educational and worthwhile. When players are attending, it is critical that the speaker know the age level. Informing the speaker of the numbers expected also helps the speaker prepare an effective presentation. Find out what equipment is needed such as an overhead projector, chalkboard, bases, bats, balls, or screen.

Facilities

It is tougher to secure facilities now with the scheduling demands on most facilities. While athletic facilities may be the most economical route, they are often not the best facilities for hearing and comfort. If the clinic is all lecture, attendees do not want to sit on bleachers.

Facilities should include a stage, so it is easy to see footwork and demonstrations. Set your date and be prepared to reserve the facility at least one year in advance. I have to reserve our facility two years in advance.

Exhibitors

This is a good source of revenue and also adds a lot to your clinic. Coaches get to see the latest in equipment and apparel and gather information on changes, advantages, and costs. Other areas to include are fund-raising vendors, pins, and photography. Exhibitors pay for the chance to meet with the attendees. Time must be allotted so that they have an opportunity to get together. Twenty-minute breaks between sessions allow time to meet. We also try to limit the amount of time they must be there. For a one-and-a-half day clinic, we have exhibitors stay through lunch the first day only. Remember, exhibitors, too, cherish their weekends.

Exhibitors must be contacted very early. Their budgets are often set in the summer months, and their advertising decisions follow. Get on their clinic schedule before their money runs out or they are committed elsewhere. Exhibitors who cannot attend in person can be given an option of providing materials for distribution for a lesser fee. Remind exhibitors that under NCAA rules, they cannot give door prizes or gifts if a school or college coach is sponsoring the clinic.

Try to obtain a clinic sponsor. For a fee, the sponsor gets title name recognition, can hang banners on the stage, and receives other special promotional opportunities. You may also increase revenue by including advertisements in the clinic brochure or an advertising flyer with your clinic mailing.

Publicity

Advertise any way you can. We do a mailing to all local high schools, youth softball leagues, and have a clinic mailing list of over 800 past attendees. We advertise on our school's softball Web site, on softball newsgroups on the Web, and in local newspapers under community services or events. We contact youth league presidents and offer league rates.

We have flyers available at athletic events—someone always knows some-one who is a softball coach, so word of mouth works effectively here. Offer a discount for preregistration. It helps with planning and also gets people to commit to attending.

Keep the Clinic Running Smoothly

Speakers must stay on schedule. Signal each speaker when there are 10 minutes remaining, then 5 minutes, then when it is time to quit. We pro-vide lunch so that we can keep everyone together and they can continue to talk softball. Use evaluation forms to find out how you can improve your clinic and to get suggestions for future speakers and topics. Include a bulle-tin board where attendees can post job openings or games needed. Use name tags that also list affiliation (youth coach, name of high school) to encourage dialogue.

Camps

Many of the logistics for running a camp are the same as for running a clinic. Reserve facilities, secure camp staff, and advertise early. For this article and to understand more about running successful camps, I contacted a variety of coaches to get their insights, tips, and suggestions. Experience is often the best teacher, and these coaches were willing to share their thoughts and recommendations.

The questions were "Why run camps? Why give up your holidays or summer vacations to spend your free time conducting camps for young softball players? And why spend the nights supervising and worrying about hundreds of young athletes when you've barely recovered from your last road trip?"

All coaches agreed that a camp is an effective moneymaker. Another rea-son most conduct camps was well said by Carol Bruggeman: "I believe it is the best thing I've done in building the program at Purdue. We have a holi-day camp in January and overnight camps in June/July. It has brought a tremendous amount of exposure to our campus and program. Four of my current teams are one-time campers."

Some of us have decided that half-day camps are the answer. When ev-eryone is tired, you all go home; insurance and costs are much less (no food or lodging costs); and there are no supervision worries. Plus, you can make more money since costs are so much lower. At Fullerton we go only four days (eliminating Fridays) because so many have weekend tournaments. You can accomplish more with overnight camps, but the risks are greater. Jay Miller confirms, "You make more money on day camps, but overnight camps help with recruiting."

There are many camps now offered, and as Bobby Simpson stated, "The nice thing now is that they have lots of choices. And camps are constantly changing. What campers wanted in the past is not what they want now." The goal of the camps he runs is "to focus on teaching campers to coach themselves when they leave. Provide a lot of information and drills and teach them how to use it in a personal way." Give an evaluation at the end of camp to find out their needs and what they want out of camp. You usually get helpful suggestions, but you never get a good grade on food!

Should You Run the Camp Yourself or Connect With an Outside Group?

The consensus was to do it yourself. Carol Bruggeman said, "You make more money and run the camp the way you want to." Jacquie Joseph wrote, "I never let an outside group run my camp. They usually don't know what they are doing and you end up doing all the work yourself." Patti Gerckens stated some benefits to connecting with an outside group such as "They do handle advertising, registration, and refunds, which can be time-consuming headaches. But you make more money doing it yourself. If the headaches outweigh the pay, then go with an outside group." One coach whose camp failed because of poor publicity felt the outside group would know better how to get the word out.

How do you publicize? Lessons learned are to start at the beginning of the year and have camp materials available at all games. Cross-advertise with baseball and do mailings together, as families have daughters, too. Make good use of the Internet, and use the NFCA listing of camps and clinics. Publicize early and often.

Some coaches incorporate, which also protects against lawsuits that could wipe you out personally. Other coaches have arrangements with their schools and may run the camps through conferences or community services that act as the middleman. Make sure you have liability insurance and secondary medical insurance to cover what their medical insurance does not.

Making More Money

Take advantage of additional opportunities to make money. Get a sponsor to donate your camp T-shirts. Have a photographer take pictures of campers with camp staff or a favorite counselor. Sell the 5 × 7 for $10 and arrange a split with the photographer. Have a camp store selling school merchandise, shorts, hats, key chains, and extra T-shirts. Dads really like the hats. Use a room in the dorm to sell snacks and food from eight to nine each evening. Sell sodas, candy, and pizza by the slice, or make a deal with a local pizza company. You get a percentage on all orders. Delegate selling to one of the instructors and give him or her 10 percent of the proceeds, or have an assistant coach be in charge and take all the proceeds.

Staffing

Campers love to hang out with college players. Get your players involved. Select players who know and love the game and would say it as you would in a given situation. As Ruth Gibbs put it, "To hear them emulate your teaching is great!" It also provides valuable experience in teaching and communicating. I also provide the staffers with letters of recommendation following the camp, outlining their responsibilities and time involved to include in their work experience portfolio. Use players as dorm counselors and hostesses. Campers want to hear of their experiences as players. The key is to get reliable people involved in both managing and teaching. Have a knowledgable trainer at all sessions as well as overnight.

Parents are most interested in safety. Will there be boys in the same building? Are the campers allowed to leave campus at any time? Everyone said a secret is to wear the campers out during the day and keep them very busy after dinner. Make evenings fun nights. Linda Wells keeps them in a hotel, so they can watch movies. Activities range from movies to talent nights, lip syncs, and ice cream socials. If showing videos, make sure they are age appropriate. Play softball games using Frisbees, Lite-Flite balls, and dodge ball on the bases. Or some camps play regular games in the evening. Have extra sessions with all the staff on the field and where campers choose the skill to work on. End late, around a quarter of ten, return to the rooms, and have lights out by eleven o'clock. Give them little time to get in trouble.

Supervision is important. Assign coaches to greet athletes and walk them to their rooms. Assign hall patrol, room checks, and wake-up calls to coaches. You need to have reliable hall supervisors. Kids get homesick and it's a long day. Have campers initial a roster to show they were checked in. Then, if they sneak out you can show the parents it was not your fault! Do a roll call every morning as well. Have one central camp office (coaches' room) that they go to in case of emergency. Have a trainer stay overnight to deal with any medical problems.

Be Organized

Alice Reen, camp director at the University of Texas, said, "Organize your camp brochure to alleviate questions from parents. Answer the questions there and eliminate many phone calls. Most of the UT programs hire a camp director to take the stress of the coaches, especially the spring sports."

Be organized at camp as well. Give a printed schedule to every camper at check-in and have plenty of copies for the coaches. Have coaches' meetings to discuss rules, responsibilities, additional assignments outside of coaching, equipment distribution, lesson plans, daily schedule, and safety precautions. Kelly Ford stated, "I have learned you need to spell it out for the coaches as well as the athletes." For large camps have one coach who oversees everything and acts as a troubleshooter. Have a bulletin board for daily plans and changes, which everyone needs to check daily. Give coaches clipboards with schedules and pencils. Synchronize their watches. Texas has the staff meet every day at breakfast to go over the day and be sure everyone is on the same page. Provide staff shirts and name tags. It looks professional.

Be prepared for everything. Always factor weather into the camp. From extreme heat to rain, plan activities for both. Be prepared as well for different skill levels, and have drills prepared in case you must simplify or be more advanced.

Here are some additional random tips and thoughts:

- Keep players at the field as much as possible. Serve lunch there to save time and cost of busing. It also helps wear them out!
- Allow time for coaches to get together and share philosophies and drills. It becomes a clinic within a clinic.
- Change instructors yearly and bring in guest coaches.
- Evaluations or scorecards? Parents like them, but they take too much time from the staff; they are also based on shallow/small evaluation and can be really wrong.
- Camp photos? Waste of time and money.
- Be disciplined early in the week and let up if you can.

Make It Fun

While moms and dads want to know what they are learning, the campers want to have fun! In the summer, campers are playing a lot of softball. As Carol Bruggeman said,

> If you simply drill them to death, they will be bored and burned out. Do lots of short stations, but also play lots of competitive games utilizing each skill. We have the softball Olympics. Events include total team baserunning, five bunts each between the cones, etcetera. There are 10 events and a total team score for each event. Teams are then awarded points for their team finish, with winners decided by overall team points. And we end the afternoon sessions with a huge water slide and each day work on a different slide. It cools them off. At closing ceremonies, each team does a skit that is the highlight of my week! Comic relief!

These are just a few simple ideas of how you can teach and make it fun.

Final Thoughts

I have run a camp in Italy for eight years. In Italy, girls and boys play baseball together until the age of eight. Then girls go into softball. At one camp, there was a little girl who did not want to leave her baseball friends to play softball. I forced her to join us and at the end of camp had a conversation with Francesca and her father. I encouraged her to stay with softball and suggested that if she worked hard she might some day play for the Italian National Team. What a thrill to be there when the Italian team qualified for the Olympics with Francesca Francolini playing first base. I did not know she was that little girl at camp until her father came up and thanked me for the encouragement given. Not all campers make an Olympic team, but we can give them the opportunity to make many dreams come true. And we can make a difference in many people's lives.

After all the hard work is done, when the camp or clinic has concluded, it is time to really evaluate and appreciate what has been accomplished. We are in softball because we love the game. Camps and clinics give us the opportunity to share the game we love and help others improve and grow. Is the hard work worth it? Look at the faces of those who attend. The answer is self-evident and a resounding *Yes!*

CHAPTER TWENTY–SEVEN

Beating the Burnout Factor

Sharon J. Drysdale and Karren J. Drysdale

Photo courtesy of Evanston Photographic Studios, Inc.

I am going to start by telling you something you already know: coaching is a challenging profession. Coaching can be stressful and burnout can result.

If you are a coach, you are a candidate for burnout. If you are an enthusiastic, hard-working coach who loves softball and kids and you want to make a difference in your players' lives, you are especially prone to coaching burnout. According to the Burnout Susceptibility Profile (Vernacchia, Level 2 USA Coaching Education Program), coaches who are susceptible to burnout are described as extremely dedicated, goal-oriented, idealistic/altruistic, high achievers, highly responsible, perfectionists, and success driven. The irony of this list is that I, as a coach, would like to be on it. I suspect many of you possess these qualities and consider them assets.

Although there is no one universally accepted, operational definition of burnout, I like the way Maslach and Leiter describe it in their book *The Truth About Burnout:* "It represents an erosion in values, dignity, spirit, and will—an erosion of the human soul. It is a malady that spreads gradually and continuously over time, putting people into a downward spiral from which it's hard to recover." Coaching burnout is a transformation from energetic, involved, accomplished, capable, *spirited* coach to exhausted, bored, withdrawn, cynical, ineffective, *burned out* coach.

Unrecognized and untreated, burnout can snuff out the fire of your coaching soul. It can undermine your professional confidence and sense of accomplishment, cause you to detach from your team, and even lead you to loathe the game and your players. It may result in total exhaustion and the loss of the will to fight back. You may even develop negative attitudes toward coaching that generalize to other areas of your life.

I'd advise you to sit up and take notice because burnout can affect anyone, at any level. In fact, all of us have probably experienced some symptoms of burnout during our coaching careers.

Signs and Symptoms of Burnout

There are varying degrees of burnout, and not everyone expresses it in the same way. Whether you are at a low, moderate, or severe level of burnout depends upon the frequency, intensity, and duration of signs and symptoms. Burnout causes physical, emotional, mental, and behavioral symptoms that may or may not be recognized by others (table 27.1).

Burnout can and probably will affect you in some way, to some extent, at one time or another. I believe that burnout is a condition that is continuously present in all of us at one level or another. The nature of the burnout experience, however, is personal and unique—different for each of us. Nevertheless, we can all end up in the same place, feeling much the same way.

The following descriptions showcase some of the more common ways burnout manifests itself. Do any of them seem familiar to you?

TABLE 27.1

Symptoms of Burnout

Type of burnout	Sample symptoms
Physical	• Depleted physical resources: weak, fatigued, tired, drained, overextended, worn down, used up, empty
	• Lack energy to face another project, person, or problem
	• Muscular tension; unable to unwind or relax
	• Cardiac problems, headache, backache, dizziness, nausea
	• Increased susceptibility to illness, psychosomatic illness, substance abuse (alcohol, drugs, food), accident proneness
	• Slow or incomplete recovery
	• Inability to sleep, interrupted sleep, or too much sleep
Emotional	• Depleted emotional resources: fragile, worried, anxious, helpless, overwhelmed, depressed, frustrated, aggravated, impatient, intolerant, fed up, angry, disinterested, unmotivated, apathetic, diminished drive, flat, complacent, indifferent, impersonal, unfeeling, distant, withdrawn, detached, isolated, dissatisfied, unfulfilled, lonely
	• Lower highs and lower lows; turn off emotions
	• Lack passion and excitement for the job; don't look forward to getting up and going to work; no longer feel challenged; uncharacteristically give days off, cut practices short, let things (i.e., bad attitudes, technique) slide, lost the edge
	• Over- or underreact to physical errors; losing; bad calls; day-to-day crises; especially if this reflects a change in your normal response and is ongoing
	• Resent anyone who makes demands on you; tired of feeling that you have to smile and be "on"
	• Take an unfeeling, distant, disinterested attitude toward coaching and your players; treat athletes in an uncaring and impersonal manner; lose positive feelings, empathy, and respect for athletes
	• Withdraw or avoid contact with players, colleagues, and perhaps even family and friends
	• Feel incapable of meeting the expectations of players, staff, administration, and yourself
	• Find your mind wanders during games/practices
	• Feel like you've had enough; feel like you're spinning your wheels

(continued)

Type of burnout	Sample symptoms
Mental	• Depleted mental resources: disillusioned, discouraged, cynical, insecure, bored, unmotivated, unchallenged, ambivalent
	• Reduced sense of personal accomplishment; feel inadequate, ineffective, indecisive; more rigid thinking
	• Lose confidence in yourself and your ability to lead your team; question your ability to get the job done and to meet the expectations of your team, staff, administration, and self; doubt your ability to make a difference in your program and in the lives of your players
	• Negative self-concept; low self-esteem; attribute poor team performance to yourself
	• Self-defeating thoughts. See "dragons on the wall," problems rather than challenges
	• Thoughts of just leaving work and going home; thoughts of quitting, finding another coaching job, or getting out of coaching all together
Behavioral	• Reduced efficiency; put in more time but get less out of it
	• Inconsistent or declining job performance
	• Late for meetings and practices
	• Lack assertiveness
	• Avoid conflict and stressful situations

The *ostrich* buries his head in the sand and attempts to cope with burnout by refusing to face it. He believes that signs and symptoms of burnout go with the territory and are an inevitable part of the job. He denies or avoids revealing to others his true reactions. He can't see anyone else burning out and continues to try to go it alone. Do you try to cope by yourself?

When the *leaky boat* springs a leak (becomes vulnerable), it begins to take on water (starts to feel burdened and increasingly stressed). Bailing (activating coping mechanisms) does not control the situation. The water keeps pouring in. Do you continue to coach with active burnout, at some level of dysfunction? Do you often feel that you're struggling to stay afloat? Do you feel increasingly exhausted and helpless?

The *balloon* takes in air (accepts more and more responsibility, works harder and longer) and begins to expand (pushes to the limit). Eventually, the pressure builds and something gives. Do you often feel that you're ready to explode?

The *barking dog* complains about anything and everything. He has no patience and becomes more intolerant. He can't seem to get control over anything and can't seem to get anyone to do what he wants, the way he wants, when he wants. Are you feeling that your players and staff aren't listening to you, that they don't hear what you're saying, that they're not buying what you're selling? Are you feeling ineffective, less productive?

The *carousel horse* spins round and round and round. Sometimes she goes up and down. She can't seem to get off the merry-go-round, and she doesn't even know if she wants to. Sometimes it seems like fun and sometimes it gets old, but she keeps going round and round. Can you get off the merry-go-round and stop to think about what you're doing, why you're doing it, and where you're going?

The *bad battery* is always low and can't seem to hold a charge. Some days he feels like his old self but is unable to retain the enthusiasm, motivation, and ambition. He can't seem to recharge. Do you go to bed early and wake up just as tired as when you went to bed? Do you feel like you just don't have it in you anymore? Are your inner resources depleted or exhausted?

The *fat cat* is content with what she has accomplished. She has less drive and enthusiasm than her athletes. Are you resting on your laurels? Have you lost the edge?

The *lame duck* is ready to retire but not old enough to retire. Are you just going through the motions?

Then there is *Charlie*—as in "Sorry, Charlie." He constantly feels down; after all "Only the best tasting tuna get to be Starkist." He feels like a failure, that he's not good enough and unable to meet the expectations of team, staff, and administrators. Do you sense rejection, lack of respect, lack of trust in your ability to lead, and lack of faith in your vision?

The coach suffering the *stock market crash* failed to heed the warning that past performance is no guarantee of future results. He has difficulty handling ups and downs, accepting risks, and riding out lows. Lows are too low—he can't stand losing any more. He can't handle slumps. Did you think things would be different and work out better?

The coach in the *stagnant pond* finds no ripples in her job. Nothing stirs her, nothing seems new and exciting. Wins and losses have lost their impact. Even during crises, the coach feels like *Been there, done that*. She feels unchallenged, sluggish, stale. Do you feel like you've stopped moving, stopped growing? Are you tired of softball practices, games, meetings, seminars, camps, clinics, interviews, books, videos, informal discussions, speaking engagements, dreams and nightmares—softball, softball, softball?

The *mighty mouse* says, "More work? Bring it on! Injuries, discipline problems, academic difficulties? No problem, I can handle it. Fund-raising, groundskeeping, event management, marketing, and promotions? It's my job and I can do it." Do you have a hard time saying no? Do you have a problem delegating tasks and responsibilities? Do you expect yourself to be the action hero and save the day?

The *stockpiler* collects negatives, carries a lot of baggage, puts together a lot of little issues and problems to make a mountain out of a molehill, and has difficulty letting go. He can be a black cloud with a long list of woes. Do you have a habit of piling up negatives?

Humpty Dumpty has fallen and can't be put back together again. She is a burnout victim. Her coping mechanisms have failed. She feels exhausted, detached, and ineffective. Do you continue coaching with active burnout, try changing coaching jobs, or make a career change?

The Path to Burnout

You begin coaching with some sense of yourself and your job—beliefs, values, expectations, concerns, and aspirations (hopes for career and team performance). You start work. You are probably enthusiastic and a little anxious but ready to go. You put in a lot of time and use up a lot of energy, but you don't mind. Stress gives meaning to your work and adds to your sense of fulfillment.

As time goes by, you and your job change. The good, the bad, nothing stays the same over time. You may experience an acute stress—for example, a death in the family or a personal health crisis. It may be that your franchise pitcher quits a week before your first game. (This worked for me!) Perhaps you have some especially difficult players to deal with, a disheartening losing streak, or a change in your administration with subsequent changes in your job requirements or expectations. Perhaps the job isn't what you expected it to be or the transition from player to coach is more difficult than you anticipated. Perhaps you are facing some serious value conflicts and realize that you cannot accomplish what you want without compromising. How you react to your experiences is very important. Acute stressors can change your perspective on your job quickly. You may become disillusioned or your job may not seem so important to you anymore.

Although any factor associated with elevated stress levels may be linked to the development of coaching burnout, it is usually a chronic response to ongoing stress and is seldom dramatic. You may experience constant, unrelenting on-the-job-frustration due to any number of stress factors. Perhaps you are wearing down from years of dealing with difficult coaching issues, injuries, fund-raising, traveling, or recruiting. You may have initially perceived stressful situations as challenging and even motivating, but now you find the situations threatening or even boring. Perhaps you are getting older and quality of life means something different to you now than it once did.

What you experience and how you experience it affect how you think about, see, feel, and express things. A change in your perception alters the match between you and your coaching job. The greater the mismatch, the greater the risk of burnout. At some point, symptoms emerge.

The path to burnout and the path to spirited coaching each has its share of bumps, dips, potholes, curves, straight-a-ways, hills, steep grades, sharp inclines, forks, and detours. How do you know which path you're on? Look within and at your behaviors.

As mentioned briefly in the introduction, a coach's own personality may drive him or her to burn out. Coaches often struggle with perfectionism. They feel they have to keep pushing, that nothing seems good enough. Extreme perfectionism may lead the coach to set excessively high standards of performance in combination with a tendency to make overly critical self-evaluations. He may not be able to set realistic long- and short-term goals and may fail to recognize and give himself credit for smaller victories. He may worry over mistakes and doubt his actions and decisions, frequently worrying about the evaluation of others.

A coach may become a workaholic, going to work early, working during meals, staying late, and taking work home. She may be reluctant to take or give days off. She may be hesitant to delegate and tries to do everything herself. Overwork is one road marker on the path to burnout. The coach in danger of burning out has too much to do and not enough time to do it. She can't seem to catch up and works longer and harder, burning the candle at both ends. The more she does, the more she is expected to do or given to do. She may have poor staff relationships with an ineffective distribution of responsibilities.

The coach may blame himself for team errors, failed strategy, and losses. He may have difficulty living with mistakes or losses or living them down. To the coach who is burning out, these events reflect personal character flaws, failures of intelligence, and lack of courage. He feels no personal identity outside of being a coach. His sense of self and self-worth is based exclusively on being a coach. Since he ties his self-worth to the team's performance and achievement, he has a hard time accepting losses and moving on. He is unable to roll with the punches.

A coach who doesn't take care of herself (diet, exercise, rest) is in danger of burning out. She may keep her burned out feelings bottled up and hidden from others, leading her to feel alone and blame herself and her own weakness. She may feel compelled to give more to others than she saves for herself. She may be reluctant, or even refuse, to take.

A coach who is burning out may feel a rewards/costs imbalance. The job provides less than he needs or want. This may lead to a diminished interest in facing the daily challenges of coaching. The game and job have lost their appeal; they're just too tiring, frustrating, and boring. Softball is increasingly becoming work, not a game. The job may have little meaning to him because he may feel he is sacrificing too much. All he sees is one crisis after another. He may have difficulty dealing with problems that defy easy solutions or answering questions that have no right or wrong answers.

The coach who takes up every cause and fights every battle tooth and nail may experience burnout. The coach's personal stressors such as self-doubt, fear of failure, and undeveloped coaching skills may become exaggerated in the face of high standards and pressure to meet the expectations of players, administrators, media, fans, parents, and himself. The tendency is to perceive coaching-related demands—such as anxiety in interacting with athletes, prospects, parents, or administrators; worry about recruiting; and fear of failure—as overly stressful.

A coach on the road to burnout may have difficulty empathizing with players and seeing things from the perspective of others. She defines what is right as what is good for her, what works for her, what she likes, or what she wants. Wrong is defined as what is bad for her, what doesn't work for her, what she doesn't like, or what she doesn't want. Her relationships with players and staff may feel nonfulfilling, and she may have continually emotionally charged interactions with players. Although she may like the job, she may have become disillusioned with the kids or athletics. A team that can't seem to get over the hump and is underachieving only intensifies the coach's feelings of burnout. She is discouraged by thinking the team has gone as far as she thinks she can take it.

A common element of the path to burnout is feeling chronic, unrelenting, perceived pressure to win. A coach under pressure may lose sight of the reasons he began coaching in the first place. He may become outcome-oriented rather than process-oriented. He feels pressure all the time and during all program phases, with no letup.

With the pressure to win, the coach may experience value conflicts. Coaches have to make difficult decisions. A coach may have to decide between what's best for an individual athlete versus what's best for the team and program. The pressure to recruit the best kids may tempt a coach to try negative recruiting. A coach may be tempted to use strong-arm tactics and bend the rules to secure players and wins. All coaches face tough decisions sometimes between family time and job demands.

On the other side, he may grow discouraged when others don't seem to care as much about his program as he does. He may feel a diminishing faith in administrators, players, and himself. A perceived lack of administrative understanding and support may highlight philosophical differences regarding the program status, budget support, and staffing. He may feel bombarded with rules, regulations, and paperwork but with little or no input into the policies that affect his program. He may be pressured by community conflicts between men's and women's sports or Olympic and revenue sports regarding facilities, budgets, promotions, and marketing. He sees no sense of shared vision with the institution, no common mission or mutual support. All he sees is an administration that is critical, expects too much, and is not open to discussing problems.

He may feel a lack of acknowledgment for his hard work, long hours, and contributions, and buckle under increasing demands to produce at even higher levels with little support in an increasingly competitive arena.

He may experience an expectations/reality conflict. The job isn't what he expected, and he may feel trapped in coaching with a lack of attractive alternatives. He is not where he feels he should be in terms of his career and team performance aspirations. The constant demand for his time and resources may lead him to believe the job demands more than he has or wants to give. He may wonder how he can meet everyone's demands.

The path to burnout is a singular path. A coach on the path may have no life outside softball and little time to pursue other interests.

Fairness and employment issues can cause stress. Low pay, few merit increases, or minimal promotions may be perceived as unjust or discriminatory on the basis of race, sex, or age, especially if she sees others making more progress personally and professionally (e.g., getting a raise, new facility, more support staff). A coach may begin to feel unrecognized, unappreciated, and devalued.

Role conflict or ambiguity may lead to burnout. A coach may feel required to play too many demanding roles, like he's being pulled in too many different directions at once. Some of these roles may not match his interests and competencies. If his job description is unclear, he may feel he's getting mixed messages or conflicting expectations from athletes, parents, administrators, boosters, and fans.

A coach who is burning out may experience loneliness, even when around players and staff; or she may have a limited, ineffective, or nonexistent support group. Her limited support group may spring from her consistently placing job before family and friends. She feels stress at the thought of neglecting her significant others and for being away from home too often.

The Pregame Plan

If you want to get on the path to spirited coaching, you must prepare for the big game. First and foremost, you must become aware. Get to know your personal versus your profressional self, and study your opponent—that is, burnout—so that you can outsmart it, just as you would an opponent on the softball field.

Get Your Act Together

Develop a personal and professional vision of where you want to go, what you hope to accomplish, and how you are going to get there. Keep it fresh in your mind. Set your sights just beyond the horizon and beware of false peaks.

Make a list of the reasons why you are coaching, what you want from coaching, and what you expect to get out of coaching. Set goals (daily practice, game, season, career) for yourself as well as your team. Review and revise them from time to time. Also be careful that the goals you set are not dead ends. Place your personal and team goals on an open-ended continuum.

Try to keep your expectations in check. "You need to define expectations of what you can do, at what pace and rhythm, for how long, with what respite. If you've never clarified and shared this with others, their expectations of you will run your life," according to John-Henry Pfifferling, PhD, director of the Center for Professional Well Being in Durham, North Carolina, and clinical associate professor at the University of North Carolina, Chapel Hill.

On a personal note, I had an anxiety attack while attending a softball session at a national physical education convention when I was a young pup. I was overwhelmed with the fear that I would never be anything but mediocre. That fear, coupled with the pressure that comes from the question What have you done lately? drives me still. Negative stressors can be powerful motivators. Critically examine why you coach and how that is related to other aspects of your life. Think about your hot buttons and who or what pushes them.

Get a Clue

You may think, "I like coaching. I won't burn out." You may treat your symptoms like a cold or flu and just wait them out, expecting them to eventually go away on their own. Unfortunately, however, some jobs are burnout time bombs. You can, in fact, be a good match for your job and like coaching but still show signs and symptoms of burnout.

You may not take symptoms seriously, believing that you've just overdone things a bit, that the symptoms are a wake-up call. With a little rest or a break, they go away and you're fine. It's just you. A vacation also helps, especially those who need it most; however, the relief is temporary. Within about three weeks, burnout symptoms usually return to prevacation levels.

You may think that the solution to the problem is to work harder, try harder, do better. Hard work is necessary, but there are limits. Working beyond sustainable limits is counterproductive.

You may accept that your symptoms go with the territory, that they are something all coaches go through and thus are nothing to worry about. It's just your job; you'll get used to it. It's a tough profession and only the strong survive. As a matter of fact, burnout is more about your job than it is about you. Contrary to this mindset, it is not inevitable, and it can be prevented, treated, and beaten.

Clueless is not a state you ever want to be in. You do not prevent, treat, or beat burnout by denying, feeling guilty, blaming yourself or others, getting mad at yourself, or working harder without giving yourself a chance to recover and recharge. Even if you are feeling good right now, in a clueless state, you are headed for trouble. It may be, too, that you have been at some level of burnout for so long that it feels normal.

Take Stock

Do a demands/resources check. On the left side of a sheet of paper, make a list of what you consider to be the major demands of softball coaching. On the right side of the paper, list the resources you believe you have within you to meet the demands. Does coaching demand more than you can give?

Do a rewards/costs check. On the left side of a sheet of paper, make a list of the rewards of coaching. Consider what you would lose if you took a coaching job elsewhere or you left coaching altogether. On the right side of the paper, list the costs of coaching, what you don't like about coaching. Does coaching provide enough or less than you need?

Increase Your Self-Awareness

Go back over the physical, emotional, mental, and behavioral features of burnout listed in table 27.1 and check off any that pertain to you. Consider that while these could be indicative of some other problem, they might be related to burnout. Be alert to recognize the signs and symptoms of burnout in you and in members of your staff, so you can address symptoms early while their intensity, frequency, and duration are minimal.

Consider seriously the manner in which you might be experiencing burnout. Do you sometimes behave like an ostrich? Might you have a bad battery? Is your pond stagnant? Are you on a carousel horse? Do you feel like a mighty mouse? These may be labels, but if the shoe fits . . .

Review the characteristics that inhabit the path to burnout. Consider each one individually, and note any that pertain to you. Jot down any suggested treatments or remedies that come to mind.

Make a list of the stresses you're facing and consider how you are reacting to them.

Next, you must engage your opponent. You have to get directly involved in the game. You will not prevail if you think you can just read this material then put it on a shelf or in a file. It will take time, energy, careful thought, and introspection. It may even take an outside reality check—feedback from others you trust. Regardless, you must become a conscious player. Light your fire, press your button, start digging, do the work, put yourself into it, and accept the challenge.

The Game Plan

The following game plan will help prevent burnout from occurring and alleviate its impact. Preventing burnout requires awareness and action. Take steps to keep burnout from zapping your coaching career.

Develop Some Work Guidelines

As soon as you realize that you are in some level of burnout, accept the fact that you are in the midst of a potentially dangerous crisis. Activate your coping mechanisms and fight back. For example, focus on the things you do well. Give yourself more credit for the things you do. When things are going well it is fine to be critical, but when you are struggling you need to support and encourage yourself just as you would a player.

Remind yourself that you direct the course of your own life. Take control. Decide how much you can realistically handle and how much you want to take on. Set priorities and follow them. Challenge your own workaholic myth and the personal myth that more work equals a better product. Even though it may feel better to work longer and harder, it isn't a smart strategy. Know when to push yourself during the season, but take advantage of opportunities for breaks.

Accept the fact that there are stressful situations that you cannot control (i.e., injuries, weather, umpires' bad calls, opposing teams' performances). Focus on what you can control—your response to these situations. I know that it is difficult, but try not to compound the problem. Choose to respond in as constructive a manner as you can.

Keep in mind that if you are not okay, it is very likely that your team and program are not going to be okay. Take care of yourself first. Just like they instruct on an airplane—put your oxygen mask on first and then attend to your child.

Don't feel guilty about retreating. Have the courage to say no at times even though doing so may put you out of your comfort zone. Stretching your limits is one thing, but pushing yourself beyond your limits is counterproductive. Delegate some of your responsibilities to others.

Try to anticipate conflict and be prepared to deal with it right away, such as announcing a change in the starting lineup or pitching rotation, an unscheduled practice, or a change in travel plans.

Choose your battles carefully. Don't invest a lot in something with little payoff. You may lose some battles, but hang in there and fight to win the war.

Get involved with your team and stay involved. Establish and maintain a bond with your players. Demonstrate that you care about them both on and off the field. Empathize with them and listen to them. Learn to read between the lines. Increase quality time and decrease quantity of time spent with athletes.

Accept change as inevitable and try to be flexible. Bend but don't break.

If you sometimes feel overwhelmed and the top of your desk is out of control, try this. Grab everything and stuff it in a bag (I call mine my black hole). Take the bag home, so you can look at it whenever you want, and you can choose not to touch it. The next day when you walk into your office, your desk looks neat and clean and things at least seem to be under control. When you take the papers and lists back out of your bag, you feel you have some control as you organize them and decide what to do next.

Believe in possibilities, not probabilities.

Develop Some Personal Guidelines

Try to develop a sense of identity that is not exclusively tied to coaching. Do not define yourself by what you do but by who you are as a person and how you do what you do.

Take care of your own health—sleep, exercise, nutrition—and don't neglect recovery. Get in shape and stay in shape. Schedule time for rest. Require that you eat meals away from your desk and work and that you exercise at a certain time each day or for a certain length of time each day.

Develop a financial plan and a retirement plan for your future.

If you have a particular interest or hobby, schedule time for it and treat that time as if it were for practice or a game. Actively search for something that takes your mind completely off work.

Change your perspective whenever possible to put a positive, optimistic spin on negative events and thoughts. Reinterpret problems as challenges. Keep in mind that faith and hope are better allies than cynicism and pessimism. Go with the good guys. Constant negativity can wear you down, undermine your confidence, and increase your risk for burnout.

Constantly strive to retain a sense of humor. Laugh as often as you can. Seek balance, challenge, and progress. Maintain your values, stay grounded, and be true to yourself. When you work, work. When you play, play. Focus on the present.

Develop and Maintain a Social Support Group

Spend time with other people. Plan more time with family and friends. Arrange to go to dinner, a movie—anything. If necessary, set dates and times, so it is more difficult to make excuses, cancel, and put work first.

It helps tremendously if you don't have to walk your path alone. Travel with people who know when you need nourishment and when you need to be challenged.

Do not hesitate to seek help from others. Share your thoughts and feelings. Start with family, close friends, and trusted colleagues who listen to you without judgment, provide emotional support, recognize and appreciate you, and challenge you to do better. At some point, you may need to confide in administrators or a professional counselor or psychologist. Do not be surprised or too disappointed if some people bail on you. Trying to help when someone is battling a severe case of burnout is not easy, and some people just don't know what to do or may even fear being pulled in themselves. Regardless, hang in there. Stay action-oriented. Resist the urge to withdraw or give up.

Live and Learn

Attend clinics, camps, and conventions. They can be motivating, give you new ideas, drills, strategies and techniques, and expand your support group. Take classes or attend seminars and clinics to improve your stress-management skills (relaxation, imagery, goal-setting, time management, assertiveness training).

Engage in group brainstorming sessions with your colleagues. Discuss the stresses inherent in coaching and talk about ways of dealing with them so as to minimize burnout. Share techniques you use to combat stress and ask burnout questions.

Schedule a coaches' caucus to discuss common issues. Meet on a regular basis if necessary. Periodically invite various administrators and support staff personnel to discuss ways to make your work more manageable and productive.

The Path to Spirited Coaching

I have been on the path to spirited coaching for over 25 years now, and it has been quite a trip. When I first started, the path was not well traveled, not for women at least, and it has changed quite a bit through the years. I'm sure that everyone who has been on the path has a different tale to tell. The following are some of my thoughts on the subject.

First, softball coaching is a people business, and a softball coach should be a people person. Softball coaching can be profitable in a great many ways, but if you expect to get rich coaching, you are going to be very disappointed. If you really are in it for the money, you won't last long because no amount of money alone is going to be worth it. The business product is not wins; the product is a team of players. A coach's assembly line consists of individual minds, bodies, abilities, and character traits. Coaches may use bats, balls, and bases, but the major work to be done is with the minds, hearts, hopes, and dreams of kids.

Coaching is not for the weak at heart or the weak of mind. Have the courage of your convictions and maintain your values no matter what. You are tested almost daily. There are always new challenges and crises as well as pressure. However, there is also the game-day excitement, the adrenaline rush, and the shared intimacy that comes with the extreme highs and lows of winning and losing as a team. Emotional stability, mental toughness, and hardiness are traits that increase your resistance to burnout. Feel the fear and succeed anyway. When times get tough, count your blessings and list the things you have to be thankful for.

Coaching is a calling for players, not spectators. You have to be connected and engaged. To stay on the path to spirited coaching, you must be actively involved with your team. The better the connection, the better able you are to deal with the adversity that inevitably accompanies athletic endeavors. I believe that this is one of the most important factors in preventing, treating, and beating burnout. It is also one of the toughest principles to abide by should your path become steep and burnout symptoms intensify. Still, you need to run to your team when you feel most like running from it.

You have to commit. After you have been a coach for a time, and you think you have a pretty good idea of what it's all about, make a considered decision about your level of commitment. Keep in mind the following: The more you invest in coaching, the more you sacrifice for coaching; the more closely you are identified with coaching, the closer you become to being entrapped. Additionally, the less you are identified with anything other than coaching and the fewer the attractive alternatives you have to coaching, the less likely you avoid burnout at some point. This can be both healthy and unhealthy. It's healthy when it compels you to work through a lot of issues when you would quit if there were an easy way out. On the other hand, remaining in coaching for the wrong reasons and continuing to coach at some level of dysfunctional burnout—just because you believe you have no other choice or you think you're helping somebody else, like your players—is bad for all concerned. You are usually better off if you are in coaching for attraction-based reasons—because you want to coach and you choose to coach, because you love it, really, really love it, especially the kids and the game. Softball is a game, but a very serious game to a lot of different people (coaches, players, parents, administrators, fans) for a lot of different reasons. Love conquers all.

There are no bad kids, just good kids who sometimes behave badly in tough situations. There are a lot of difficult issues that you, your staff, and your players must deal with through the course of a season (i.e., failure, disappointment, slumps, intrateam conflict, coach-athlete conflict, loss of confidence, injuries, pressure of big games). There are also a lot of behaviors that are going to bug you. Try to identify behaviors that cause you to react with strong or exaggerated negative feeling. One way to do this is to think about your athletes' behaviors and make a list of those that bother you most. Learn to live with a degree of negative attributes in your athletes, so you can enjoy the rewards of their positive contributions. You can reject specific behavior patterns without necessarily rejecting the whole person. Once you begin to lose faith in your players or you become disillusioned, you must take immediate action. This aloofness can be very serious. If you are not okay, I doubt that your kids will be okay.

Recruiting is a game within itself. I know that when I'm evaluating talent, I feel that all my competitors see what I see and that they all want whom I want. At times I have felt intimidated, stressed, and powerless. Now I realize that everyone gets kids. They may not always be our top choices, but recruiting is somewhat like buying stocks and mutual funds—there is no guarantee of future results. Developing a ball player is like making a pie. You need to have certain ingredients, but some cooks do a whole lot more with what they have to work with than others. The basic key is to make the recruits that you get better.

Once you get your recruits and add them to your team, keep in mind that if you expect more than they are capable of giving, you are going to be disappointed. You may be disappointed because you believe they are underachieving and that reflects negatively on your leadership, or you may be disappointed because you overestimated their ability and that reflects negatively on your judgment. This kind of thinking is counterproductive. For most of us, recruiting is a crapshoot. We make educated guesses, but they are guesses nonetheless. Accept your players and your team where they are at any given time. Try to help them to get better. If what you are doing doesn't seem to be working, change your perspective.

It is not an exaggeration to say that the evaluation phase of recruiting can be injurious to your health. Sitting on bleachers in extreme heat with limited access to food and water for as many as 15 hours at a time for several days throughout the summer is enough to test an Olympian's mettle. You are also expected to be on throughout the ordeal.

You can tell how much time a coach has spent on the recruiting trail by his or her recruiting habits. A coach who sits in the shade on a chair with a back has been around for a while, especially if he or she has a personal supply of bottled water and a mister. I used a small umbrella once. I used it only once because it made me feel 20 years older, but I highly recommend it, provided you can take a little ribbing.

On a more serious note, there is a great burnout risk associated with the recruiting evaluation process. What needs to be changed is not you but the nature of the process itself. Everyone is ready, willing, and able to recruit, but at the same time, everyone is also vulnerable. Therefore, I advise the following: Coaches, pool your resources. Set up a tent, tables, and chairs. Invest in some community coolers, ice, and drinks. Organize and work together to make this part of your job more bearable.

Burnout is a function of the nature of the job and the nature of the person doing the job. Some time ago, the question was raised at the NFCA about the adoption of a recruiting calendar. At the time, I was vehemently against this motion. I felt that it was un-American to legislate work ethic. I believed that any coach who wanted to gain an advantage by outworking opponents should be allowed to try. Since then I have changed my mind. I have come to the conclusion that my colleagues would take the risk of burning out before they would ever let me outwork them. This is a battle that nobody can win. The lesson I have learned from this experience is that burnout is not a personal weakness, a lack of mental toughness. On the contrary, it is the trait of mental toughness, coupled with extreme drive, determination, motivation and passion that can become a spirited coach's Achilles' heel. I realize that it may still be possible to outrecruit and out-work an opponent. In the process, however, some very good coaches are going to suffer from burnout. I would hate to see these coaches continue to work with active burnout, or be driven out of the profession by unrealistic work requirements. We must try to find ways of making our jobs more do-able, especially when it comes to evaluating prospects on the summer re-cruiting trail.

It's not whether you win or lose, it's how you play the game . . . but, you do need to win sometimes. Use this philosophical yardstick to measure yourself and your accomplishments. I know that I will always remember certain wins and losses, but more importantly, I try to focus on the coach-ing experience and its payoffs—like relationships with my players and colleagues, funny stories to tell, and experiences of overcoming adversity and rising to meet challenges. What a rush! I don't believe that winning is everything or that winning is the only thing. It sure does give you a buzz, but that may not be enough to keep you or your players in the game over time. Winning makes everything and everyone but a selfish person feel better. Winners laugh and smile more, hang closer together, are more posi-tive and communicative, and are lower maintenance. It is a fact that we compete to win. On any given day, however, half of the teams that play are going to lose.

Be process-oriented rather than outcome-oriented. Emphasize behaviors and performances that are indicative of progress. When you concentrate on the process of coaching and competing rather than on the outcome, you have many more victories along the way.

Other things can help prevent burnout. Getting off the beaten path and doing something a little different can be stimulating and provide a little wind at your back. For me, it was writing bylaws for the NFCA, rules for the NCAA, books, and articles. These healthy diversions kept me on the path and in the game by providing me with an avenue to feel good about myself whether coaching was doing it for me or not.

When you are struggling, it is nice to see the smiling faces of people who want what you have to offer, appreciate what you are doing, and respect you for it. Think about the environment in which you can place yourself to get these positive strokes that are so necessary to recharge your battery. Consider conducting a seminar or clinic for parents who coach, for younger players, or for your colleagues in other parts of the country. (I suggest an-other part of the country because a change of scenery can be a welcome relief. Also, I have found that you can be taken for granted at home.) Go where you need to go to get the feedback you need to feel good about your-self and put a smile on your face.

Find some classes that might be of interest to you so you, can be the sponge for a change. Sit and think to yourself, "Teach me if you can!" You are on the receiving end of instruction, and you might enjoy the role reversal. If you are an older coach like me, you might find something like a bridge club helpful. It worked for me because I was the youngest player and a rookie, a nice position to be in for a change. Other things that helped me to extend my career are heaters in the dugout, a room of my own on road trips, and buses (no more driving). If you travel in vans, consider taking along designated drivers. It may cost a little more, but I think you will find it worth the money and safer, too.

Keep things in perspective. It's not all about you. In fact "An outlook based on self-centeredness, self-design, self-struggle and self-importance leads to self-destruction" (source unknown). Keep in mind that you learn to perceive stress in your own unique way. You also have a unique burnout threshold. Some can take more unrelieved stress than others before they burnout. Some can also continue to coach effectively despite active burnout.

Imagine that I am standing in front of you with an empty glass jar. I fill the jar to the top with rocks. Do you think it's full? I then add as many small stones as the glass will hold. Do you think it's full now? Next I add sand until it is level with the top of the jar. Is it finally full now? I add water until it reaches the brim. Is it full now? For the purposes of this exercise, the answer is yes. What is the message of this exercise? Is it that when you think you've done enough, you can always do more? Is it that there is always room for more? Could be, however, the message I would like to send to you is that if you want to put big rocks in your jar you had better put them in first or they will not fit. In other words, set priorities. Make sure there is room in your life for what you value most. Take care of the big things first and the little things last. View problems as challenges and challenges as opportunities. View failures as temporary setbacks.

Lighten your load and lose the baggage. There's an old Zen story that illustrates this point. Two monks were traveling together in a heavy downpour when they came upon a beautiful woman in a silk komono who was having trouble crossing a muddy intersection. "Come on," said the first monk to the woman, and he carried her in his arms to a dry spot.

The second monk didn't say anything until much later. Then he couldn't contain himself anymore. "We monks don't go near females," he said. "Why did you do that?"

"I left the woman back there," the first monk replied. "Are you still carrying her?"

As you travel along your path to spirited coaching, travel light. Lose the baggage that is counterproductive.

Take control. Do not allow softball to run your life. Imagine that your life is a 16-ounce glass. It only holds so much. In fact, it likely does not hold as much as you would like or feel you need to pour into it. You must make choices. If the only thing you pour into your glass is coaching, you are going to lead a one-dimensional life. This may work for some people for some time but not for many for long. Most of us require diversity. We want to have a personal, social, family, recreational, and professional life. To accomplish this balance, I believe it makes sense to set priorities but to be flexible. Sometimes the glass may be filled to the brim with coaching. Another time it may be filled with family, friends, and recreational endeavors. Vary the nature and quantity of that which you choose to pour into your glass. If you let softball dictate your life, you are going to put yourself at risk for burnout.

Try to do the right thing. You may not always do the right thing, but try, try, try. Trying is the key. Things may not always turn out as you like, but don't let it be for lack of motivation and effort. When you follow this advice, you find it easier to accept yourself and others, as well as the consequences of your actions.

Consider the following story as told by Gordon B. Hinckley in his book *Standing for Something*. An older boy and his young companion were walking along a road that led through a field. They saw an old coat and a badly worn pair of men's shoes by the roadside, and, in the distance, they saw the owner working in the field. The younger boy suggested that they hide the shoes, conceal themselves, and watch the perplexity on the owner's face when he returned. The older boy thought that would not be so good. He said the owner must be a very poor man. After discussing the matter, they concluded to try another experiment. Instead of hiding the shoes, they would put a silver dollar in each one and, concealing themselves, see what the owner did when he discovered the money.

Soon the man returned from the field, put on his coat, slipped one foot into a shoe, felt something hard, took it out, and found a silver dollar. Wonder and surprise showed in his face. He looked at the dollar again and again, turned around and could see nobody, then proceeded to put on the other shoe where, to his great surprise, he found another dollar. His feelings overcame him and he knelt down and offered aloud a prayer of thanksgiving, in which he spoke of his wife being sick and helpless and his children without bread. Then he fervently thanked the Lord for this bounty from unknown hands and evoked the blessing of heaven upon those who had given him this needed help. The boys remained concealed until he had gone. Then they quietly walked along the lane and one said to the other, "Don't you have a good feeling? Aren't you glad we didn't try to deceive him?"

Finally maintain your values and stay on the path. Find the positives, give the benefit of the doubt, practice objectivity and fairness, and accept responsibility. Don't compromise, get negative, become argumentative, or blame others if things don't go as you like. Most importantly, don't give up on yourself, your staff, or your players. Keep trying to do the right thing!

Final Thoughts

If you are just beginning your journey as a coach, you have a path to choose. It needs to be a conscious choice. You must be an active player in your chosen profession. You can go down the path to burnout or self-actualization.

If you are already coaching, you are already on one of these two paths. Nobody wants to be a burned out coach. Take time every now and then to think about who you are and where you are along your path. Where are you headed? What are your goals? Are you still committed or do you feel trapped? Are you still involved with your players or have you become more detached and impatient? Do you still feel that you have control over your situation or are you feeling more and more helpless and resigned? Are you still optimistic, or are you becoming more cynical and disinterested? Don't wait until you are so far down the wrong path that you are lost or so exhausted and isolated that you don't have the strength to act, or that there is no one to whom you can turn for help.

Somebody told me once that my stubbornness would keep me alive but stop me from getting better. I believe that my stubbornness has kept me in the game. The connection has been my lifeline. As I now move along my path to spirited coaching, I am not as physically strong as I once was, but I like to think I counter that with experience and a measure of wisdom. I am a burnout battler, and I am better for it. You can be, too.

Remember, at the same time that you become increasingly aware of burnout and you fight it, you are on the way to becoming a spirited, dynamic coach. Care and be aware. Coach with pride, principles, and love. Enjoy a satisfying, productive, long-term run as a spirited coach, someone who makes a difference in a meaningful endeavor.

As your coaching career comes to an end, I think you'll find that your path has led you up a mountain. "Climb slowly, steadily, enjoying each passing moment; and the view from the summit will serve as a fitting climax for the journey" (Harold V. Melchert).

ABOUT THE NFCA

The National Fastpitch Coaches Association (NFCA) is the sport's leading professional growth organization for coaches at all competitive levels of play. The NFCA has more than 4,000 members, most of whom are high school, travel-team, and collegiate coaches.

The NFCA provides a forum for discussing matters of interest to its members and works to formulate guiding principles, standards, and policies for conducting competitive fastpitch softball programs for girls and women. It recognizes outstanding members through its Victory Club and Coach of the Year awards programs, in addition to All-Region, All-American, and Scholar-Athlete awards programs for members' college and high school players. All members receive the association's newspaper, *Fastpitch Delivery,* and enjoy discounts on softball coaching clinics, videos, and books. They also have access to the NFCA job bank, camp network, and other professional networking opportunities.

The NFCA headquarters are located in Columbia, Missouri, where executive director Lacy Lee Baker and her husband, University of Missouri head softball coach Jay Miller, and their daughter, Nikki, also reside.

Jacquie Joseph became the head softball coach at Michigan State University in 1994 after serving as head coach for five years at Bowling Green State University. In 1997, she led the Spartans to their first Big Ten Tournament appearance in school history and their first bid to the NCAA Tournament. She served as president of the National Fastpitch Coaches Association from 1994-1998 and has a career record of 389-346 in her 12 years as a head coach.

ABOUT THE CONTRIBUTORS

Rayla J. Allison is the former vice president and league director of Women's Professional Fastpitch (WPF), as well as the former executive director of the NFCA. She was a professional catcher for the Conneticut Falcons, the most successful team in the International Women's Professional Softball Association. In 1999, Allison was inducted into the NFCA Hall of Fame. She is currently an attorney.

Rayla J. Allison

Dianne Baker, head coach at Texas Woman's University since 1996, has built a winning record of 96-53-1 (.643). Her coaching career began at Stephen F. Austin State University, where she led her team to their first and only NCAA Division II title in the school's history and enjoyed a successful 15-year tenure. With an overall record of 596-345-2 (.633), Baker is one of the winningest active Division II coaches in the NCAA. She has collected numerous Coach of the Year awards and was a 1998 inductee into the NFCA Hall of Fame.

Dianne Baker

Gayle Blevins has been the head coach at the University of Iowa since 1988. From 1989-1998, her teams placed in the top three in the Big Ten Conference, winning the conference title four times. Blevins came to Iowa from Indiana University, where she led her teams to the College World Series three times in seven years. With an impressive career record of 846-409-5 (.671), Blevins is the sixth all-time coach to achieve 800 victories. She has been named the NFCA Mideast Region Coach of the Year six times and is a member of the NFCA Hall of Fame.

Gayle Blevins

Carol Bruggeman

Carol Bruggeman is head coach at Purdue. In the team's inaugural season in 1994, she led them to a 21-17-1 (.545) record. In 1997, she brought them to their first-ever Big Ten Tournament, returning in 2000. Bruggeman came to Purdue from Michigan, where as an assistant coach (1989-1993) she helped lead the Wolverines to back-to-back Big Ten championships (1992-1993), earning them their first two postseason trips to the NCAA Tournament.

Mike Candrea

Mike Candrea, head coach at the University of Arizona since 1989, has the highest career winning percentage (.805) in the history of Division I softball with a record of 879-212. For 11 consecutive seasons, he led the Wildcats to the College World Series and claimed the title five times, including in 2001. He also claimed the Pac-10 championship title five times. In 12 seasons, Candrea was recognized 13 times with conference, regional, or national Coach of the Year awards. In 1996, he was inducted into the NFCA Hall of Fame.

Sharon J. Drysdale

Sharon Drysdale resigned as head coach at Northwestern after the 2001 season. After 23 years at Northwestern and four years at Kansas, her career record is 684-504-3 (.574). Drysdale led the Wildcats to five league titles, two regional playoffs, and three consecutive College World Series from 1984-1986. She was named Big Ten Coach of the Year three times and has been inducted into the NFCA Hall of Fame. **Karren Drysdale** works at Aurora Community Hospital as the purchasing coordinator.

Karren J. Drysdale

Bill Edwards is head coach at Hofstra University with a record of 387-177-2. In his 11 consecutive winning seasons, his teams have won two East Coast Conference Championships, three America East Championships, one North Atlantic Conference Championship, and an ECAC Championship, as well as making four NCAA Tournament appearances. His efforts have been recognized with the North Atlantic and Mid-Atlantic Region Coach of the Year awards. Edwards came to Hofstra from Commack High School (New York), where he coached for nine years.

Bill Edwards

Judi Garman is the retired head coach for Cal State Fullerton. In her 20-season tenure, she led the Titans to postseason play 18 times. Her teams won or shared eight conference titles and seven regional championships. They attended the College World Series 7 times and brought home the championship in 1986. Garman's Cal State record totals 913-376-4 (.708), but her overall career record of over 1,100 wins places her as the nation's winningest coach by victories. Garman was elected to the NSCA Hall of Fame in 1993. She is the head coach/manager of the Italian National Team.

Judi Garman

Yvette Girouard is the head coach at Louisiana State University. She is a recent addition to the LSU coaching staff, coming from a successful 20-year stint at Louisiana-Layfayette. She led Louisiana-Layfayette to 19 consecutive winning seasons with 10 NCAA regional appearances and three College World Series. With an overall record of 758-252 (.750), Girouard is a two-time NCAA Division I Coach of the Year, a five-time South Region Coach of the Year, and a nine-time Louisiana Coach of the Year.

Yvette Girouard

JoAnne Graf

JoAnne Graf, head coach at Florida State University (1979-present), has an impressive career record of 1055-312-6. She was the first coach in Division I softball to reach 1,000 victories, earning each one at Florida State. She has led the Lady Seminoles to eight ACC championship titles, 13 NCAA regional tournaments, and five appearances in the NCAA College World Series. In 11 of the past 15 seasons, her teams have finished among the top 13 in the nation. Graf has received the ACC Coach of the Year award three times.

Betty Hoff

Betty Hoff is the head coach for Luther College (1973-present). Within Division III coaching, she has accumulated a 444-251 career record. Her teams won the Iowa Conference championships from 1985-1988 and advanced to the NCAA Division III finals three times. Since 1985, she has brought Luther College softball to postseason play eight times.

Carol Hutchins

Carol Hutchins has been the head coach at the University of Michigan since 1981. In addition to posting a 704-294-4 record with the Wolverines, she has led her teams to seven Big 10 regular season championships, five Big 10 post-season tournament championships, and five regional championships. Under Hutchins, Michigan has been ranked among the top 10 Division 1 teams five times.

Jeff Janssen

As one of the nation's top Peak Performance Consultants, **Jeff Janssen**, MS, helps athletes and coaches develop the mental toughness and team chemistry necessary to win championships. Janssen has worked with many of the nation's top teams including Mike Candrea's Arizona program, winners of six national championships. A popular and frequent speaker nationwide, Janssen has authored numerous videos and books on peak performance including "Championship Team Building" and "The Seven Secrets of Successful Coaches."

Margo Jonker has been head coach at Central Michigan University since 1979. Her career record stands at 730-393-5 (.649), ranking her 10th in victories among active coaches in Division I softball. She has won nine Mid-American Conference titles and made 10 NCAA regional appearances. Jonker has earned many honors including being named the Mid-American Coach of the Year seven times. In addition, she has served as the assistant coach for various USA Softball teams including the Olympic team that competed in Sydney in 2000.

Margo Jonker

Cheri K. Kempf is owner and pitching instructor at Club K, the largest indoor training facility for female fastpitch softball players in the country. She was a member of a five-person panel assembled by the Amateur Softball Association (ASA) and the United States Olympic Committee to develop universal standards by which to teach fastpitch pitching. Kempf has played and coached softball at all levels, including four years as a NCAA Division I coach. She has been inducted into the NAIA Collegiate Hall of Fame, the Missouri State ASA Hall of Fame, and the Missouri Western State College Hall of Fame.

Cheri Kempf

Brian Kolze, head coach for the Pacific Tigers, holds a career record of 271-230-1. At Pacific, his totals are 128-125-1. In 1998, Kolze led his team to its first of two consecutive NCAA appearances. For his success, he was named the Big West coach of the year, earning this title again in 2001. Prior to Pacific, Kolze was assistant coach at UNLV, followed by Sacramento State. He has also coached internationally, serving as the assistant coach for the Canadian Renegades.

Brian Kolze

Jay Miller

Jay Miller, head coach at the University of Missouri (1988-present), has compiled a career record of 680-382. He was an assistant coach for Missouri from 1982-1984, during which time the Tigers won the Big Eight tournament and took one trip to the NCAA College World Series. After three years as head coach at Oklahoma City University, Miller returned to Missouri as head coach, where he led his teams to another Big Eight championship, two more trips to the College World Series, and a Big XII championship. All told, he has made eight NCAA appearances during his time with Missouri. He has been recognized for his achievements with conference and regional Coach of the Year awards. Miller has also coached internationally, serving as one of six head coaches for the USA National Teams during the summer of 2001.

Deb Pallozzi

Deb Pallozzi is the head coach at Ithaca College. After spending her first year rebuilding the team, she began a run of 11 straight winning seasons. She brought her team to the NCAA regionals a total of four times, twice placing second and twice winning the regional title and advancing to the NCAA championships. Prior to Ithaca, Pallozzi was head coach at Rensselaer University and an assistant coach at the University of Missouri and at Albany.

Rhonda Revelle

Rhonda Revelle is head coach at the University of Nebraska. For six consecutive seasons, she has led her teams to the NCAA Tournament, which includes four straight "Sweet 16" appearances and one Big 12 Conference Tournament title. She has been honored with the Big Eight and Big 12 Coach of the Year awards (1995 and 1998 respectively) and was inducted into the Nebraska Softball Hall of Fame in 1997.

Lori Sippel is the assistant coach at her alma mater, the University of Nebraska. As a player at Nebraska, she was a four-time All Big Eight performer and led her team to the College World Series three times. Internationally, she played in the World Tournament and helped to qualify Canada for the Olympics in both 1996 and 2000. Sippel has been inducted into both the Softball Canada Hall of Fame and the Nebraska Softball Hall of Fame.

Lori Sippel

Elaine Sortino has been the head coach at the University of Massachusetts since 1980. She has an all-time record of 688-314-3 (.685). Sortino has led the Minutewomen to 13 Atlantic 10 regular season and championship titles, as well as taking them to the College World Series three times. She has never had a losing season at UMass, and she has been recognized with four Northeast Region Coach of the Year awards and five Atlantic 10 Coach of the Year honors.

Elaine Sortino

Mona Stevens, head coach at the University of Utah, has a record of 150-89 (.628) with the Utes. In 2000, she guided her team to Mountain West Conference regular season and tournament championship titles and was named Coach of the Year. Prior to Utah, Stevens spent three years at UMass, where her teams claimed the Atlantic-10 Conference regular and tournament championship titles twice, as well as advanced to the NCAA Tournament. Stevens has coached internationally and has been honored with the United States Olympic Committee National Softball Coach of the Year award. She is the author of *The Fastpitch Softball Drill Book*.

Mona Stevens

Denny Throneburg coached for 22 years at Casey-Westfield High School. In that time, he brought home six Class A state softball championships and was named National High School Coach of the Year twice. His career record for the Warriors is 647-56 (.920).

Denny Throneburg

Linda Wells

Linda Wells, head coach at Arizona State (1990-present), has a 349-271 (.563) record with the Sun Devils, and has led her teams to seven NCAA Regional appearances in 10 seasons—including her first trip to the College World Series in 1999. Before Arizona State, she coached 15 years at Minnesota, where she earned Big Ten Coach of the Year honors in 1988 while claiming the Big Ten championship. In addition, Wells played 18 years of women's major fast-pitch. She is a former president of the National Softball Coaches Association (NSCA) and is a member of the NSCA Hall of Fame.

Marge Willadsen

Marge Willadsen, head coach at Buena Vista University (1979-present), has a record of 465-280-2 in 20 seasons. Five of those seasons resulted in regional championship titles, and her team earned one NCAA Division III National Champion title. Willadsen has been recognized numerous times as Coach of the Year at the conference, regional, and national levels. She serves on the NCAA Sportsmanship and Ethical Conduct Committee and the NCAA Softball Rules Committee.

Teresa Wilson

Teresa Wilson is the head coach at the University of Washington. In the nine-year history of Husky softball, Wilson has built the program from the ground up and led the team to two Pac-10 Conference Championship titles and five straight College World Series appearances. She has accrued a 399-141 (.739) record with the Huskies, bringing her cumulative 14-year coaching record to 603-302 (.666). Prior to Washington, she coached at Oregon and Minnesota. At all three universities, Wilson led her teams to postseason play. She has been named Coach of the Year by the NCAA (1989), the Big 10 (1991), and the Pac-10 (1989, 1996, 2000).